Detecting Detection

Detecting
Detection

International perspectives
on the uses of a plot

Edited by
Peter Baker and Deborah Shaller

continuum

Continuum International Publishing Group
80 Maiden Lane, Suite 704, New York, NY 10038
The Tower Building, 11 York Road, London SE1 7NX

www.continuumbooks.com

© Peter Baker, Deborah Shaller, and contributors 2012

Library of Congress Cataloging-in-Publication Data
Detecting detection : international perspectives on the uses of a plot / edited by
Peter Baker and Deborah Shaller.
p. cm.
Includes bibliographical references.
ISBN 978-1-4411-4936-7 (hardcover : alk. paper) – ISBN 1-4411-4936-8 (hardcover : alk.
paper)– ISBN 978-1-4411-0078-8 (pbk. : alk. paper) – ISBN 1-4411-0078-4 (pbk. : alk. paper)
1. Detective and mystery stories–Authorship. 2. Plots (Drama, novel, etc.) 3. Fiction–
Technique. 4. Fiction–Authorship. I. Baker, Peter, 1955– II. Shaller, Deborah.

PN3377.5.D4D48 2012
808.3'872–dc23
2012002427

ISBN: HB: 978-1-4411-4936-7
PB: 978-1-4411-0078-8

Typeset by Fakenham Prepress Solutions, Fakenham, Norfolk NR21 8NN
Printed and bound in the United States of America

CONTENTS

CONTRIBUTORS

Sofia Ahlberg teaches comparative literature at La Trobe University, Australia. She has published on transnational and transhemispheric issues in the *Journal of Modern Literature*, and *Comparative Literature Studies*, among other journals and collections of essays. She is currently working on a book that contrasts scenes of instruction in twentieth-century transatlantic literature.

Peter Baker is the author of three books of criticism, including *Deconstruction and the Ethical Turn* (1995), and the editor or co-editor of three other volumes. Along with co-editors Rod Smith and Kaplan Harris, he is editing Robert Creeley's *Selected Letters*. He teaches literary theory, modern literature and cultural studies at Towson University, Maryland.

Kim Toft Hansen is Teaching Assistant Professor in the Department of Culture and Global Studies, Aalborg University, Denmark. Hansen has in connection with the cross-disciplinary research programme, "Crime Fiction and Crime Journalism in Scandinavia," published extensively about crime fiction. His book *Mord og metafysik* (*Murder and Metaphysics*) discusses a tendency within fiction to discuss the absolute, the divine, and the supernatural. He has co-edited the two anthologies *Fingeraftryk* (*Fingerprint*) about crime fiction and criminality, and *Kulturtrafik* (*Cultural Traffic*) about aesthetic expressions in a global world, as well as the first issue of the academic journal *Academic Quarter* about *Flesh*. He is the co-editor in chief of *Academic Quarter* and the editor in chief of the online review journal *Kulturkapellet*. Recent publications range from articles about Chinese crime fiction as well as religion and metaphysics in crime fiction to specific articles about authors such as Henning Mortensen and Philip Kerr. Hansen has published many reviews of Scandinavian crime fiction.

Amadou Koné, novelist, playwright and essayist, taught African literature for many years at the National University of Côte d'Ivoire. He currently is Professor of African Literature and Culture in the French Department of Georgetown University in Washington, D.C. His most recent work is *L'Oeuf du monde* (2010).

Sheng-mei Ma is Professor of English at Michigan State University in Michigan, USA, specializing in Asian Diaspora/Asian American studies and East–West comparative studies. His five single-authored, scholarly books in English are: *Asian Diaspora and East–West Modernity* (2012); *Diaspora Literature and Visual Culture: Asia in Flight* (2011); *East–West Montage: Reflections on Asian Bodies in Diaspora* (2007); *The Deathly Embrace: Orientalism and Asian American Identity* (2000); and *Immigrant Subjectivities in Asian American and Asian Diaspora Literatures* (1998). He co-edited and translated *Chenmo de shanhen* (*Silent Scars: History of Sexual Slavery by the Japanese Military—A Pictorial Book*, bilingual edition, 2005), as well as co-edited *The City and the Ocean* (2011). *Sanshi zuoyou* (*Thirty, Left and Right*) is his Chinese poetry collection (Shulin, 1989). He also published numerous articles and book chapters on literature, film, and global culture.

Ana-Maria Medina was a Visiting Assistant Professor of Spanish for two years at the University of Houston Downtown, before starting as an Assistant Professor at Metropolitan State College in August 2011. She holds a PhD in Peninsular Literature from the University of Houston, an M.A. in Peninsular Literature from Saint Louis University and a B.A. in Hispanic Studies from the University of Texas at Austin. Her dissertation, *Manuel Rivas: A Revolution in Contemporary Galician Literature & Beyond*, a study of narrative and film from the feminist perspective in the context of twentieth- and twenty-first-century Spain, delves into the pressing questions of cultural conflict and assimilation, union and disunion, historical memory, feminine space, and trans-cultural and multilingual artistic production in the Peninsula. Dr Medina teaches beginner and intermediate language classes, heritage language courses and twentieth- and twenty-first-century peninsular literature, film and culture courses. She has published in various mediums, including scholarly journals, collections, and magazines, and has presented at national conferences.

Heta Pyrhönen is Professor of Comparative Literature at the University of Helsinki. Her books include *Murder from an Academic Angle* (Camden House, 1994), *Mayhem and Murder: Narrative and Moral Problems in the Detective Story* (University of Toronto Press, 1999), and *Bluebeard Gothic: Jane Eyre and Its Progeny* (University of Toronto Press, 2010). Her essays have been published in such journals as *Mosaic*, *Textual Practice*, *Contemporary Women's Writing*, and *Sign System Studies*.

Michelle Robinson is an Assistant Professor of American Studies at the University of North Carolina in Chapel Hill. She completed her doctorate at Boston University's American and New England Studies Program, with a dissertation titled "Places for Dead Bodies: Race, Labor and Detection in American Literature." Her essays have appeared in *Studies in the Novel* and *Modern Drama*.

Rossitsa Terzieva-Artemis is an Assistant Professor in the Department of Languages and Literature at the University of Nicosia, Cyprus, and works in the fields of modern English and American literature, psychoanalysis, and continental philosophy. She holds an M.A. in English Language and Literature, University of Veliko Turnovo, Bulgaria (1993); an M.Phil. in Gender Studies, Central European University, Hungary (1998); an M.Phil. in the Human Sciences, The George Washington University, USA (2000); and a PhD in the Human Sciences, The George Washington University, USA (2005). She is the author of the book *Stories of the Unconscious: Sub-Versions in Freud, Lacan, and Kristeva* (Peter Lang Publishers, 2009) and several articles in English, American, European, and postcolonial literatures. At present she is editing a volume of essays on Ford Madox Ford's novel *The Good Soldier* (Rodopi Press) and a special journal issue on Julia Kristeva for *Studies in the Literary Imagination* (Georgia University Press, due in 2013), and also writing articles on Kristeva, the postmodern novel as a genre, and the intersections between psychoanalysis and literature.

EDITORS'
INTRODUCTION

The detective story's proliferation compels us to ask questions much as the detective story itself compels us to seek clues. For, regardless of the questions we ask, we are agreed that as a story, the detective narrative is ubiquitous; it effortlessly crosses media and national boundaries, embeds itself in other stories, lurks in the corners of vastly different cultural landscapes. Its pervasiveness, however, challenges us not to generalize about its possibilities, but to particularize, not to round up the usual suspects, but to begin sketching very specific portraits in time and location—though assembling the usual suspects, of course, is not entirely without its pleasures. It is, after all, where so much contemporary criticism of the detective novel so fruitfully began—with Tzvetan Todorov's narrative typologies[1] or James Cawelti's formulae,[2] topoi with such enduring relevance that no matter where we currently travel, these territories continue to define much of the world we critically inhabit.

To see the detective story as narrative topology or formula is to engage with repetition not as fault, but as opportunity: the stories we tell—and tell repeatedly—offer insights into the worlds we like to imagine and the people we like to think we are. When readers demand the same story—whether in classical, hard-boiled, or hybrid forms—they necessarily demand that we take those preferences seriously, that we take them, as readers, seriously. In becoming part of the story, readers expand the boundaries of the text into the social, cultural, and ideological realms that it inhabits. And, indeed, when criticism of the detective novel began to apply structural analysis, it offered one of the first distinct counterpoints to any remnants of New Critical orthodoxy. For the realm of the popular—vexed and elusive of definition as the word may be—demands that critical readers ask not simply "what?" but "why?" Why this form, why this persistence, why this moment?

At the same time, variations in repeated forms sharpen our eye for the significance of difference, whether it occurs when the classic story gives way to the hard-boiled narrative, the least likely suspect changes shape, or women detectives bring gender and genre into elegant collision. Repetition and variation thus enter into dialogue, cross-textual exchanges that writers are free to engage explicitly or implicitly, depending as they do on the knowledge of their readers to note the selections. As we notice writers' choices, we agree to read several works at once, to understand not only the kinds of choices made but something about the reasons for their selection. The detective narrative becomes, then, about writing and about reading—reading the clues, reading the world, reading the detectives among us. And there are so many detectives among us. Contemporary anthologies find them in post-colonial and transcultural sites, place them in ethnic, racial, and economic context, expanding the range of our deductions and uncovering detectives at work in expected places.

Those unexpected places seduce our own gaze here as various essayists look not so much for detectives, but for detection itself, textual traces of a plot often found hidden in other plots. As Fredric Jameson elsewhere reminds us, "the literary past ... offers abundant examples of plots that would no longer work for us today" (365).[3] The detective plot, far from losing efficacy in our time, seems to animate it, to be useful in an increasing number of ways to an ever-growing body of literary and cultural work. It seems important, then, to take note of both the vibrancy of the narrative form and its willingness to be used for a variety of purposes. Exploring detection within other narrative frames helps us in two broad ways. First, it continues to foreground the contours and the purpose of the detective plot itself and so offers commentary on detective texts wherever we find them. The insights from essayists in this collection thus easily weave back into the general discussion of detective fiction as genre or sub-genre. Second, and at the same time, detective plots here burrow into other plots; as they do, they reshape those plots and thus tell us something important about the nature of modern narrative.

The essays in this collection are both provocative in subject and unusually rich in context. The writers here explore the detective plot within densely woven arguments that rely on deep knowledge and broad reference, equally at ease with contemporary material and historical description. Each essay is therefore a resource in itself, an invitation into the past, the present, the near and the far.

* * *

Reading the detectives, guiltily

Readers and detective stories have long been linked in their own conversations as writers of the genre engage readers in battles of wits, intertextual games, subtle invitations to tread often treacherous territories whose dangers are not the crimes themselves, but the moral and ethical choices readers make as they follow clues, take sides, imagine innocence and guilt—particularly imagine them as comfortably separate categories and as categories from which they are happily excluded. But readers of detective fiction are never innocent, and the writers' capacity to construct and reveal the reader's guilt is one of the genre's most compelling qualities.

As readers of Ann-Marie MacDonald's *The Way the Crow Flies*, Heta Pyrhönen writes, we have been caught out, discover we have guessed badly, misread, taken ourselves too seriously in all the wrong ways. We have been inadequate detectives because we have let "our advantages in knowledge and the narrator's confidentiality create in us a sense of superiority that has blunted our alertness and critical capacities." We are witnesses, argues Pyrhönen, but what, after all, do we see? What, after all, do we ever see? Linking detective plots to trauma narratives, Pyrhönen's essay traces MacDonald's use of a detective plot to raise complex questions about personal and national trauma, about reading, witnessing, and understanding; in doing so, it asks us to consider our role as readers of the past and the present, the local and the world.

Peter Baker's analysis of Roberto Bolaño's *The Savage Detectives* finds in the novel a work whose structure challenges our notions of existing genres as it engages epistemology, aesthetics, and ethics. Detection, Baker writes, provides occasion to consider—much as Pyrhönen has suggested—our role as witnesses, to uncover what is at stake when we agree to accompany Bolaño's detectives on their quest. For Bolaño, Baker claims, witnessing demands "investment in those who suffer and die." As readers, we investigate by necessity but also at our own peril, for adopting the quest is nothing less—or less important—than implicating ourselves in its crimes. The relationship between personal and national trauma, "the dark vision that haunts all of Bolaño's work," writes Baker ("Is *The Savage Detectives* a Detective Story?") "stems from the primal trauma of what happened to his country of Chile on September 11, 1973," even, or perhaps especially, in the novels Bolaño sets outside of Chile, like *The Savage Detectives*, and among detectives who may not be occupying a detective novel at all.

If you want to write a political novel

In his recent interview with National Public Radio, Greek detective fiction writer Petros Markaris was asked the inevitable: why detective fiction? Without hesitation, Markaris replied, "If you want to write today a social or political novel, you have to turn to the crime novel," making explicit an implicit attraction of the form.

Indeed, as Ana-Maria Medina makes clear in her essay "Detectivism as a Means of Resistance in Juan Marsé's *El embrujo de Shanghai*," political repression in Spain both suppressed and eventually animated the detective novel. In her survey of the genre's history in Spain, Medina travels through its nineteenth-century emergence, as a form based on the foreign influences of Poe and Conan Doyle, to its twentieth-century iterations as a distinctly Spanish creation that would only flourish in post-Franco, post-censorship Spain. But Medina is primarily interested in the detective narrative's influence not on detective novels, but on contemporary Spanish literature; to that end, Juan Marsé's novel provides a postmodern instance of "resistance and recuperation." In fact, it is interesting to see *El embrujo de Shanghai*, writes Medina, "as a conversation among writers of contemporary post-[Spanish] war narrative," enlivened by the generic freedoms of postmodernism, engaged "in the boom of globalization and the entrance of foreign cultures in a country once isolated from all exterior influences."

Two men, Ignatius Reilly and Burma Jones, walk into *A Confederacy of Dunces*, and by means of a secondary detective plot, "transform social arrangements," so that the janitor Jones emerges with both the visibility and economic access that have otherwise been denied him as a black man in New Orleans. And thus, in "Two Men Walk into a Bar," Michelle Robinson detects a role for detection that while it does not solve every problem for the characters it engages, Robinson claims, does act as a "foil for the dubious practice of activist 'ethnojournalism' exemplified by the works of Howard Griffin's 1961 book *Black Like Me*," a practice parodied in the novel by Reilly's *Journal*, and a form of activism that offers little or no opportunity for real social transformation. In an essay that digs deep into American, African American, and detective literatures, Robinson offers a critically engaged and engaging tour of the territory, using the occasion of Burma Jones' social change to inspect political action itself.

In an essay willing to explore WikiLeaks, Vietnam, Cuba, and contemporary terror alerts, Sofia Ahlberg sees in Graham Greene's *The Quiet American* the anticipation of a "world in which detection is ubiquitous in the art of narration as a way of grappling with questions of commitment, judgment, and belief." With Walter Benjamin, Ahlberg wonders at the very possibility of storytelling as a way of encountering truth, ultimately arguing that today, "we think of truth along the lines of how we become aware of it, not necessarily by what it is." The "how" of our encounters, however, is itself formed by narratology, within which detection occupies a special place. Using *The Quiet American* as example, Ahlberg argues that Green's detective emerges as an opportunity for both moral engagement and narrative renewal—as we, the novel's readers, negotiate a world in which such moments are increasingly difficult to penetrate and to claim.

What's a nice plot like you ... ?

Similar questions of epistemology pervade Julia Kristeva's novel *Possessions* and "promote," writes Rossitsa Terzieva-Artemis ("The Stories We All Tell: The Function of Language and Knowledge in Julia Kristeva's Novel *Possessions*") "that ontological questioning which further renders problematic the very idea of one solid subjectivity." Amidst her better-known work in philosophy and psychoanalysis comes a trio of detective novels and the promise of a fourth. Easily aligned with psychoanalysis, the detective genre nevertheless compels certain practices that Kristeva must "surmount" "by applying dense intertextuality" that pulls readers away from what is often the centerpiece of narrative detection, its plot. If we read these works as parodies of the conventional form, however, Terzieva-Artemis argues, we understand them as providing "insights into the workings of desire and language, of desires in language, of desires in the silences between language and speech." As such, the narratives offer Kristeva a medium for exploring the territories that intrigue her elsewhere.

Sheng-mei Ma's essay, "Zen Keytsch: Mystery Handymen with Dragon Tatoos," takes a playful, but deeply serious, look at the role of Eastern "handymen" in a range of contemporary and historical narratives from Charlie Chan to *The Matrix* and to the tattooed hero of Steig Larsson's enormously popular series of books. Ma creates the term "Zen Keytsch" to describe "Orientalist kitsch," tropes that represent "popular culture's wishful duplications of what alleges to be the transcendental from Eastern mysticism." Here, the larger narrative these detectives occupy—and to some extent disrupt—is modernism itself, particularly the post-Enlightenment imperative to separate reason and affect, logic and emotion, a move that, according to Ma, displaces such characteristics as intuition onto the non-West. Ma is equally at home with TV, film, and literatures past and present; the essay effortlessly gathers its players into a convincing collage of Western and Eastern Zen keytsch, a convincing picture of, as Ma writes, "Orientalist images as discursive handymen, mysterious yet kitschily functional in inducing an aura of awe, ever so elusive while dutifully serving at the pleasure of the West."

Swedish writer Arne Dahl's *Morkertal* (*Hidden Numbers*) begins Kim Toft Hansen's broad and rich assessment of the detective novel's history. What Hansen calls "the backside history of crime fiction" challenges our notions of the detective novel as modernist text—that is, as a narrative that asserts the role of reason and rationality while exiling the religious and supernatural. His historical vision moving backwards in time and eastward in direction, Hansen traces detection in China and the Arab world, then comes forward to encompass twentieth- and early twenty-first-century works like *The Da Vinci Code*. "Religion, metaphysics and supernaturalism, which savage modernity and the hard secularism it has strived to cleanse from public sphere," has been, Hansen argues, an "undercurrent or side stream" throughout the detective narrative's history; if we look far enough, we see it not as a disruption of metaphysics, but as proof that, contrary to many claims, "post-secularism has never really come about."

Finally, Amadou Koné's essay is firmly situated in the realm of African oral tradition, specifically three Fulani initiation narratives. He wants to claim that by examining these narratives in depth "one becomes aware that this type of narrative functions in reality by using motifs that are similar or at least analogous to the motifs of detective stories." Mystery is very important in these initiation narratives: "There is the mystery that stems from the places the action takes place, from the characters in the narrative, from the scenes that one witnesses during the story." The candidate for initiation functions much like the traditional detective when he searches for the master initiator and most importantly when he strives to interpret the symbols that have been presented during the journey. A key difference is that there is no initiating crime, and so the solution to the mystery is very different: "It is rather a matter of achieving an understanding of the elements of the global mystery of the functioning of the world and society."

The ubiquity of the motifs of detection in works of modern fiction finds a suitable corollary here in the sheer variety of the provenance of the authors and the works under consideration. Indeed, it may well be that in addition to solving individual mysteries and following the various plots to their conclusion we are in fact witness to something like the "global mystery of the functioning of the world and society."

Notes

1   Tzvetan Todorov, *The Poetics of Prose*. Trans R. Howard. Oxford: Blackwell, 1977.

2   John G. Cawelti. *Adventure, Mystery, and Romance*. Chicago: University of Chicago Press, 1976.

3   Fredric Jameson, "Realism and Utopia in The Wire," 2010: http://muse.jhu.edu/journals/criticism/vo52/52/3-4.jameson.html.

1

The detection plot as a means of testimony in Ann-Marie MacDonald's *The Way the Crow Flies*

Heta Pyrhönen

"The description of the victim had been matched to a list of missing teenagers in the area. A half hour later, a man was brought to the scene to identify her. As he looked at the body, a father's anguished howl filled the night. The victim's name was Eve Drake. In the past year, two other black teenagers, both living in the poorer sections of town, had been murdered and dumped in similar fashion in community gardens" (9–10). Taken from the opening chapter of George Pelecanos's *The Night Gardener* (2006), this scene describes a typical starting point in contemporary detective fiction: the discovery of a murder that causes inconsolable pain to the victim's family as well as disrupting communal life. Numerous detective narratives use the detection plot in order to probe crime as a traumatic event addressing both individuals and their societies. In these novels the detection plot emerges as a means of giving testimony, for the investigator's work aims at bringing to attention a violent event that has taken place—of which the body is the concrete proof—but that is nevertheless experienced as inexplicable in its context. Given the current general awareness of trauma, it is surprising that so far scholarly literature has not studied detective fiction from this perspective. What strengthens this link between the detective plot and the manifold issues raised by trauma is the fact that this plot structure plays a major role in contemporary non-detective novels as well. In such works as Kazuo Ishiguro's *When We Were Orphans* (2000), Ian McEwan's *Atonement* (2001), and Michael Ondaatje's *Anil's Ghost* (2000) traumatic events compel protagonists to act as accidental or incidental detectives, and the detection plot serves the ends of testimony.

To claim that the detection plot may function as a vehicle of testimony about traumatic events is a potentially problematic claim. By definition, trauma ensues from a dreadful event involving threats to life as well as bodily and psychic integrity. While such an event is taking place, the subject is not able to experience it fully and to integrate it into consciousness. If trauma is a break in the mind's experience of time, then recovery necessitates the translation of that break into narrative memory, understood as the ability to construct mental schemas that make sense of experience (Kacandes 91). The process during which a traumatized person narrates traumatic events is called witnessing or giving testimony. Because the event defies her cognitive and emotional capacities, narration often falters. Literary scholars of trauma fiction agree that representing trauma and giving testimony place specific requirements on literary expression. Anne Whitehead, for example, observes that narrating traumatic experiences demands a literary form which departs from a conventional linear sequence. She maintains that the impact of trauma "can only adequately be represented by mimicking its forms and symptoms, so that temporality and chronology collapse, and narratives are characterized by repetition and indirection" (3). Thus literary techniques ought to reflect the effects of trauma. In this view, traumatic experiences are neither knowable through traditional frameworks of knowledge nor can they be represented by conventional historical, cultural, and autobiographical narratives (83).

In this context the detective plot may appear unsuitable, even inappropriate, for giving testimony, because it relies on the shapeliness, unity, and cohesion familiar from the nineteenth-century realist literary tradition. This plot is committed to ordering facts so as to produce an explanation in the form of a coherent narrative. In so doing, it reduces the impossible to the possible, for the process of making understandable is thematically that of the detective plot itself. Yet, as was already pointed out, this genre focuses on crimes that are not only experienced as traumatic but also depicted as such. This obvious similarity suggests that detective and trauma fictions may not be incompatible. One notable parallel, however, is that witnesses and detectives must go over the past: both dig out what is left after in order to reconstruct this past. The witness makes fragments of memory and symptoms yield a narrative about devastating events, while the detective gathers and interprets clues to put together a story about a shattering crime. For both the discovery is about uncovering missing links. Both are committed to a truthful reconstruction of the past, whose importance surpasses the witness.

The novel I discuss in order to show how one contemporary author relies on the detection plot as a structure for giving testimony is Ann-Marie MacDonald's *The Way the Crow Flies* (2003). This is an expansive novel with multiple generic ties: it is first and foremost a historical and psychological novel but has elements of the murder mystery and spy story. The events it recounts—sexual abuse at school, the murder of a girl, and buried wartime crimes surfacing in Ontario, Canada—defy the cognitive and emotional capacities of Madeleine McCarthy, its nine-year-old protagonist. While the novel's first parts deal with the build-up leading to murder and its aftermath, its last parts trace the adult Madeleine's reconstruction of the past. What gives special weight to MacDonald's book is that it was inspired by the so-called Truscott case. An adolescent called Steven Truscott was sentenced in 1959 in Ontario, for having allegedly raped and killed his classmate, a verdict that was later pronounced a miscarriage of justice. Thus MacDonald's novel invites readers to consider how a fictional work may testify to a real-life murder case. Moreover, as Susanne Luhmann points out, it has other significant ties to Canadian history: most notably, it refers to the Holocaust and its resonances in post-war Canada, the cruel treatment of Aboriginal children, and the silence surrounding childhood sexual abuse prior to the 1970s (93). By engaging with a host of difficult issues, argues Luhmann, MacDonald offers a trenchant critique of the dire consequences of national blindness to and forgetting of trauma-inducing historical events (91).

The detection plot relies on a specific structure of communication between authors and readers: authors deviously hide clues in their texts while readers try to make sense of them in order to put together a solution. In this process the figure of the detective serves as both a help and hindrance: in "reading" clues the detective exemplifies the reader's role, yet the author often uses this figure as one means of obfuscation. As regards the testimonial function of the genre, the detective serves a similar exemplary function: this character illustrates the witness's role for readers. Given that the job involves encounters with trauma, the detective may be designated as a professional witness. Such a role calls for a commitment to the truth and technical neutrality, but these qualities are not the same as moral neutrality (Herman 135). Also this function of the detective as a professional witness is submitted to the author's communication with readers about traumatic experiences in the narrative world. Part of the readers' task is to evaluate how the detective functions in the role of witness. In order to probe the intersection of detection and testimonial plots, I will focus on the multi-layered rhetorical transactions in MacDonald's novel. This perspective addresses the ways in which the implied author, on the one hand, and the narrator, on the other hand, invite their respective audiences to serve as detectives and witnesses. More specifically, it entails probing the relationship between the narrator and the narrative audience or the observer position readers are encouraged to assume within the narrative world as well as the relationship between the implied author and the authorial audience or the author's ideal reader from the dual viewpoints of detection and witnessing (Phelan 2004, 631–2). In engaging the reader's intellect, psyche, emotions, and ethical values, these transactions provide a fruitful context in which to explore these acts in MacDonald's book.

The narrative audience as detectives and witnesses

The Way the Crow Flies is set for the most part in the year 1962–3 in Centralia, a fictional military training camp in Southern Ontario. It inter-weaves three separate series of events so that eventually they form a tragic whole. One plot line concerns Madeleine McCarthy whom her teacher, Mr March, orders to stay in an after-school "exercise club" during which he sexually assaults its members. This crime turns Madeleine into a child-detective who desperately tries to understand what is happening to her and why. The second series of events deals with Madeleine's father, Wing Commander Jack McCarthy. He agrees to help First Secretary Simon Crawford, a former British squadron leader who taught Jack to fly. Simon's request concerns a secret British–American operation to help a rocket scientist defect from behind the Iron Curtain and hide him in Canada before transferring him to the United States. Without authorization to act in this operation, Jack's participation is a military offense. The murder of a schoolgirl forms the third plot line that welds the other two plot lines together. Unbeknownst to each other, Madeleine and Jack happen to see the victim just before she disappears; thus, the murder investigation concerns them both, although in a different manner.

The novel opens with a fragment headed by a picture of a crow in flight. The first sentence reads "The birds saw the murder" after which the book's narrator supplies scant information about the location. The fragment sets a tone of confidentiality between the book's third-person narrator and the narrative audience (the observer role actual readers are encouraged to take). This narrator is located above and outside the events of the narrative world; she focalizes events from multiple perspectives and has access to the consciousnesses of various characters.[1] This type of a narrator shares a lot of crucial information with the narrative audience, creating a sense of real intimacy and trust.

Of all the birds present at the murder scene only the crows show interest in the event, thanks to the victim's glinting bracelet. The narrator establishes from the start a specific task for the narrative audience by assigning them a double role: they are the only human witnesses of the murder scene, and they are also placed simultaneously in the detective's position by being invited to investigate this event. The opening is thus an instance of the peculiar temporality of the detective plot, for it reveals what Robert Champigny calls its "what will have happened" motivation: the detective cannot stop the murderer because the murder has already occurred (13–14). Thus the narrator asks the narrative audience to scan the ensuing story about the life of the McCarthy family for clues in order to elaborate the murder story which they know will take place at some point. What is more, the literally bird's eye view of the opening fragment specifies the textual level as that on which not only detection but also witnessing primarily takes place. As only the narrative audience is privy to these fragments, they belong to what Irene Kacandes calls the circuit of textual witnessing as the level where communication about trauma happens. This circuit addresses the novel's discourse, and it involves the narrator's transmission of the characters' traumatic experience to the narrative audience (97, 111). The specificity of MacDonald's novel lies in the way it combines detection and witnessing at the textual level, and I will now take a closer look at how this is done.

The teacher's abuse of his pupils and the narrator's strategic placement of the fragments elaborating the murder story make it seem reasonable for the narrative audience to link these two events together and conjecture that the as yet unidentified victim is one of the schoolgirls. For a while the audience fears it is Madeleine herself, until they learn that it is Claire McCarroll, a schoolmate. Likewise, the teacher seems a good candidate for the perpetrator. But the narrator asks the narrative audience to play detective in another sense as well. Ignorant of sexual matters, Madeleine has no conceptual context that would enable her to explain what is happening to her. The most she can do is contrast Mr March's interpretation—that she is a distracted student in need of special attention—with her sense of uneasiness and shame, which convince her that she is being mistreated. By drawing attention to the young victims' inability to get a handle on this traumatic event, the narrator underlines a key similarity between detectives and witnesses: both must name and classify events as well as assessing what role characters play in them. Both sort out various conceptual frameworks—or, try to devise such frames of reference—that would explain traumatic events, and the narrative audience must do likewise. In this instance they have no difficulty in naming Mr March's actions as sexual abuse as well as assigning him the role of perpetrator and the girls the role of victim. By confiding in the narrative audience the narrator makes sure they understand much more than the characters about the events.[2]

At this stage no one other than the members of the "exercise club" knows about the abuse in the narrative world. The picture of a crow heading each new fragment of the murder story reminds the narrative audience that the community has not properly witnessed the event. Witnessing and detection take place solely at the textual level between the narrator and the narrative audience. Thus the audience is the only witness not only to the murder but also to the suffering of the schoolgirls. The narrator's confidentiality draws the audience's attention to the traumatizing effects of sexual abuse. A particularly harmful consequence is the fact that the abuse destroys a child's ability to serve as an intrapsychic witness, that is, to create an internal interlocutor with whom to review painful events. Without this psychic structure no one can begin to mend a wounded psyche (Kacandes 99, 101). The narrator also shows how Mr March's intimidation of the girls turns the abuse into such a compelling secret that they keep it hidden even from themselves. They are bound in a common belief in being an elected group united by muteness (see Felman 229).

In order to illustrate to the audience how a traumatic event disrupts the normal flow of time, the narrator frequently uses the present tense, as the following excerpt from a scene after Mr March has penetrated Madeleine illustrates:

> Right now [Madeleine] is more worried that her head may not return to normal size. The moment she left the school, it began to swell and expand until it became huge, like the grey cloud that has become the sky this afternoon. If she closes her eyes she can feel herself growing impossibly tall and weightless, her head ballooning up up and away, her feet far below and tiny on the ground in their scuffed Mary Janes. (233)

Throughout the narrator makes the narrative audience aware of the formation of traumatic symptoms and the way they take on a life of their own. The abuse overwhelms Madeleine, leading to a state of altered consciousness characterized by emotional detachment and sensations of bodily fragmentation. Although she tries to split off these painful experiences, they nevertheless live on in an abnormal form of memory, which keeps breaking spontaneously into consciousness. For example, Madeleine has crying fits, is bewildered by explicitly sexual thoughts invading her mind (321), and compulsively smells her hands (281, 292, 662). Thus by inviting the narrative audience to probe the crime, the narrator also makes them explore the formation of trauma. The narrator's frequent use of the present tense intensifies the depiction of scenes of trauma. It immerses the narrative audience into whatever is narrated be it an event, a perception, an attitude, or a belief. This strategy encourages audience participation, instead of, for example, observing and judging, by fostering a sense of deeper understanding of what is revealed (see Phelan 635).[3]

The centrality of the textual circuit of witnessing is strengthened by the narrator's account of Madeleine's failed attempts at interpersonal witnessing, that is, at finding another person with whom she could share her painful experiences (Kacandes 105). As is to be expected, she turns to her parents for help. Neither Mimi nor Jack is tuned to hear Madeleine. They want to spare their children from all unpleasant things in life. "Think nice thoughts," is their motto, which convinces Madeleine of their innocence.[4] Confiding in them seems a violation of their outlook on life: "Games where you are trapped between [Mr March's] knees are not good. Her father is too innocent to know it's a bad game. Dad doesn't know what could happen ... Madeleine presses her back against the good bark and cries with her forehead on her knees. The tree hears her. *Poor Dad. Poor Dad*" (197). A gross crime continues unnoticed by the community, and the narrator underlines the smarting nature of its blindness. Having fought in the Second World War, the military personnel could be expected to know that horrible things can happen in unlikely places committed by improbable persons. That they never even consider this possibility, the narrator suggests, demonstrates how the relief at the war's end immediately led to a denial and determined forgetfulness of its horrors. The community views the military and political victory as sufficient, and in not wanting to know about the witnesses and victims of genocide, it refuses to be on their side. "The Allies," writes Felman, "[were] involved in making history by not looking at it, and in particular, by overlooking hell" (191). Luhmann argues that two distinct strategies shape the community's response to the traumatic past: Mimi exemplifies the effort to ignore trauma and to focus optimistically on the present and the future, while Jack illustrates the attempt to master trauma through historical knowledge. He, however, understands history, including the Nazi terror, as something cut off from the present—it exists solely in the past (95–6). MacDonald's narrator elaborates this blindness by linking it with the post-war ideological climate of the Cold War: the adults ascribe the cruelties of war and the human propensity for evil to the Nazis and the Communists, while they hold the West as the champion of democracy and decency. This ascription involves breaking former ties and forging new ones: (West) Germany, the former enemy, is now a partner in the fight against the former ally, the Soviet Union. The Centralia community wholeheartedly subscribes to this post-war ideology of the Cold War, a conviction that leads to complacency with tragic consequences. The implication is that the refusal to deal with wartime crimes is intimately connected with the communal blindness to crimes in its midst.

The confidentiality between the narrator and the narrative audience is enhanced by the novel's subplot dealing with Jack's participation in the covert operation to bring a rocket scientist to the West. This subplot engages the narrative audience in further detective work, because parts of it are told through a series of expanding narrative fragments. This time each fragment is headed by a picture of a mountain; the pieces are parts of a fairy tale about a treasure buried within. While this tale delves much further back in time than the murder story, it too deals with a crime, for the audience learns from the start that slaves are digging up the treasure (120). Again, the narrator confides in the narrative audience over the characters' heads by linking the fairy tale fragments with the Nazi rocket program and, through this link, to the defector. The mountain with its treasure serves as another reminder of the post-war reluctance of the Allies to witness to the Holocaust.[5] As regards detection, the main and subplots position the narrative audience in the same way, but they diverge when it comes to witnessing. The former subplot records Madeleine's traumatization, while the latter tracks Jack's moral downfall. The narrative audience follows how Jack's credulity, uncritical admiration of his mentor, and a naive belief in Western Cold War propaganda suck him into events over which he has little control. To this list must be added his view of the past as cut off from the present; consequently, he cannot even envision that the past could encroach upon the present in the form, for example, of a war criminal trying to evade discovery (Luhmann 97). Jack believes he is acting for the cause of the West, helping the free world to win both the arms race and the race to the moon. The narrator's openness about Jack's involvement and the contemporary audience's general knowledge of Nazi history make them privy to Jack's mistaken assumptions: he thinks the defector is a committed scientist, grateful for being freed from Soviet oppression, whereas to the narrative audience his German name (Oskar Fried) betrays his nationality, suggesting his sinister role in the war.[6] The narrator's gradual elaboration of the fairy tale contextualizes Jack's convictions and actions, showing the narrative audience the larger picture that Jack refuses to know. The exploitation of natural resources and the crimes against humanity committed during the manufacture of the rockets place the Cold War race for space in a horrifying light. With the fairy tale material the narrator ensures that the narrative audience perceives the cynical callousness of the West in using Nazi scientists and their know-how in this race.

We are now in a position to ponder the reasons for the narrator's welding together the acts of detection and witnessing at the textual level before and after the discovery of Claire's murder. As was already mentioned, the narrative audience assumes the role of detective from the first, for no one in the narrative world appears either to know of or to care about the depicted crimes. Donning the detective's garb affects the narrative audience's role as witnesses. It not only creates empathy and solidarity with the young victims whose vulnerability and loneliness are underlined but also engenders a sense of troubled uneasiness, thanks to the collective evasion of the legacy of the Second World War. Consequently, this double perspective enables the narrative audience to perceive that personal traumas may be intimately linked with national traumas. As Luhmann observes, one of this novel's merits is that it illustrates the intertwining of family and state histories (93). Further, by placing this audience on a par with the crows, the narrator makes them aware that they cannot overstep the barrier separating the textual level from the narrative world. The crows can dive down to tug at the victim's bracelet, but the audience has no chance of intervention. This setup leads to profound and frustrated helplessness which strengthens the deeply tragic nature of the events. Once the victim is identified and the investigation begins in the narrative world, the narrative audience's burden as detectives and witnesses grows even heavier. They know of the innocence of the accused teenager, Rick Froelich, but must powerlessly look on to see an ever widening circle of trauma when the whole Froelich family is sucked into, and maimed by, the events.[7] Now the subplot is braided with the main plot: one of the connecting links is Henry Froelich, Rick's stepfather. Henry accidentally bumps into the defector Oskar Fried, identifying him as a former vicious warden at Dora, an underground work camp for the manufacture of rockets, where Henry slaved during the war. Unsuccessful in harming Froelich then, Fried now unwittingly destroys him through Jack's thoughtless actions.

The narrator uses the narrative audience's sense of helplessness in the face of human suffering and gross injustice to create yet another function for intertwining detection and testimony. Investigating crimes and being privy to suffering prompt the audience to consider whether there is anything they can do. No one in the narrative world acts on behalf of the abused girls. No one confesses to any of the crimes. No one cares about the unprecedented agony during the war. The narrator uses this impossible situation to suggest that the narrative audience assume responsibility. Given the impossibility of intervention, the narrative audience is invited to commit itself to the truth. In this situation knowledge of the truth emerges as the only available means of ensuring that at least some justice is done to the victims. Consequently, the narrative audience attempts to achieve a careful reconstruction of the events and a realistic judgment of guilt and moral responsibility. This commitment underlines truth as a value in and for itself. Simultaneously it reminds the audience of the fact that no other work—healing, for example—can be undertaken unless historical reality is reconstructed to fit what really took place and this reconstruction is (re)affirmed. Detection and witnessing are bound together by the narrative audience's search for the truth.

The narrative audience as failed detectives and witnesses

The novel's two final parts take place 20 years after the tragedies at Centralia. They change the narrative audience's role and in so doing compel real-life readers to reconsider the narrator's invitation to act the role of detective and witness while reading. Another way of putting this idea is to say that we are reminded of the fact that narrative transactions take place at two levels: the narrator–narrative audience relationship is framed by the implied author's relationship to the authorial audience. To recapitulate, the implied author posits a hypothetical authorial audience who discerns a text's intended force (Phelan 1996, 147). The readjustment called upon by the implied author makes us realize that the novel's exceptionally powerful narrator has enticed us to enter so deeply into the narrative audience position that we have failed to maintain our simultaneous participation in the authorial audience. The novel's concluding parts, as we shall see, show us that there is a significant gap between the narrator's assumptions about her audience and the author's assumptions about hers. When the reading experience is viewed from the perspective of the authorial audience, we must reconsider our understanding of the narrative audience's role. I now reflect on what is at stake in this readjustment.

Twenty years later panic attacks compel the adult Madeleine to seek a therapist's help. The narrative audience now follows a process of witnessing in the narrated world: in the therapist Madeleine finally finds an interpersonal witness who helps her to give testimony to herself about past trauma. While reconstructing the past, Madeleine engages actively in detection work. Besides probing her memories, she consults the transcripts of Rick Froelich's court hearings. Her detection yields the same conclusion as the narrative audience's—the teacher is the murderer. A phone call to the police officer in charge of the murder investigation reveals, however, that Mr March had an unshakable alibi. By carefully reconsidering the evidence, Madeleine concludes that Claire was murdered by two classmates, Grace and Marjorie, who were among the girls Mr March abused. This realization is followed by the last fragment dealing with the murder, only this time the event is told in full and it corroborates Madeleine's conclusion.

Knowledge of the correct solution compels us to review how we have acted as detectives and witnesses while assuming the position of the narrative audience. This assessment in itself joins us with the authorial audience. Reviewing the narrative in hindsight, we perceive that the narrator has actually given us all the needed clues to arrive independently at the solution. In a typical detective story-like manner, these clues have been shown to us inconspicuously, separately, and disconnectedly. Joining the authorial audience makes us as members of the narrative audience perceive that the narrator has purposefully encouraged immersion as well as fostering the sweeping emotional force of her narration in order to make the narrative audience overlook these clues. Joining the authorial audience makes us realize that, as members of the narrative audience, we have acted poorly as detectives. We have let our advantages in knowledge and the narrator's confidentiality create in us a sense of superiority that has blunted our alertness and critical capacities. In hindsight we perceive the many instances when acting as detectives has enticed us to jump into hasty conclusions. The odious Mr March and his disgusting tactics of intimidation and bribery have made us overlook such telling clues as the butterfly pattern of Claire's underwear that links with Grace's beautiful drawing of butterflies as well as the missing streamer on Claire's bike that later adorns Grace's bike, to mention just two key clues. Assuming the authorial audience's perspective reduces our self-satisfied smugness that we have enjoyed as members of the narrative audience.

The solution of the crime adheres to generic conventions of the detective narrative according to which the more surprising and shocking the solution, the better. To be sure, when the story of Claire's murder is finally told in full, the narrative and authorial audiences are profoundly shaken. The possibility of considering the two girls as murderers has not entered the narrative audience's mind. The authorial audience perceives that the murder is the culmination of parental neglect, ongoing abuse, jealousy, envy, and an attempt to deal with trauma by acting out, to name its most obvious motivating factors. The final fragment shows that, in fact, Mr March is the murderer in a roundabout way, because Grace and Marjorie impersonate him while intimidating, raping, and finally strangling Claire. Their inability to act as intrapsychic witnesses shows in the fact that it takes them awhile even to understand that they have killed their classmate: it has all been a repetitive acting out of what goes on in class after school.

The implied author does not aim at cheap shock effects, however, but uses the detection plot to throw the difficulties involved in the act of witnessing into sharper relief. In light of the solution we must admit that, as members of the narrative audience, we have not been good witnesses. In reviewing the court transcripts Madeleine wonders "Why was there no one to hear [the children]?" (761) and in assessing our reception of the narrative we must pose this question to ourselves. In so doing we realize that, as members of the narrative audience, we have fallen into some of the typical hazards of witnessing. Dori Laub lists among such dangers foreclosure through facts and listeners who know it all in advance (73). To this list may be added feelings of impatience with, even anger at, the schoolgirls for not telling about the abuse. We recognize that we have made hasty conclusions about the victims without really seeing and hearing them. There are, for example, indications of internal strife among the "exercise club." Before Claire's murder Grace and Marjorie team up; they act aggressively toward others, once even giving Madeleine a beating. Had we joined the authorial audience earlier on, we would have been able to compare two different coping strategies adopted by the traumatized girls. Madeleine falls back on her strong sense of humor and her acting abilities which enable her to survive the abuse. She even impersonates a figure of a golfing clown, modeled after Mr March. This figure later evolves into Maurice, one among the stand-up comic roles that make the adult Madeleine famous. In addition, she has a good home with caring parents. In contrast, Grace is the class reject, and no one wants to befriend Marjorie, an infuriating busybody and know-it-all. Both suffer from gross parental neglect. The violence they resort to even before the murder is evidence that they have no psychic resources with which to deal with the intolerable situation: they can only repeat what has been done to them. The awareness of having partially failed in the roles of detective and witness places readers alongside the blind community. Being a witness is not a matter of mastery, but of willingness to listen and keep oneself in the background. It requires from the witness openness to another and sensitivity. These characteristics apply to witnessing in the legal context as well, because giving testimony about traumatic incidents always calls for psychic investment of the witness.

This shift from being an informed witness to a fallible one is one of the didactic points the novel's implied author aims at by creating a narrator who immerses the narrative audience in the narrative world, making them forget the authorial audience's role. This lesson prompts the authorial audience to consider the extent of their knowledge as members of the narrative audience. It would be wrong to say that the narrative audience's actions as detectives and witnesses have been wholly misplaced. Much of what they have achieved is valid and valuable. Rather, the point is the challenging difficulty of seeing the whole picture: all the details, foci, and facts that comprise a human situation. As I understand it, the novel's implied author not only underlines the fact that detection and witnessing are demanding tasks, but also exhorts the authorial audience to look beyond the novel's confines and consider their own contexts. If we have been blind while reading a book, the details of which are nevertheless the result of an author's careful design, what are we blind to in our indefinable daily lives? Is there bitter heartache, even irreparable tragedy, brooding at our doorstep of which we—like the Centralia community—are unaware or even willfully ignorant?

This chastising of the narrative audience close to the novel's ending explicitly invites us to join the authorial audience. Hence in the last proper chapter, titled "My Huckleberry Friend," Madeleine (re)assumes the lead as an exemplary detective-witness. Madeleine has now reconstructed the traumatic past: she was abused by her teacher; Grace and Marjorie killed Claire, and her beloved father, participating in a shady political operation, helped convict an innocent boy of Claire's murder, by not verifying his alibi, although he was the only one who could have done so. Jack's moral cowardice led to Henry Froelich's murder, as Jack confided in Simon Crawford the fact that it was Henry who had recognized Oskar Fried as a war criminal. Crawford then ordered Henry's murder. As the only one cognizant of what happened 20 years ago, Madeleine's detective work has given her a position no one else in the narrative world holds. The authorial audience follows closely her actions, for having failed previously we are awakened to the difficulties of detection and witnessing. I shall now detail how Madeleine handles these tasks, and in so doing, I shall pay special attention to her commitment to the truth, comparing it to the way in which we as members of the narrative audience performed this pledge.

Judith Lewis Herman explains that reconstructing the trauma story always involves a systematic review of its meaning not only to the survivor but also to the important people in her life. Such an assessment rests on the survivor's understanding of the truth: it includes her inner experience of what happened and why as well as her examination of the moral questions dealing with guilt and responsibility. This inner experience may not always tally point for point with the facts, for the reconstruction of the traumatic event is invariably inflected by the survivor's interpretation of its significance for him or her. Going over the past enables Madeleine for the first time to assess where the blame lies. She concludes that Mr March alone was responsible for the abuse; it had nothing whatsoever to do with the girls' characteristics or abilities, for, to begin with, they were a miscellaneous group. Also, he looms large in Claire's murder. This realization enables Madeleine to deal with the fact of her own survival. Cathy Caruth observes that traumatic events are unbearable in two ways: because they are intolerable as experiences, living through them is excruciating for the survivor (7–8, 64). One significant effect of reconstructing the past is that it allows the survivor to claim her survival as uniquely that of her own. Madeleine has felt guilty for having lived through her childhood, while Claire did not. Although Claire's fate partly overlaps with hers, knowledge of her death enables Madeleine to differentiate herself from Claire: she knows she would have fought back Grace and Marjorie.

Dealing with the past compels Madeleine to readjust her notions about her father, a task that involves moral assessment. The man whom she believed to be a stalwart embodiment of morality is revealed to be a coward who trusted that his daughter's court testimony would release him from the obligation of telling the truth. Madeleine's evaluation is blunt: "He's a criminal" (740), yet she forgives him. While forgiveness does not extend to Mr March or Simon Crawford, her understanding reaches her fellow victims, Grace and Marjorie. Upon pondering the court transcripts she perceives that their testimony was about the teacher's abuse, but the girls lay the blame on Rick in order to cover their own tracks. Madeleine's musings invite the authorial audience to ponder the extent to which a neglected 9-year-old, mishandled at home and at school, is able to take responsibility for her actions.

Madeleine's evaluation invites the authorial audience to compare her reconstruction of the past and her choices with those of a fictional detective. The subgenres of detective fiction vary as regards to the degree to which a detective's solution tallies with the truth. Classical detective fiction, for instance, represents this solution as a faithful rendition of the truth, while the hard-boiled variant acknowledges that the solution is always colored by the sleuth's interpretation. Moreover, having solved the crime, fictional detectives decide what is to be done. In principle, they ought to place the case in the hands of the legal authorities. Yet such a move does not always take place, even if the protagonist is an official representative of the law. The genre leaves ample room for a detective's private moral assessment and individual choices about modes of action. In contrast, although in mainstream non-detective fiction the accidental or incidental detectives such as Madeleine have engaged in detection, they are not detectives. Their decisions rest primarily on their status as survivors, who need to decide whether to take action as regards the injustice they have suffered. Ideally, reporting such crimes as sexual abuse and rape leads to legal intervention and social restitution. In reality, as Herman observes, survivors encounter a legal system that may be indifferent or even hostile to them (165). Madeleine resolves to engage in three kinds of action. First, she reports the abuse to the police, but Mr March is dead and thus beyond the reach of the law. Moreover, the retired police investigator who was in charge of the case is no longer interested. Second, Madeleine confides in her mother about the abuse and is gratified by the mother's empathetic response. Finally, she tries to locate Grace and Marjorie, learning that Grace has gone missing for almost 20 years, while Marjorie refuses to talk to her. Although Madeleine's attempts to try to effect a public reinvestigation do not turn out as she wished, taking action is in itself important, because it confirms the ethical beliefs and values she holds dear—including her reverence for the truth. Such action helps her to reclaim herself, that is, to rebuild a faithful notion of who she really is.

With no chance of obtaining restitution from the legal system, yet in possession of the solution, Madeleine acts like a conventional detective by contacting the persons whom the crime still addresses, Ricky Froelich and his sister, Colleen. The book's last chapter resembles the final conference with the suspects, familiar from detective stories. In a detective-like fashion, Madeleine's task concerns both pointing out the criminal and lifting the shadow of doubt from the wrongly suspected. In this instance, the latter mission involves verifying the scapegoat's innocence. Madeleine accosts the Froelich siblings as a detective-witness, as the following excerpt illustrates:

[Madeleine] "I've brought you something."
[Colleen] "What?"

Something that belongs to you.
Neither has moved. As though each is waiting for the other to jump from the teeter-totter.
A story.
Madeleine goes to her car and reaches into the back seat.
What remains?
Story. Yours, or one like it, in which, as in a pool, you might recognize yourself.
...
Madeleine holds up her father's air force hat.
Memory breeds memory. The very air is made of memory. Memory falls in the rain. You drink memory. In winter you make snow angels out of memory.
So much remains.
One witness.

Tell. (804)

By far, the most important decision Madeleine makes is to contact the falsely convicted Rick in order to acquaint him with her reconstruction of the past. Madeleine's situation as the sole person in possession of this story literally demonstrates Felman's characterization of the witness's appointment as something from which she cannot free herself by any delegation, substitution, or representation. This situation makes the witness's burden an inherently solitary one (3).

With Madeleine's decision the implied author explicitly revisits the notion of truth as a value in and for itself. This notion is elaborated by showing its concrete meaning for the survivors. Telling the truth has restorative power, for, as Herman points out, in the telling the trauma story becomes testimony. Knowledge of the truth makes past trauma more present and real by confirming and verifying not only the events as they happened but also the victim's experience of them (181). If the traumatized person is the victim of violence or injustice, the perpetrator takes care to refute or crush his or her experience of the event. With the truth the perspective shifts to the events as the survivors know them, restoring thereby their dignity. Herman explains that truthful telling has the ritual power of healing with a private dimension, which is confessional and spiritual, and a public aspect, which is political and judicial (181). In this particular instance, however, whatever healing takes place in the narrative world happens in the private realm. Hence as the testimonial telling of the truth reinforces the values and beliefs that are generally held vital in any human community, it does so primarily within the small circle that has unwaveringly held on to the truth, the Froelichs and Madeleine.

While the last chapter evokes the context of the detective narrative, it also surpasses its generic conventions. In confronting the suspects, detectives have their official standing as their insulating backing. Be they private detectives or members of the police, they act in the institutional role of an investigator. It is in this (semi-)official capacity that they make decisions. Madeleine, in contrast, lays herself on the line, an act that makes the authorial audience aware of her courage. As a child, she stuck to the truth in court, although her father and Colleen were hoping she would provide Rick with an alibi. As an adult, she prizes the truth, although, given the past events, she cannot expect Rick and Colleen to receive her favorably. In telling the truth she confirms Rick's innocence, but her account assigns heavy blame to Jack whom the Froelichs have held as their staunch supporter. When she contacts the siblings, Madeleine has no way of knowing how her narrative will be received. She relies on the value of truth and the experience of its redeeming power to guide her. Her action demonstrates Felman's observation about witnessing as an act that breaks the confines of the witness's loneliness, thanks to the fact that the witness accepts the appointment to speak for and to others. Consequently, the witness's speech transcends her, conveying her and her hearers to a reality beyond the witness (3). In this sense, witnessing is taking responsibility for the truth of the events. Thus it goes beyond the personal and has general (nonpersonal) validity and consequences (Felman 204).

Madeleine's unwaveringly courageous detection and witnessing invite the authorial audience to reconsider their performance in these roles as members of the narrative audience. To be sure, what differentiates both the narrative and authorial audiences from the protagonist is that the latter functions as an intra- and interpersonal witness, while the former can only act as textual witnesses. This dissimilarity in status, however, is not what is at stake. A forceful effect of the novel's conclusion is to emphasize the fact that readers can never be witnesses in the same sense as characters. Such an erroneous assumption accounts for the narrative audience's misfired attempt to serve as witnesses to the suffering depicted in the novel. While immersion in the narrative world enables us to get a powerful feel of the effects of trauma, that trauma is not ours, even if we may have had similar experiences. It belongs to the characters, while our contribution pertains to the level of reading—in engaging with the novel as a textual and narrative artifact. Kacandes reminds us of this fact in bringing forth the crucial differences between witnessing in a therapeutic setting, for example, and in literature. The role of readers is to respond to literature as texts-as-statements, which means that reader-witnesses must always engage with the various representational strategies of literature (98). The social dimension of trauma fiction emerges only by considering its mediated character, an aspect to which we now turn.

Reading as witnessing

The copy of *The Way the Crow Flies* that I have at my disposal is a paperback with "exclusive extras" such as the author's brief interview, an account of what growing up in an air force base is like, and a short account of the Steven Truscott case. The Author's Note begins with this line: "The ordeal of Stephen [sic] Truscott, his spirit and courage, have been a major inspiration in the writing of this book" (819). This section also includes Pierre Burton's poem, "Requiem for a Fourteen-Year-Old" that he wrote six days after Steven Truscott was sentenced to hang. The poem was published on October 5, 1959, in the *Toronto Star*, and it was part of the public outcry against Truscott's death penalty. The sentence was changed into a life imprisonment, and Truscott served ten years before being released.[8] It was only in the year 2007 that Truscott was acquitted of the charges, an apology made by the Attorney General on behalf of the Government of Ontario, and a compensation paid. Published four years before the official acquittal, MacDonald's novel powerfully states the author's belief in Truscott's innocence as well as indicating her conviction that the case was neither properly investigated nor witnessed when it happened. While the novel heavily leans on this case, citing many of its details, it also departs from it in crucial ways. For one thing, the solution MacDonald draws up differs from the widely shared suspicion that a local man, whom many in the community knew to be a pedophile, was the culprit. Further, connecting this case with the plot line concerning the defecting scientist with a criminal record from the war is the author's invention, although it is based on factual evidence of war criminals hiding in North America. It also accords with the fact that the governments of these countries in some cases chose to ignore the documented knowledge of the past of these persons, because their presence was seen as advantageous for various reasons. Finally, through Ricky and Colleen the novel illustrates the prejudices many Aboriginal children had to deal with, whereas the sexual abuse of children was a hushed-up subject for a long time. These links give special weight to the reading experience, observes Luhmann, inviting readers to ponder how ignored and repressed national traumas keep haunting a nation, until people are willing to witness them (97). Yet I believe MacDonald is not only concerned with engaging readers in comparisons between the novel and real life even in its immediate Canadian context. In fact, one of the topics the novel prompts readers to consider is MacDonald's choice to use a real-life murder case and information about former Nazis as "new" Canadians as the foundation for a fictional work. Why is the novel anchored in reality, while it is also an independent work of the imagination? And why does it couch its examination of the past in terms of detection and witnessing?

Such questions as these belong to what Kacandes calls the literary-historical and transhistorical-transcultural circuits of witnessing. The former circuit considers how a text communicates to the actual flesh-and-blood readers of the culture and time in which it was written. Given the recent publication of MacDonald's novel in 2003, contemporary readers approach its witness statement at this circuit. Yet it also evokes the transhistorical-transcultural witnessing that includes the previous circuits. At this circuit readers from a culture other than the one in which a text was written (such as I myself as a Finnish reader) and/or from a later time period cowitness to the trauma articulated in and through the text (Kacandes 116–17). In this case witnessing is initiated by the readers' realization of the absence or insufficiency of literary-historical witnessing. Successful witnessing at this circuit consists partly in learning "what happened" in the sense of noting both the incomplete previous attempts at witnessing and/or the absence of attempts altogether (Kacandes 133). In my view, the novel activates this circuit as well through its references to the historical situation 50 years ago, suggesting that neither the murder case, the legacy of the Second World War, nor the manipulation of Canadian immigration laws by war criminals were properly dealt with at the time of their occurrence. For the sake of simplicity, I discuss both circuits under the most comprehensive transhistorical-transcultural one. These levels address directly the task readers have as witnesses. In Kacandes' account, if readers are to serve as witnesses while reading, this act is enabled by their interpretive response to the text as a witness statement. Thereby readers facilitate the flow of testimony that the characters, text, and author communicate (135).

The novel's focus on crime directs attention to the way testimony is given through its detection plot. I have already demonstrated that the use of this plot structure actively guides both the narrative and authorial audiences, inviting them to take the role of witness.[9] I would now like to consider the impact of the detection plot on the novel's overall design and the wider implications of its use as a vehicle for testimony. In this context there are two specific issues to ponder. First, there is the fragmentary nature of representing clues which eventually yields to a cohesive narrative closure. This issue is directly connected with the tension between the discourses of realism (portraying crimes, the solving process, and characters in life-like terms) and modernism (the fragmentary discourse that shatters temporal continuity) that characterizes the whole genre. Second, we need to consider the patterns of knowledge on which detection and the solution rely. These questions target key issues in studies of trauma fiction, especially the question of whether the depiction of traumatic events requires what Michael Rothberg terms "new regimes of knowledge" (6) and non-traditional representational schemata.

When the detection plot is considered as a vehicle for witnessing, the way an author uses clues enjoys a special standing. Among all the clues, the most significant is, of course, the body, a mark of deadly violence. The murder victim is the annihilated witness whose experience is never directly available to us. The clues point to whatever details are still available of his or her story. Speaking of an author's mode of employment of clues alludes to the specific use to which he or she puts them: clues can either serve as stereotypes or clichés, in which case they simply function as the necessary building blocks in constructing the typical detection plot, or they can be used as *traumatic indexes*, in which case they embed a claim of referring to the real while simultaneously acknowledging that traumatic extremity makes realist representation impossible (Rothberg 106). The concept of a traumatic index is an inherent part of Rothberg's theorizing of what he calls traumatic realism, a representational strategy for portraying historical extremity, in particular the Holocaust. Testimonial narratives include details (akin to clues) that indirectly refer to reality, while at the same time recognizing that this reality cannot be directly accessed and known. In Rothberg's words, such a detail "does not embody the real but evokes it as a felt lack, as the startling impact of that which cannot be known immediately" (104). Yet through its indirect reference, this detail nevertheless insists on its status as an object of knowledge and an effect of the real and, in this way, moves readers toward the site of trauma (103–4). Rothberg explains that the aims of traumatic realism are twofold: it attempts to construct access to a previously unknowable object and to instruct an audience how to approach that object. Thus it is inherently epistemological and pedagogical (103).

As I see it, the clues operate according to the principles of traumatic realism in *The Way the Crow Flies*, and those referring to Claire's body best illustrate this use. The authorial audience learns of her body through fragments dispersed throughout the narrative: first Claire is present as her charm bracelet, then as her hand, her head covered by underpants, her bulging eyes, her body covered by bulrushes, her broken hymen, her stomach contents, and so on. In themselves, these clues are commonplace details of everyday life such as children's jewelry, the butterfly design of underpants, a girl's dress, and the form of the body of a 9-year-old. Yet the violence done to Claire inflicts the clues with extremity, removing them from the reach of the quotidian. To apply Rothberg's notions, these clues are simultaneously held together and kept apart through the unassimilable mixture of the everyday and the extreme. What is more, it is precisely this irreconcilable character of the traumatic index that serves as the call to the authorial audience to take the position of the (surrogate) witness to the trauma in and of the narrative (129–30, 136).[10] It also accounts for the emotional impact the clues have. Because the extreme cannot be fitted to the everyday, this audience is called on to witness to the painful and distressing rift between them. Rothberg describes such witnessing in the following way: "When we try to grab hold of the extreme with language, as in testimony, history or other genres committed to some notion of realism and reference, it slips away, leaving the grounds ghostly empty. When we try to avoid it, it returns, or rather, reveals that it was there all along" (136).

In considering the cohesive force of the detection plot, it is useful to link its role to the patterns of knowledge employed in investigating crimes by characters in the narrative world, on one hand, and by the authorial audience, on the other. In this context, the term refers to the conceptual frameworks employed to make sense of crime as a traumatic event and experience. Studies of trauma fiction claim that highly painful incidents require both new modes of representation and new schemes of knowledge. MacDonald's novel seems not to meet this requirement, if that is what it is. This book relies on widespread contemporary knowledge of sexual abuse and its consequences as well as on current information about the Nazi science programs and the fates of war criminals after the war; it also instructs readers about these issues. The narrator's manipulation of the narrative audience's assumptions, however, is a strategy to prompt the authorial audience to consider not only what characters in the narrative world think they know about the issues the novel deals with and how that knowledge is accessible to them but also how these same questions pertain to the authorial audience. The inquiry into assumptions about sex offenders is a case in point. The authorial audience follows with incredulity the flippancy with which the Centralia community assumes that a responsible, caring, and respected youth may turn into a murderous rapist overnight. This sudden change relies on a scapegoating mechanism according to which anything departing from the mainstream, such as being of Métis origin, evokes suspicion and leads to expulsion from the community. But the spotlight turns equally on the beliefs of the narrative audience, for the implied author ultimately challenges the authorial audience to rethink many notions such as, for example, our beliefs about children and childhood. Is childhood a particularly happy period? What are children capable of, especially if they are mishandled and neglected? Does childhood suffering teach girls to grow up persevering and patient, as traditional girls' books would have it?[11] MacDonald's use of the detection plot reminds us that approaching extreme events and their traumatic consequences is not only a matter of new strategies of representation but also a matter of probing familiar cognitive schemes and adjusting them to fit particular cases. In fact, the detection plot makes at least one contribution to trauma literature and witnessing by using the familiar, the well-known, and that which goes without saying to question our supposed familiarity with such things. It forces readers to re-examine their assumptions, beliefs, and ways of thinking.[12]

The employment of familiar discourses and frameworks of knowledge plays a part in creating narrative cohesion in detective fiction. Another contributing factor is the solution that characteristically ties the narrative fragments together so that they form a unified whole and provide a satisfying sense of closure. Thus all the major details find their place in the plot line; consequently, the mystery is dispelled and explained away. This genre is thus a far remove from trauma fiction which prizes strategies of rupture, fragmentation, deliberate incompleteness, and open endings. In MacDonald's novel, too, the detection plot structure yields a sense of rounded closure: all disparate clues are integrated into the plot, their inter-locking nature is revealed, and all the major mysteries are explained. The objection leveled at this effect of the detection plot stems from its suggestion that traumatic experiences can be thoroughly known, which, in turn, leads to the assumption that trauma may be expelled.[13] I would argue, however, that considering the typical tension between realist and modernist repre-sentational strategies of the detective plot modifies the conclusion made above. First, the plot of *The Way the Crow Flies* builds on such numerous sets of coincidence that they begin to test our credulity. Everything that can go awry, does so; for example, if Oskar Fried had not arrived on a particular day, Jack would have remembered his resolve to see Mr March, and he would have caught the teacher in the act of abuse. Or, if the sun had not glinted in Jack's face, Rick would have been able to recognize him, and consequently, could have identified the key witness to the police. These sets of coincidence as well as the way they interlock remind the authorial audience of the novel's constructed nature: they loudly proclaim its status both as narrative and as fiction. The novel's constructed nature is enhanced by the manifold epitaphs at the beginning of each chapter. Almost without exception they are taken from various sources of the late 1950s and early 1960s such as schoolbooks, women's magazines, popular songs, newspapers, television shows, political speeches, and so on. Not only do they condense the gist of each individual chapter, but they convey wonder-fully a sense of the period. Further, the author's couching of the plot dealing with the history of the Nazi rocket program (and of Oskar Fried's past) in terms of a fairy tale is jarringly incongruous with the subject treated. Thus the tendency of the detection plot to render a realist depiction of events and experiences is at each turn undercut by the novel's multiple representational strategies that bar the authorial audience from viewing the narrative as a simple reflection of reality. The tension between the realist and modernist discourses is crucial to the novel's witness statement, because it keeps in view its anchorage in reality (especially the Truscott case and the post-war legacy), while reminding us of its imaginative, fictional nature. This strategy ensures a probing of the probable reasons behind the crimes while simul-taneously taking care not to usurp the stories of real people and speaking for them.

Even this brief analysis shows that as a narrative structure the detection plot is not in itself incompatible with witnessing and testimony. On the contrary, its basic structure may be made to convey the same kind of unknowability we experience in trauma fiction. Furthermore, some of its emphases parallel those of trauma fiction: identifying and naming events accurately and truthfully—for example, sexual abuse instead of after-school exercises—assessing the distribution of guilt and moral responsibility, and a commitment to truth. Thus the detection plot may invite readers to bear witness to various violent crimes that continue to speak through manifold symptoms in Western societies. As Kacandes points out, though testimony may lack any personal psychotherapeutic healing, there is, nevertheless, a societal benefit to narrative witnessing (135), such as, for example, consciousness raising. Luhmann states that the contribution MacDonald's novel makes is to call on readers to keep the victims' suffering in the (inter) national consciousness. In so doing, it exceeds remembrance strategies such as merely knowing about and memorializing traumatic events. Instead, it asks us to consider how knowledge about these events is passed down to us and what we are doing with it now (98, 102).

The novel ends with a fragment capping the story of Claire's murder: an old air-raid siren in Centralia goes off unexpectedly, after which it is taken out. In the authorial audience's ears the wailing siren sounds like a death bell commemorating all the victims; it is also reminiscent of the perpetually distressed Grace's terrible bawling. The fragment closes with these words:

> Municipal workers from the nearby town of Exeter climb the pole to clear away the nest and remove the siren altogether. Bits of tinfoil, bottle caps, a key glint amid the straw—the shiny things that crows collect. And a tiny silver charm. A name.
>
> *Claire.* (811)

The witnessing crows did come away from the murder scene with a trophy, a charm from Claire's bracelet. The narrative and authorial audiences take the intellectually and emotionally demanding reading experience with them on finishing this novel. This last fragment emphasizes the eulogizing timbre of the narrator's voice. Besides reminding us of the waiting crows in the beginning, the piercing sound of the siren alerts us to the fact that the events of this novel forcibly call upon readers to think about whose suffering we care about, for such allegiance actually defines ourselves and our communities.

Notes

1   In narratological terms, the novel has an extradiegetic-heterodiegetic narrator.

2   Simultaneously the narrator draws attention to a major difference between professional witnesses such as detectives and ordinary people. Detectives know to expect bad things in life: it is part of their job. Hence for them

everyday life is infused with potentially traumatic events. Moreover, these events do not address them as private persons but as professionals. Their traumatic impact concerns the lay characters. Part of this impact derives from the fact that during such experiences everyday life shows its unpredictable and uncontrollable side.

3   A focus on experiencing and participation, observes Phelan, is typical of lyricality. The timbre of MacDonald's narrator's voice may in many places be characterized as lyrical.

4   The mother, Mimi McCarthy, is committed to keeping the children from coming into contact with anything unpleasant. For example, she does not let them watch news about the Cuban missile crisis and hides newspapers dealing with Claire's murder. In spite of her efforts, she nevertheless communicates her anxiety to the children, for whenever she is worried, she starts chain smoking and acting in an irritated manner. Such behavioral traits are one way of passing on an unconscious legacy to children.

5   Another feature connecting the main and subplots is the fairy tale of the "Pied Piper of Hamelin" that the narrator relates to both plots. The use of this fairy tale foregrounds the tragic consequences of communal neglect of children's experiences and needs.

6   The narrative audience sees Jack's slowness to realize that Henry Froelich is a German Jew and a concentration-camp survivor. They cringe on Jack's behalf when he treats Henry as a beer-drinking, sausage-eating German with whom he nevertheless shares war experiences.

7   The Froelich family is hit hard: the innocent Rick is sentenced to prison, where he is repeatedly raped. He is subjected to years of therapy the purpose of which is to force him to own to his crime. He is also used as a guinea pig for new drugs that damage his memory and cause MS. His father, Henry Froelich is murdered by some American government agency that covers up for secret operations. Rick's sister Elizabeth dies of grief some years after Rick's sentencing.

8   Pierre Burton's poem is an example of a testimony taking place at what Kacandes calls the literary-historical circuit of witnessing. In examining this circuit we consider how a text communicates to the actual flesh-and-blood readers of the culture and time in which it was written. Often this is the circuit about which later readers will have the least information (115). Seven years after the poem's publication Isabel Le Bourdais published *The Trial of Steven Truscott* (1966) in which she argued that the police and the justice system had handled the case badly. She cited numerous oversights as well as producing new evidence against the verdict. In March 2000 the television program *the fifth estate* (on CBC) presented the results of the journalist Julian Sher's two-year investigation into the Truscott case. It also included an interview with Truscott. Later on Sher published a book based on his research, *"Until You Are Dead": Steven Truscott's Long Ride into History* (2001). (See http://www.cbc.ca/fifth/truscott/ for further details.) The case has spawned other testimonial accounts as well; for example, the Canadian rock group, Blue Rodeo, made a song titled "Truscott" for their 2000 album

The Days in Between, while Beverly Cooper based her play, *Innocence Lost* (2008), loosely on this case (see http://en.wikipedia.org/wiki/Steven_Truscott).

9   The question of the extent to which the authorial audience's position overlaps with the literary-historical and transhistorical-transcultural circuits is a tricky one. It seems safe to say that the authorial audience's position resides in the literary-historical circuit, because the (implied) author produces his or her text within a specific literary-historical context. But at what point does this circuit change into the next one? Is this simply a temporal question, or does it include, for example, the availability of documents and data about the period in which the text was written? Furthermore, given the belated character of our response to trauma, it is possible that contemporary readers, who are to position themselves as the authorial audience, may not be able to receive a text's testimony, thanks to, for example, a historically exceptional political situation. There are many instances of such works; Kacandes' example is Kolmar's *A Jewish Mother* to which neither author nor original audience was able to bear witness fully. Consequently, it is possible that readers at the transhistorical-transcultural level are the first ones to hear a text's testimonial statement.

10 Does the murdered Claire refer to Lynne Harper, the girl Steven Truscott supposedly strangled? The murder in MacDonald's novel resembles the real-life case, but is not identical with it. The crucial differences between the novel and real life suggest that the novel is not a literary adaptation of the case, but an independent work of art. By writing a novel the author underlines the fact that she does not know the persons involved and will not usurp their experience.

11 See Laura Robinson's excellent article on MacDonald's questioning our assumptions about childhood in her "Remodeling an Old-Fashioned Girl: Troubling Girlhood in Ann-Marie MacDonald's *Fall on Your Knees*" (*Canadian Literature* 2005, Autumn, 186: 30–45).

12 The juxtaposing of crimes in the present with those in the past presents a challenge to the authorial audience, for they have to figure whether these offenses are related. The conclusion is that Mr March's abuse and the consequent murder in no way stem from the aftermath of the Second World War; yet its legacy contributes to communal insensitivity and indifference, thus enabling him to carry on. What is more, the ways in which the past is handled is familiar from the larger cultural context. As Rothberg points out, since the 1990s there has been an intense preoccupation with the "postmemory" of the Holocaust—people haunted by the memories they have inherited from their families and from the culture at large—in North America (181–6). Thus the authorial audience is able to identify relatively easily the book's message of the troubling and far-reaching consequences of our not having come to terms with this legacy. The audience is reminded of our strategies of denial, self-imposed forgetfulness, and outright exploitation of this past. This is not to downplay the seriousness with which the issues are handled, especially, the callously cynical advantage taken of the Nazi science as well as the general deadening effect that the untreated war legacy has on general culture. Rather, the point is that readers are pushed to consider the structures of knowledge with whose help they are handled during reading.

13 Madeleine and Rick Froelich are portrayed in a heroic light—another
emphasis alien to trauma fiction—which suggests that in some crucial
aspects the novel is not quite satisfactory. Rothberg, for instance, observes
that "'deliverance' and 'heroism' are concepts difficult to attribute to most
examples of survivor testimony" (228). Yet it is also true that some people
preserve their moral fiber better than others in the midst of hardship. For
example, many commentators have marveled at Steven Truscott, whose
pleasant character seems not to have been damaged by his ordeal.

Works cited

Caruth, Cathy. *Unclaimed Experience: Trauma, Narrative, and History.*
Baltimore: The Johns Hopkins University Press, 1996.

Champigny, Robert. *What Will Have Happened: A Philosophical and Technical
Essay on the Mystery Story.* Bloomington: Indiana University Press, 1977.

Felman, Shoshana. "Education and Crisis, or the Vicissitudes of Teaching; Camus'
The Plague, or a Monument to Witnessing"; "The Betrayal of the Witness:
Camus' *The Fall*; and "The Return of the Voice: Claude Lansman's *Shoah.*"
In *Testimony: Crises of Witnessing in Literature, Psychoanalysis, and History.*
Shoshana Felman and Dori Laub. New York: Routledge, 1992.

Herman, Judith Lewis. *Trauma and Recovery: From Domestic Abuse to Political
Terror.* Reprinted with a new afterword. London: Pandora, 1998.

Kacandes, Irene. *Talk Fiction: Literature and the Talk Explosion.* Lincoln:
University of Nebraska Press, 2001.

Laub, Dori. "Bearing Witness or the Vicissitudes of Listening." In *Testimony:
Crises of Witnessing in Literature, Psychoanalysis, and History.* Shoshana
Felman and Dori Laub. New York: Routledge, 1992. 57–74.

Luhmann, Susanne. "Ill-Fated Lessons: History, Remembrance, Trauma and
Memory in Ann-Marie MacDonald's *The Way the Crow Flies.*" *Topia:
Canadian Journal of Cultural Studies* 16 (2006): 91–109.

MacDonald, Ann-Marie. *The Way the Crow Flies.* New York: Harper, 2003.

Pelecanos, George. *The Night Gardener.* New York: Back Bay, 2006.

Phelan, James. *Narrative as Rhetoric: Technique, Audiences, Ethics, Ideology.*
Columbus: Ohio State University Press, 1996.

—"Rhetorical Literary Ethics and Lyric Narrative: Robert Frost's 'Home Burial.'"
Poetics Today 25.4 (2004): 627–51.

Rothberg, Michael. *Traumatic Realism: The Demands of Holocaust
Representation.* Minneapolis: University of Minneapolis Press, 2000.

Whitehead, Anne. *Trauma Fiction.* Edinburgh: Edinburgh University Press, 2004.

2

Is *The Savage Detectives* a detective story?

Peter Baker

As Marcela Valdes points out, Roberto Bolaño, in his "Last Interview," said that if he hadn't become a novelist, he would have wanted to be a homicide detective:

> I should like to have been a homicide detective much better than being a writer. I am absolutely sure of that. A string of homicides. I'd have been someone who could come back to the scene of the crime alone, by night, and not be afraid of ghosts. Perhaps then I might really have become crazy. But being a detective, that could easily be resolved with a bullet to the mouth. (Valdes 9; *Interview* 122)

Motifs of detective fiction run throughout his works, some of them more closely approximating the genre than others. His one novel that could be fairly described as a detective novel, *The Skating Rink*, offers a crime and an investigation by police, but ends in unresolved fashion. One source of the lack of resolution is that the novel is narrated by three different characters, one of whom successfully shelters the presumptive killer, and one of whom hears a confession from an entirely different character that may or not be completely plausible. In his last work, his great masterpiece *2666*, the fourth and longest of the five sections is an extended police procedural, or *Reportaje* (cf. Goodman 2010), that lists in excruciating detail more than a hundred mainly unsolved murders of women and girls in the fictional city of Santa Teresa, standing in for the very real series of murders in the 1990s and beyond in Ciudad Juarez. Many of his other short novels and short stories feature investigations, crimes, political violence, to the point where one could plausibly claim that elements of the detective genre haunt his entire collected works. *The Savage Detectives* is a genre-defying work that involves epistemological questions of how one knows anything, various aesthetic investigations, and finally an ethical dilemma that revolves around an unresolved trauma, perhaps the defining trope of Bolaño's fiction.

In *The Savage Detectives* the question of genre is complicated by the structure of the novel itself, with two framing narratives that together form a continuity in what might be called the "present" time of the novel, and a long central section that primarily follows the two protagonists through a series of third-person interviews with people who knew them in the twenty-year period after they return from the desert (at the very end of the frame tale and so of the novel). The two protagonists, Arturo Belano and Ulises Lima, are involved in two detective-like activities. In their role as literary detectives they are attempting to track down the works of an elusive precursor, Cesárea Tinajero, who anticipated their literary movement, "visceral realism," almost fifty years earlier, and eventually to track down the author herself. In the other strain that dominates the end of the first part of the frame tale and the entire second part, Belano and Lima are pursuing their researches in the Sonora Desert in the company of two young people, one of whom, Lupe, is a prostitute attempting to escape from her pimp. Here the "metaphysical" or literary detective thread is constantly threatened by what seems like a bad Mexican gangster movie. How this all plays out in the Sonora Desert of Bolaño's imagination constitutes the unresolved trauma that in a sense the whole central section of the novel circles around, the question being: what happened to the boys in the desert?

The sheer exuberance of the writing and the wildly picaresque mini-narratives in *The Savage Detectives* certainly go a long way in explaining the seductive quality of the narrative. Having taught the novel in an (English) course on post-war world fiction, I can attest that the work holds the attention of a wide variety of students. But it is too simple to say, as Valdes does in her otherwise remarkable "Alone Among the Ghosts," that "*The Savage Detectives*, with its carousing characters, is Bolaño's novel of friendship and adventure" (17). Again, the experience of teaching the novel was instructive to me in that regard. While totally exuberant enjoyment and wild laughter at times characterized the classroom experience during the first few classes, as time went on all the students seemed to share my sense of the deepening dread in the novel, almost akin to free-floating anxiety. The Mexican gangsters are only a part of this sense of threat. One of the main characters, Quim Font, who precipitates the gangster narrative by encouraging young Lupe to leave her pimp, is interviewed throughout the second part of the novel from a series of mental hospitals. One of Ulises's companions in the second part of the novel, an Austrian who narrates his own section, is clearly a mentally-diminished psychopath and almost certainly a murderer. Arturo Belano (a transparent stand-in for the author as he repeatedly attested) has several scrapes involving a knife when he gets himself involved with some bad company. I think it would be fair to characterize Bolaño's overall aesthetic as one that utilizes humor, absurdity and eroticism as a cover for the "traumatic kernel of the Real" in Lacan's sense, the primal trauma that dominates the realm of the Imaginary but can never be reached directly.

Asking questions

"Concepts lead us to make investigations; are the expression of our interest and direct our interest." (Wittgenstein *Philosophical Investigations* I, § 570)

The two main characters of *The Savage Detectives*, the visceral realist poets Ulises Lima and Arturo Belano, provide the main focus for all three parts of the novel. Bolaño's narrative strategy to use a much younger affiliate of the movement, 17-year-old García Madero, as narrator of what I am calling provisionally the frame tale is a brilliant stroke that guarantees Lima's and Belano's activities, beliefs and writings are always viewed from a remove— there will be proximity but never an intimate access to the main characters' thoughts or motivations. What's more, García Madero (he wants to be called by his first name, Juan, like everybody else, but is repeatedly rebuffed (SD 29, 42 *et passim*)) functions as the naïf, what Wallace Stevens called the "ephebe" or the "idiot questioner." Not exactly an investigator (he's too lazy for that) and far from a detective, there are still things he strives to know. The first lines of the novel (the first and last sections are represented as García Madero's dated journal entries) indicate the focus of his inquiry, with Bolaño's trademark humor:

NOVEMBER 2
I've been cordially invited to joint the visceral realists. I accepted, of course. There was no initiation ceremony. It was better that way.

NOVEMBER 3
I'm not really sure what visceral realism is. (SD 3)

This is only the beginning of Bolaño's running joke at the expense of the reader. Of course we want to know what García Madero does, precisely the role of the naïf in the standard detective plot. But unlike the canonical detective sidekick stand-ins for the reader, who eventually learn the answers to their mysteries, we readers of *The Savage Detectives* are never really clued in to what exactly "visceral realism" is. What might be called the epistemological question is broached ... and then left open, or shifted to the realm of aesthetics.

As Stanley Cavell reminds us, there are really two related questions at the root of epistemological inquiry: How do I know what I know? and, How do I know that I know? (*Little Did I Know*). And since epistemology is so often evoked in the literature on detective fiction, I think it might be instructive to dwell for a moment on the words of a professional philosopher. In these related questions, Cavell addresses knowledge as content (what I know) and as process (that I know), moving from a more traditional approach (at least as old as Kant in its classical iteration) to something more like his avowed interest in the later works of Wittgenstein, with their emphasis on knowing, we might say, as opposed to knowledge (cf. Baker 1986, 119–35). What I believe to be important when discussing the relationship of detection to epistemology is that the two operations are, strictly speaking, *analogous*, as when Cavell states:

> The discrepancy between an ordinary case of investigation (as revealed in the case of the detective) and the investigation of the epistemologist does not show the latter to be meaningless; the very fact that his question is analogous (showing exactly a discrepancy) with the detective's case, goes to show that it is (to some unmeasured extent) quite meaningful. (Cavell 363)

As much else in Cavell's discussion goes on to show, he is actually only mildly interested in the traditional questions associated with classical epistemology and much more interested in what so-called "ordinary language" can tell us about how human beings go about understanding the world. And this too finds a parallel with the world of *The Savage Detectives*, for it is never so much a question of what visceral realism is (knowledge as content) as it is the various activities (forms of life, or *lebensformen*) of its practitioners and, of course, much of what they do is talk.

Framed by the two first-person narrative sections, Part II "The Savage Detectives (1976–1996)," presents itself as interview transcripts with multiple people either associated with the visceral realists during their time in Mexico City, or those who encounter them later in their peregrinations, mainly in Europe, but also in North America and Africa. One of the clearest versions of the mystery involved is narrated by Luis Sebastián Rosado (1983), a highly literate, and high-strung, gay writer who is obsessed with his on-again, off-again affair with one of the original visceral realists, Luscious Skin. As Rosado recounts the germ of the story:

> Everything had begun, according to Luscious Skin, with a trip that Lima and his friend Belano took up north, at the beginning of 1976. After that

trip they both went on the run. First they fled to Mexico City together, and then to Europe, separately ... After he'd spent several years in Europe, Lima had returned to Mexico. (SD 327)

I'm deliberately skipping some of the fuller narrative here, to come back to in the final analysis, but the kernel of the story is here: trip to the desert, mysterious events, flight. Rosado then presses Luscious Skin on his source for the story and this is also worth examining:

Then how do you know all this? Who told you this story? Lima? Luscious Skin said no, it was María Font who'd told him (he explained who María Font was), and she'd gotten it from her father. Then he told me that María Font's father was in an insane asylum. Under ordinary circumstances, I would have started to laugh right there, but when Luscious Skin told me that the person who'd started the rumor was a madman, a shiver ran up my spine. And I felt pity too, and I knew I was in love. (SD 327)

So, even in this relatively straightforward account of what happened and what the mystery is, there is the compounding difficulty of a classic unreliable narrator, or even perhaps layers of unreliable narrators. Bolaño also shows his gift for the quick shift of subject and mixing of levels in the last sentence. All of this adds up to a tangled plot that will seek resolution only in the final section.

To the question of *what*—what I know about what happened in the desert—we can also add the question of *who*—in this case not the who of whodunit (that comes later), but who wants to know. Any reader of the long central section of *The Savage Detectives* will inevitably have to ponder the question of who is interviewing these more than 50 people, some of whom are interviewed repeatedly over a span of 20 years. One tantalizing possibility is that the implied interviewer (something like Genette's narratee) is Arturo Belano. Bolaño hints in this direction when one interviewee, Andrés Ramírez (1988), begins his life-narrative (one of the strangest in the whole book, about someone endowed with a weird ability to piece together numbers seen at random on the street into winning soccer lottery numbers) by saying: "I was destined to be a failure, Belano, take my word for it" (SD 360), the only instance in 400 pages of interviews of a named interlocutor. This possibility is also strongly supported by a note Bolaño made that was found among his papers associated with his final novel: "The narrator of 2666 is Arturo Belano" (2666 898). To this seemingly definitive statement, I would add a marginal note I added next to Ramírez's statement above, "Belano [is] the narrator of all my books," but I may have imagined this quote.

Ultimately the question of the narrator's identity is less of a riddle (susceptible to a solution) and more of a puzzle (a structural conundrum), and what is more, a puzzle that cannot be finished, similar to a book with no definitive ending such as the one under examination. I want to suggest that Bolaño's ever-expanding narrative strategy, as well as the ever-proliferating narratives of 2666, may be compared to a work Bolaño clearly admired, Georges Perec's *Life a User's Manual* (Bolaño *Last Interview*, 118). Not only is Perec's story (in Genette's terms the *histoire*, or totality of what happens) centered on a complex puzzle scheme that comes to dominate the lives of the central characters, but the ordering of the book's 99 chapters (Genette's narrative, or the actual order of the text) is presented in an open form that expands exponentially. Or as Perec put it in an interview from 1978, the year the book appeared: "I always imagined this puzzle game as a machine for destroying the novel. Instead I realized to the contrary that it is a machine that makes it proliferate into infinity" (*Entretiens et conferences* I, 261; my trans.). Bolaño was also clearly obsessed with this paradox. In his short story "Dentist" he gives one of his more profound iterations of this idea: "We never stop reading, although every book comes to an end, just as we never stop living, although death is certain" (*Last Evenings* 207). And as the reader of the present piece may have already anticipated, epistemological questions inevitably raise the possibility that the aesthetic realm will raise questions that may call for different kinds of investigation.

Aesthetic inquiry

"My aim is this: to teach you to pass from a piece of disguised nonsense to something that is patent nonsense." (Wittgenstein *Philosophical Investigations* I, § 464)

So if we try to answer the question of what "visceral realism" is, at least part of the answer will lie in the nature of their aesthetic positions, whom do they admire, what are the tenets of their movement, do they have a manifesto, do they run a closed shop and only admit and retain fellow members who share their beliefs? Oddly, or perhaps not, since they are after all "savage," one defining trait of their movement is what they are opposed to. I have it on good authority that Spanish *salvaje* like the French *sauvage* has a greater range of meaning than the English *savage*, which is pretty much limited to the range of fierce and lawless, whereas the former languages admit a range of meanings that includes wild, untrained and closer to nature (I'm particularly thinking of Truffaut's *L'Enfant Sauvage* (1970), usually translated as *The Wild Child*). Belano and Lima are less the fierce and lawless young men engaged in savagery, and more the undertrained and uncouth young men who are always outside the norm and perhaps, like Rimbaud, one of Bolaño's constant touchstones, destined to remain that way. One way they demonstrate that their movement is outside mainstream culture is their constant denigration of that leading man of Mexican letters, Octavio Paz. This reaches such a point that in one of the early meetings between Luis Sebastián Rosado and Luscious Skin, the latter says he has something important to tell him about their plans and the overheated, hypersensitive Rosado imagines the following:

> For a moment, I admit, the idea of a terrorist act passed through my mind. I saw the visceral realists getting ready to kidnap Octavio Paz, I saw them breaking into his house (poor Marie-José, all that broken china), I saw them emerging with Octavio Paz gagged and bound, carried shoulder-high or slung like a rug, I even saw them vanishing into the slums of Netzahualcóyotl in a dilapidated black Cadillac with Octavio Paz bouncing around in the trunk, but I recovered quickly. (SD 155)

So perhaps the two ranges of meaning for our "savage detectives" are equally possible, at least in more sensitive and refined minds.

I want to remain for a moment with the pair of poets, Rimbaud and Octavio Paz. And this is because one of the most salient features of *The Savage Detectives* as a novel is the nearly constant stream of references to an astonishing range of poets from all the major Western traditions. In one interview, Bolaño says, "Basically, I'm interested in Western literature, and I'm fairly familiar with all of it" (*Last Interview* 63). But even more than Bolaño demonstrating his erudition, the near constant flow of poets' names and the discussion of poetry centers the narrative by demonstrating that these wild and uncouth young men actually care deeply about poetry. This, in turn, helps to provide a grounding and a context for the specific act of literary sleuthing that Lima and Belano are engaged in. Before turning to their specific literary sleuthing, I want to make a few comments about Rimbaud and Paz, since in a sense they represent two poles of a Western poetic tradition. What's more, they are the only two poets to be represented by whole poems in the text. That crazy-like-a-fox Bolaño has García Madero "discover" a poem he claims is by someone named Efrén Rebolledo called "The Vampire" ("El vampiro"), a fairly straightforward sonnet in Petrarchan form that provokes the young teenager into a marathon masturbation session (SD 11). Only in the acknowledgments to the English translation do we find that this is a poem by Octavio Paz, interestingly translated by Samuel Beckett (not very well). So, while Bolaño the author is clowning around and slamming Paz every chance he gets, he sneaks in an early and not terribly representative Paz poem. Does he assume his Spanish readers know Paz's œuvre so well that they will spot this relatively obscure early poem? The Rimbaud poem, "Le cœur volé," is recited from memory and in French by Ulises Lima in one of Luis Sebastián Rosado's descriptions of a visceral realist reunion.

Before introducing the poem, Rosado asks his interviewers, or the readers, to guess who the author is ("Éstos eran los versos, a ver si ustedes lo adivinan ..." 155), explicitly playing the literary riddle game. Whereas Paz represents everything Bolaño despises about the literary establishment, Rimbaud becomes something of a template for the character of Arturo Belano, including the last sighting of Belano (1996) disappearing in Africa (SD 517).

From the heights of nineteenth- and twentieth-century poetry, we turn to the extended interview that Belano and Lima conduct with another "writer," Amadeo Salvatierra. Salvatierra is interviewed in January 1976, while "the boys" (as he calls them) are wandering around in the Sonora Desert, so the encounter that he describes had to have preceded (and in some ways motivated) their journey. The interview with Salvatierra (but he repeatedly asks them to call him Amadeo, so I guess I will too) is anomalous among all of the other interviews in the book. While Amadeo is interviewed in 12 of the 26 chapters in the book (the Spanish edition has a helpful list of the interviews as part of the index at the end), he alone among the characters who are interviewed multiple times is interviewed on the same date each time, essentially constituting one long interview divided into 12 parts. Spreading out his interview over the span of nearly 400 pages of text in the book helps heighten the suspense of this literary sleuthing. Because what Ulises and Arturo are here to ask Amadeo is for any help he can give them in identifying Cesárea Tinajero, a putative member of a literary group from nearly 50 years earlier that also bore the name of "visceral realism." At first they ask for any memories Amadeo has of her and then they ask if he has any examples of her works. Memories he has plenty of and his storytelling is consistently marvelous in its meandering, sentimental blend of literary history and emotional investments (especially with regard to Cesárea Tinajero). He himself was a member of her group or circle, but quickly came to realize that his talents in poetry were limited. At the time of the interview he is in his working office where he works as a "writer," in that he writes for hire for people who come in to him for anything from letters to lawyers to love letters to letters to family members. Despite his lowly status, he does however maintain a prodigious archive in addition to his capacious memory.

Before arriving at the archival discovery, Amadeo and the boys down a bottle of "Los Suicidas" mezcal, and at least two additional bottles of tequila. Amadeo in the end is having trouble staying awake, walking, or even focusing on his two young interlocutors. Such is his state when he reveals to them the first issue of the earlier visceral realists' journal, called *Caborca*, with what he says is the only surviving poem by Cesárea Tinajero. When he shows it to them, one of them responds, "Not only was it interesting, he said, he'd already seen it when he was little. How? I said. In a dream, said the boy, I couldn't have been more than seven, and I had a fever" (SD 353). This shocks Amadeo, who reaches out to see it again, and here is what he sees (in my approximate version):

Sión

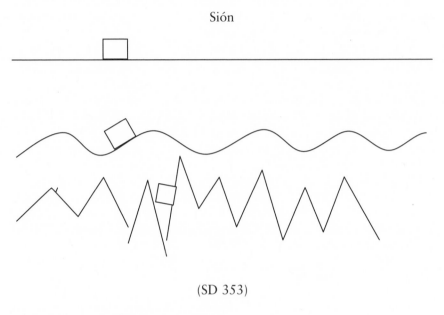

(SD 353)

Then we have the following exchange:

> And I asked the boys, I said, boys, what do you make of this poem? I said, boys, I've been looking at it for more than forty years and I've never understood a goddamn thing. Really. I might as well tell you the truth. And they said: it's a joke, Amadeo, the poem is a joke covering up something more serious. But what does it mean? I said. Let us think a little, Amadeo, they said ... Well, then, I said, what's the mystery? Then the boys looked at me and said: there is no mystery, Amadeo. (SD 354)

So, by now the roles are well-established. Amadeo serves as the truth-teller, saying he can't understand what it means (exactly what my wife said the first time she saw it). The boys are either enjoying their roles as provocateurs or their understanding exists on some level of Dada intuition. But is there another possibility?

I think it is possible that we are dealing with an instance of what Wittgenstein called "private language." When Belano (presumably) says he has already seen this in a dream when he was a child, he is echoing another text of Bolaño's, *Antwerp* (*Amberes*), written in 1980 but not published for the first time until 2002. As he says of the work, "The only novel that doesn't embarrass me is *Amberes*, maybe because it continues to be

unintelligible" (*Last Interview* 117). This is where we read the following
passage: "'When I was a boy I used to dream something like

this'... 'The straight

line is the sea when it's calm, the wavy line is the sea with waves, and the
jagged line is a storm'" (30). The next section of *Antwerp* contains several
more drawings, one of them almost identical to the further elucidation that
the boys give to the "poem" when their conversation with Amadeo resumes
after another 30 pages or so. Among their explanations is to give the little
"house" or whatever it is in the original poem a three-sided sail, and then
it becomes a boat in calm seas, a boat in wavy seas and a boat in the storm;
whereas before it was a house on the plain, a house in the hills and a house
in the mountains (SD 373–7). Is this completely convincing, or is it possible
that these various meanings exist for Bolaño, or his stand-in Belano, alone.
Here is Wittgenstein in one of his clearest statements of what he means by
"private language":

> But could we also imagine a language in which a person could write
> down or give vocal expression to his inner experiences—his feelings,
> moods, and the rest—for his private use?—Well, can't we do so in
> our ordinary language?—But that is not what I mean. The individual
> words of this language are to refer to what can only be known to
> the person speaking; to his immediate private sensations. So another
> person cannot understand the language. (*Philosophical Investigations*
> I, § 243)

By bringing his readers as close as possible to a "private language," I believe
Bolaño is trying to get us to think about the very limits of interpretation,
perhaps even its ultimate value.

In the desert of the real

"The philosopher's treatment of a question is like the treatment of an
illness."

(Wittgenstein *Philosophical Investigations* I, § 235)

Of course, when one has exhausted the possibilities of interpretation or even
the possibility of interpretation itself, "read all the books," as Mallarmé
says ("La chair est triste et j'ai lu tous les livres"), then there is only one
solution and that is to move along, hit the road, go for an ocean voyage.

As Mallarmé does in his "Brise Marine," a poem brilliantly invoked by Roberto Bolaño in his essay, "Literature + Illness = Illness":

> Books are finite, sexual encounters are finite, but the desire to read and to fuck is infinite; it surpasses our own deaths, our fears, our hopes for peace. And what is left for Mallarmé, in this famous poem, when the desire to read and the desire to fuck, so he says, are all used up? Well, what is left is travel, the desire to go traveling. And maybe that's the key to the crime. ("Illness" 133)

So, when the boys are finished harassing a drunk old man and tormenting him with their private dreams passed off as interpretations of a hermetic "poem," the only thing left is to follow out his clues as to the whereabouts of Cesárea Tinajero and hit the road. But this is where the literary detective story starts to intersect with the Mexican gangster movie playing in the background. As mentioned previously, a mentally unstable Quim Font has encouraged young Lupe to leave her pimp, Alberto. On New Year's Eve, 1975, everyone is gathered at the Font compound, with Alberto and his accomplices lurking outside the gated fence in their yellow Camaro, and no help in sight, when Belano and Lima arrive and, together with Quim, hatch a plan to escape. After García Madero wins a brief scuffle with Alberto at the gate, he jumps in the car with Ulisses and Arturo and Lupe, and Quim's white Impala proceeds to take them north away from Mexico City and toward the Sonora Desert with the gangsters in hot pursuit (SD 123–4). Belano and Lima have succeeded in combining Quim Font's plan to liberate Lupe with their own plan to find Cesárea Tinajero and the result is Part III, "The Sonora Desert" (1976).

Bolaño, in the essay on literature and illness, counterpoises Baudelaire's "Le Voyage" to Mallarmé's "Brise Marine." While there is much to be said about the poem and Bolaño's trenchant commentary, time is short and the gangsters may be gaining on us, so let's cut to the last line, which he also uses as the epigraph to his final work, *2666*: "An oasis of horror in a desert of boredom" ("Une oasis d'horreur dans un desert d'ennui"). Of which Bolaño says:

> In that line alone there is more than enough. In the middle of a desert of ennui, an oasis of fear, or horror. There is no more lucid analysis of the modern illness of humanity … All the indications are that every oasis in existence has either attained or is drifting toward the condition of horror. ("Illness" 138)

This is the dark vision that haunts all of Bolaño's work and I think it stems from the primal trauma of what happened to his country of Chile on September 11, 1973 and the terrible years that followed. If Arturo

Belano is an extremely disturbed individual in his early twenties, drifting through Mexico with only the wildest of literary dreams, and now being chased by gangsters, it starts with his condition of exile from his native land. The last section of *The Savage Detectives* ends with a specific trauma, but the effects can be generalized to account for all of Belano's (and to some extent, Lima's) troubled wanderings in the long central section of the novel, wanderings that often involve encounters with other deeply troubled individuals, encounters that often involve extreme violence.

The four young people in the white Impala do quite a bit of wandering, while Belano and Lima search for traces of Cesárea Tinajero. The two poets investigate library archives and school records, interview one of her former rooming house mates, and even track down a former bullfighter who knew another bullfighter with whom Cesárea was briefly involved after leaving Mexico City. When they finally succeed in locating her, where she is living in a shack not far from the U.S. border and selling herbs at the local markets, they find that she is nothing like the willowy intellectual who captivated Amadeo Salvatierra. She is a large, heavy, deeply aged woman who is barely subsisting and almost totally merged with the Indian culture that surrounds her. But she is gracious and gentle and the four young people spend some time with her before the gangsters show up and provoke a confrontation. As García Madero says: "We found Cesárea Tinajero. In turn, Alberto and the policeman found us" (SD 569). In the final confrontation, there are the two cars parked in the desert. Cesárea is with the four young people and Alberto has his policeman. When Alberto makes a move to recuperate Lupe from the car, Belano jumps him: "With one hand he seized Alberto's gun arm. His other hand shot out of his pocket, gripping the knife he'd bought in Caborca. Before the two of them tumbled to the ground, Belano had buried the knife in Alberto's chest" (SD 572). Lima makes a move to tackle the policeman and then García Madero recounts:

> I saw the policeman and Lima rolling on the ground until they came to a stop at the edge of the road, the policeman on top of Ulises, the gun in the policeman's hand aimed at Ulises's head, and I saw Cesárea, I saw the huge bulk of Cesárea Tinajero, who could hardly run but was running, toppling onto them, and I heard two more shots and I got out of the car. I had trouble moving Cesárea's body off the bodies of the policeman and my friend. (SD 572)

So, in the end, Alberto and Cesárea are dead and the policeman is bleeding to death. As García Madero reports, "I heard Belano say that we'd fucked up, that we'd found Cesárea only to bring her death" (SD 573). The ending of the book comes quickly. Belano and Lima take charge of the bodies and drive off in the yellow Camaro, leaving Lupe and García Madero with Quim Font's white Impala. "The boys" will show up again in the long central section of the book, from which Lupe and García Madero are absent. (García Madero's name is mentioned once or twice, but nobody can remember who he is.) Without his friends and their projects, García Madero's final journal entries drift into a realm of virtual non-existence.

For readers coming to the end of the book, the sense of anxiety and foreboding that has been building throughout the long, central section finally has a traumatic event to latch onto. But I want to suggest that this trauma is actually repeated in the central section, or echoed, as if Lima and Belano are so scarred by what happened to them that they cannot help but involve themselves in repeated incidents that likewise expose them to the kind of violence they experienced in the desert (something that, for me, suggests Nietzsche's "eternal return"). Likewise, in the fuller works of Roberto Bolaño, the central trauma of his young life finds expression in several works that deal with various aspects of Chile's long nightmare under Pinochet, notably *Amulet*, *By Night in Chile*, and *Distant Star*. I want to suggest here that the trauma in the desert in *The Savage Detectives* is in some sense a placeholder for the larger sense of trauma that Bolaño experienced with the "loss" of his country, or a representation of trauma that stands in for something that is strictly speaking unrepresentable. That's because none of us can really access the deepest elements of what Lacan calls "the Real" and that remain with us nonetheless. This is similar to what Giorgio Agamben discusses as what he calls the "unlived" part of one's experience:

> What remains unlived is therefore incessantly sucked back toward the origin without ever being able to reach it. The present is nothing other than this unlived element in everything that is lived. *That which impedes access to the present is precisely the mass of what for some reason (its traumatic character, its excessive nearness) we have not managed to live.* (Agamben 17; my italics)

One particularly haunting aspect of the final section of the book, aside from the violence at the end, is the desperate poverty in which Cesárea lives and the accompanying stark solitude she endures for so many years after having left the cosmopolitan surroundings of Mexico City. One might term this an aspect of the "unlived" nature of her experience, as well, one that almost calls for the cataclysm of violence in which she dies.

How does the violent ending of *The Savage Detectives* fit with our idea that the novel utilizes elements of the detective plot while standing outside the genre, properly speaking? Here we might invoke the ethical dilemma that the detective faces at the end of so many narratives in the genre. As one particularly apt example in this context, we might remember the dilemma that Holly Martin faces at the end of *The Third Man* (dir. Carol Reed 1949). After he discovers that his friend, Harry Lime, once thought dead, is actually alive and has faked his death, Martin also is made aware of Lime's criminal activities. After one deal with the British major to essentially trade Lime for the freedom of Lime's German girlfriend falls through, Martin is ready to call it quits. But then the major gives Martin a tour of a hospital where the young victims of Lime's criminal dealings in shoddy antibiotics are housed. Martin faces the ethical dilemma of whether to aid the police directly in Lime's capture. Not only does he do so, but in a fitting twist, he actually fires the fatal shot resulting in Lime's death. Do Lima and Belano face a similar ethical dilemma here, having at least indirectly caused Cesárea's death (even worse than kidnapping Octavio Paz)? Is there a question of culpability to be figured out and guilt to be assigned? Here I am drawn to Umberto Eco's reflection on the subject at the end of his "Postscript" to *The Name of the Rose*, where he says:

> It seems that the Parisian Oulipo group [which included Georges Perec; *my note*] has recently constructed a matrix of all possible murder-story situations and has found that there is still to be written a book in which the murderer is the reader.
>
> Moral: there exist obsessive ideas, they are never personal; books talk among themselves, and any true detection should prove that we are the guilty party. [... *e una vera indagine poliziesca deve provare che i colpevoli siamo noi.*] (533; trans. 535)

I think that Bolaño moves very close to this idea that "we are the guilty party"; but that sense of guilt alone is not enough as a guiding idea here. Bolaño shows his protagonists to be culpable on one level, because on another level we are all responsible parties.

Bolaño's early work returns obsessively to the events in Chile in 1973 and the years following. The great works of his maturity, *The Savage Detectives* and *2666*, stage their scenes of trauma elsewhere, but the sense that we are all meant to be witnesses persists. As Robert Harvey has recently argued, "All 'life' consists of subsisting in that mid position *between* forgotten 'trauma' (birth, my past) and the oblivion of death (my future). We are necessarily witness by virtue of the midst; that is, our balancing above the abyss" (45). The abyss Harvey invokes here is the unresolved trauma, the "oasis of horror" that Bolaño locates in Baudelaire's poem, and that he stages in the Sonora Desert in the final section of *The Savage Detectives*. I believe he does mean to implicate his readers in the responsibility to bear witness to the most painful events of the recent past (thousands of disappeared in Chile, hundreds of murdered women and girls in Ciudad Juarez). His narrative puzzles cannot be resolved through the exercise of reason and logic, but demand an investment in the imagined realities of those who suffer and die (in this way, once more, they are very similar to the works of Georges Perec). As Harvey says, "The puzzle's solution is a world of witnesses to be read, one by the other, rather than be compelled to speak. The enigma is lifted by a witness who has no higher ambition than to *bear* witness—not by virtue of speech, but in the literal sense of *taking on* that burden ..." (130). Just as we are all invited along to participate in the savage detectives' dual quest, so we are all implicated, at the very least as witnesses, in the crimes, both real and imagined, that they see and perpetrate, because this is quite simply the world we find ourselves in.

Works cited

Agamben, Giorgio. *Nudities*. Trans. David Kishik and Stefan Pedatella. Stanford: Stanford University Press, 2011.

Baker, Peter. *Modern Poetic Practice: Structure and Genesis*. New York: Peter Lang, 1986.

Bolaño, Roberto. *2666*. Trans. Natasha Wimmer. New York: Farrar, Straus and Giroux, 2008.

—*Antwerp*. Trans. Natasha Wimmer. New York: New Directions, 2010.

—*Last Evenings on Earth*. Trans. Chris Andrews. New York: New Directions, 2006.

—*The Last Interview*. Brooklyn: Melville House, 2009.

—"Literature + Illness = Illness." In *The Insufferable Gaucho*. Trans. Chris Andrews, New York: New Directions, 2010. 121–44.

—*Los detectives salvajes*. Barcelona: Anagrama, 1998 (Edicíon "Compactos").

—*The Savage Detectives* (SD). Trans. Natasha Wimmer. New York: Farrar, Straus and Giroux, 2007.

—*The Skating Rink*. Trans. Chris Andrews. New York: New Directions, 2009.

Cavell, Stanley. *Little Did I Know: Excerpts from Memory*. Stanford: Stanford UP, 2010.

Eco, Umberto. "Postille" (1983). In *Il nome della rosa* (1980). Milano: Bompiani, 1984.

—"Postscript." In *The Name of the Rose*. New York: Harcourt, Brace, 1983.

Genette, Gerard. *Figures III*. Paris: Seuil, 1972.

Goodman, Robin Truth. *Policing Narratives and the State of Terror*. New York: SUNY Press, 2010.

Harvey, Robert. *Witnessness: Beckett, Dante, Levi and the Foundations of Responsibility*. New York and London: Continuum, 2010.

Lacan, Jacques. *Écrits*. Paris: Éditions du Seuil, 1966.

Perec, Georges. *Entretiens et conferences* (2 vols). Paris: Éditions Joseph K, 2002.

Valdes, Marcela. "Alone Among the Ghosts." Introduction to Bolaño, *The Last Interview*. 9–40.

Wittgenstein, Ludwig. *Philosophical Investigations* (1953). Trans. G. E. M. Anscombe. Oxford: Blackwell (3rd edn), 2001.

3

Detectivism as a means of resistance in Juan Marsé's *El embrujo de Shanghai*

Ana-Maria Medina

With works such as *Encerrados con un sólo juguete*, (1960) Últimas tardes con Teresa (1966), *La oscura historia de Montse* (1970), *Si te dicen que caí* (1970) and *El embrujo de Shanghai* (1993), Juan Marsé (Barcelona, 1933) has established himself as an author representative of narrative realism in Spanish contemporary literature. As such, he delves into the societal factors that surround specific characters during a particular time and elicits a fictional reality that grants readers the opportunity to see the intra-history of society. It is in *El embrujo de Shanghai*—his initial exploration of postmodernist writing—that Marsé first utilizes the motif of detection to denounce the socio-cultural performance of Catalonian people under Franco. It is the goal of this article to present how detectivism is used as a narrative tool in the elaboration of *El embrujo de Shanghai* and how it is through this motif that, the, at first glance, discursively simple novel becomes an artifact that serves to promote a greater understanding of the virtue of childhood and its loss during the turbulent times of the post-Franco era through a retrospective vision of inner exile. Initially, this article presents an outline of Spanish detective fiction or *novela negra* from its inception in Spain to the publication of *El embrujo de Shanghai*. A chronology is provided in order to offer an understanding of the development of the genre and thus the literary lineage that precedes Marsé's work. Second, it seeks to expose the use of the detective motif in *El embrujo de Shanghai* and the narrative aesthetics the author employs through detectivism to formulate a seemingly silent resistance that takes shape when the reader in the act of reception of the dialogic discourse becomes detective and participates in what Gosselin identifies as "inadvertent learning."

The detective genre in Spain

In order to portray the evolution of detectivism in Spain, it is important to understand that, although the true core of the detective novel in Spain was produced in the post-Franco years, the detective novel is found as early as the nineteenth century, albeit as mere replication of the popular British and American novels. The earliest suggestion of the Spanish detective novel appears 13 years after Poe's initial work in Pedro Alarcon's *El clavo y otros relatos de misterio y crimen* (1853). However, the work does not entirely fit the detective novel structure because it concludes with a moral deliberation or *moraleja*. However, it is nearing the end of the century that Emilia Pardo Bazán publishes *La gota de sangre* (1893–8), which is clearly influenced by the foreign genre. As Cate-Arries points out,

> The narrator-protagonist Selva himself is constantly aware of Sherlock Holmes's influence ... Early on, the narrator acknowledges the pre-existing literary model that generates his own text, and motivates his decision to follow in the footsteps of the fictional amateur detectives that have gone before him: "Quizá me ha sugerido tal propósito la lectura de esas novelas inglesas que ahora están de moda, y en que hay policías de afición, o sea detectives por sport. Ya sabe Ud. que así como el hombre de la Naturaleza refleja impresiones directas, el de la civilización refleja lecturas." ["Perhaps the reading of those English novels that are now so in vogue have suggested such a purpose and in that there are police hobbyist, that is detectives for sport. You already know that as the man of nature reflects direct impressions; of civilization, reflects readings."] (205)

As such, Pardo Bazán, although integrating a new genre into her work, truly did not advance the detective discourse into a Spanish detective novel within its own right but replicated the previously established mold.[1] It was only in the early twentieth century that Spanish authors actively began to write their own versions of the detective works, most noticeably the publication of the series by Joaquin Belda and Manuel A. Bedoga.[2] These novels, although not unique in plot line, do begin to locate their action in Spain and to use recognizably Spanish characters and the two of them go on to establish the parameters that the detective novel will develop within the peninsula. Jose Colmeiro enumerates some of the aspects that these works began to establish in *La Novela Policíaca Española: Teoría e Historia Crítica*:

> ... la burla paródica de la rigidez formal del patrón clásico, la mezcla heterodoxa de lo policiaco y lo humorístico, la ausencia de tratamiento serio (racionalista, científico) del método de encuesta y el intento de superación de la esquemática formula policiaca por medio de su "literaturización" (estilización, autorreflexividad, expresividad del lenguaje, penetración social o psicológica, costumbrismo, ambigüedad moral). [... the paradoxical mockery of the formal classical pattern, the unorthodox mixture of the detective and the humoristic, the absence of serious treatment (rational, scientific) of the scientific method and the effort to overcome the schematic detective formula by means of its "literaturization" (sterilization, self-reflexivity, expressiveness of language, social or psychological insight, literary treatment of local customs, moral ambiguity).] (105)

These novels thus set the initial parameters for what would become the Spanish detective novel. They were followed by a number of kiosk series in the early part of the century.[3] Although the majority were translations, three authors and their work become exceptions: the novel *El Collar de Nuria* (1927) by Cesar August Jordana, Merce Redodera's novel *Crim* (1936) and the trilogy by E. C. Delmar; El secreto del contador de gas, Piojos grises, and *La tórtola de la punalda* (1932–7) (Hart 25). In spite of this, with the rise of the Second Republic (1933–6), the Spanish Civil War (1936–9) and the subsequent Franco dictatorship (1939–75)—during which the publication of literature as a whole was truncated—the detective novel did not develop a plot line nor unique characterizations, thus it did little more than once again imitate the British and American models. However, the genre itself was very popular due to the translations brought in by publishing houses that, as some critics believe, truncated the rise of an authentic Spanish detective novel (Vazquez de Parga 28).[4] It was only starting in the 1950s that a group of detective novelists began to publish what would later be termed the "novela negra" ("crime novel"), a detective novel that is very similar to the American "Hard-Boiled" novel.[5] Two authors that are representative of this in Castilian-speaking Spain are Mario Lacruz, author of *El inocente* (1953), and Francisco García Pavón, creator of the detective character Plinio, first presented in a short story in *Ateneo* followed by subsequent novels, the first of which was *Los carros vacíos*. In

Cataluña, however, the detective novel had taken center stage before the 1950s. This reality has gone relatively unnoticed because they were not easily accessible to the Spanish-speaking public as they were not translated from Catalan. As such, many studies focusing on peninsular literature have left them at the periphery of the canon. As Craig-Odders writes:

> Catalan writers, including Manuel de Pedrolo, Jaume Fuster, Guillem Frontera and Lorenc Capella, among others have made important contributions to the detective canon in Spain. The linguistic inaccessibility of these works to many readers outside of Catalonia and the scarcity of translations account, in part, for the fact that they have not achieved widespread recognition. (xviii)

It was the Catalan writers that were able to advance the detective genre novel before the 1950s, which is a focus of Craig-Odders' work, as well as Patricia Hart's and Joan Ramon Resina's. All of them agree that the Spanish detective genre was greatly influenced by the multiple series published in Catalonia and that "the 'boom' of detective fiction in the late 1980s was, in large part, made possible by the Catalan publishing houses and the reading public of Cataluña" (Craig-Odders quoting Resina 19).[6]

On a broader scale it is unquestionable that the detective novel boom of the 1980s is seen as a direct response to the death of Franco and the demise of restrictive writing practices. As such, the Spanish detective novel exposes and criticizes issues of concern linked to the modernization and Westernization of Spain which only became possible during the transition period. Because of the socio-cultural events that led to the detective novel boom and the comparable aesthetic characteristics it shares with the Hard-Boiled American detective novel it is important to acknowledge the social-cultural parallel both countries faced. In the United States in the years following the Prohibition Act, which was increasingly unpopular in large cities, the financial demise and the Depression in the 1930s, there was an observable increase in violence and organized crime. As a result, the detective novels representative of those times comprised "una estética *hard-boiled*, de lenguaje y personajes endurecidos y de las instituciones, exponiendo la injusticia, violencia, corrupción e hipocresía que sostienen el estado de cosas" ("a *hard-boiled* aesthetic of language and hardened characters and of institutions, exposing injustice, violence, corruption and hypocrisy that support the status of things") (Colmeiro 212). Almost half a century later, similar circumstances are taking place in Spain after the death of Franco, the establishment of democracy and the restoration of liberties that will lead Spain into the globalized age. Although this change has been perceived through a retrospective idealism, the reality is that it gave way to a social crisis that stemmed from the legacy of poverty, a static economy, a social conditioning constructed by an extremely rigid ruling system and a repressive society which led to, among other things, political unrest, socio-economic instability and new conflicts, such as a new wave of crime and criminality that played out as a response to having to adapt abruptly to a globalized age, something for which neither Spain's economy nor its citizens had had time to prepare.

As a result of the events of the "transition" and the disappearance of extreme censorship of narratives, the detective genre was able to truly flourish. This was due to the genre's inherent need to provide a social reality and a plot line intertwined with criminality and crime-solving. Colmeiro underscores that the genre thrived because the "novela negra ... se distingue por su presentación de ambientes urbanos donde prevalecen la violencia, el crimen y el miedo, su testimonio crítico de la sociedad y su denuncia de los abusos y de la violencia del poder" ("the crime novel ... is distinguished by its presentation of urban settings where violence, crime and fear, its critical testimony about society and its condemnation of the abuses and violence of power") (215). Thus the circumstances of the events happening in Spain provided the backdrop necessary to write truly authentic Spanish detective novels. Moreover, Colmeiro establishes that the novel's thematic relevance provides not only a way to criticize but also a way to collectively escape from the criminality that has begun to weigh so heavily on the collective imagination of the Spanish nation:

> ... sirve simultáneamente como medio de crítica social y como válvula de escape colectiva a los conflictos y tensiones provocados por choques de intereses en la sociedad y por ambiguas posturas con respecto a ciertos valores morales y particulares ... esta novela propone una lectura crítica de la realidad social pero típicamente no crítica de su posible función escapista o reintegradora. Por esta razón, la novela policiaca negra corre el serio peligro de perder su poder incisivo, de atenuar y ver mermada su capacidad crítica; debido a la repetición sistemática, a la mecanicidad de su propia estructura formulaica, la carga corrosiva de esta novela tiene a devaluarse. [... serves simultaneously as a medium of social criticism and as a collective escape valve for the conflicts and tensions provoked by the conflicts of interest in society and by ambiguous stances on certain moral values and issues ... this novel proposes a critical reading of the social reality but typically does not criticize its possible escapist or reintegrative function. As a result, the detective crime novel runs the serious risk of losing its incisive power, to mitigate and see depleted its critical capacity; as a result of the systematic repetition and the mechanicalness of its formulaic structure the caustic indictment of this novel tends to be underrated.] (220)

Although the thematic relevance of the post-Franco detective novel becomes attuned to Spanish circumstances, the stringent parameters of the hard-boiled detective plot, typically represented in the Spanish detective novel, do not change, thus causing the narrative artifact to lose its relevance as a symbolic representation of the space in which it is created. However, it has been established that in the postmodern age the Spanish detective novel has become more heterogeneous and malleable. In the presentation of *Manuscrito Criminal: Reflexiones sobre novela y cine negro* (2008) Javier Sánchez Zapatero and Àlex Martín Escribà underlined that:

> Si algo caracteriza al género negro es su agilidad. Su apego a la actualidad, muy superior al de otras formas literarias y cinematográficas, hace de él un escenario adecuado para que los autores puedan captar y enjuiciar los cambios de la realidad social. Los nuevos contextos a los que han de enfrentarse los autores no permiten fácilmente la inclusión de figuras prototípicas como la del detective sin suponer una afrenta contra la verosimilitud que se le exige a una forma artística que enlaza con lo realista y lo social. [If anything characterizes the crime genre, it is dexterity. Its attachment with current situations, superior to other literary and cinematographic forms, makes it a suitable stage for authors to capture and indict changes in the social reality. The new contexts which authors must confront do not easily permit the inclusion of prototypical figures, like that of the detective, without assuming an affront to the credibility that is required of an art form linked to what is realistic and social.] (1)

It is possible then to denote how in a representation of an era where everything has changed from what it was, not only politically but culturally, there is a need to incorporate the new technologies and the divergences in everyday life that cause distinct changes in the way members of society relate to each other. As a result of the new possibilities for Spanish detective novels, publication, in the last four decades, has been consistent and has provided a fertile ground for scholarly research.[7] Of greater interest for this article, however, is the analysis of the repercussions of the proliferation of detective works and how these works have influenced contemporary Spanish literature, in particular *El embrujo de Shanghai* by Juan Marsé, which although not a Spanish detective novel does show definite influences of the detective motif within its narrative aesthetics. The detective novels that precede *El embrijo de Shanghai* provide its setting while the narrative itself reflects postmodern form and preoccupation. As the postmodern world tears down the delineating and constraining limitations of what a genre is and is not, Marsé encounters the freedom to create a dialogic discourse that utilizes the detective genre as a means of resistance and recuperation. As we will see in the next section, Marsé's novel differs from formulaic and escapist ideals, focusing on attenuating their critical and 'resistance' potential.

The detective motif: resistance and recuperation in *El embrujo de Shanghai*

El embrujo de Shanghai speaks to a part of Catalonian literature that was created in a period of new-found liberation conditioned by the vitalizing revival of traditional cultural factors that had long permeated the arts there and that now served as a means to enter the postmodernist era. Authors new and old began to establish dialogues with other genres and global popular culture, and it was a period in time when the re-encountering of the one-time silent past became significant. Marsé exemplifies this in *El embrujo de Shanghai* through a play of narrative voices that vacillate from a young group of boys, one of whom is the narrator—Daniel—to that of an elderly man who seeks to end the stench that reeks from Barcelona's underground during the post-war. This occurs alongside a storyline that is based on the suspenseful tales of Nandu Forcat, a *maqui*-exile who has returned to Spain permanently after several visits to see his dying mother and to live with Susana and her mother Anita, both of whom are indebted to him for safekeeping Kim: a legendary man whose story is told to Daniel by Blay and then by Forcat to both Daniel and Susana. It is Forcat who narrates Kim's post-war chronicle to the children and exposes them to his experiences while living in exile in France as a *maqui* in name of the Republican cause, returning periodically to check on his daughter and to inquire about his mission in Shanghai. It is not until the end of the novel that the reader is informed by a minor character, Dennis, a comrade of Forcat's and Kim's, that the events Forcat narrates in reference to Kim are lies. As a result of the true story being told and the mystery being resolved, the world known by Daniel and Susana is destroyed. The destruction resulting from the interplay of storylines and the climatic disclosure of the truth gives way to a fertile ground for the analysis of the motif of detection. The motif is concealed between the narrative discourse and the narrators' stories through the use of symbolic essentialism and the mixing of the imaginary and the real that Daniel, Susana, Blay and Forcat provide.

Marsé's work follows the motif of the classic detective formula which has the following elements as basic boundaries: the reconstruction of a hidden or lost story (that is, the crime); and the process of reconstructing (that is, detection), which, in its turn, is also usually hidden in essential respects from the reader (Hühn 453). Inasmuch as the reader believes that he or she knows the "true story" the double entendre lies in the detection which originates from the reconstruction of a hidden or lost story within the narration. As Peter Hühn highlights in reference to the reader as detective, extracting the "'true' story from the (invariably distorting) medium of discourse is a feasible as well as valuable enterprise ... when the detective finally narrates the 'true story' of the crime, thus correcting its previous misrepresentation in discourse, the listeners are presented with merely another version of discourse (which, however, purports to be congruent with the story line itself)" (452). Both Daniel and the reader are told a story that is based on what Daniel believes to be reality; however, retrospectively throughout the discourse he acknowledges to the reader the lack of veracity of what he is retelling and what is being told to him:

> Nosotros no podíamos en aquel entonces ni siquiera intuir que el personaje [Forcat] era improbable, lo mismo que el Kim: inventado, imaginario y sin fisuras, un personaje que sólo adquiría vida en boca de los mayores cuando discutían, reticentes y en voz baja, sus fechorías o sus hazañas, según el criterio de cada cual. [We could not at that time even intuit that the character [Forcat] was improbable, like Kim: invented, imaginary and without fissures, a character that only takes on life through the voices of the adults when they argued, reticent and in low voices, their misdeeds or their exploits, according to each individual's criteria.] (17)

It is because of the presupposed discourse of truth in Forcat's storytelling to Daniel and Susana, and the experiences that Daniel has with Blay, that will be seen later in this article, that the detective motif is portrayed. The suspense of these events lies in the fact that the "truth" stands within the narrative discourse: the reader is detective and must decipher the truth from the imaginary within a fictional work. The narrator enables the detective motif throughout the text as he foreshadows and leaves the reader guessing about what might happen or not. As such, the reader, while attempting to ascertain the true story, becomes detective and partakes in inadvertent learning seen in multicultural detective fiction.[8] Two examples of this will be seen: first through the story of Blay and next through the analysis of the storyline involving Forcat and the telling of his mysterious relationship with Kim.

However, before the analysis it is necessary to define "inadvertent learning." Inadvertent learning is the result of having to interpret the symbolic essentialism Marsé so often utilizes. Maria Esperanza Dominguez Castro exemplifies this essentialism by detailing how Marsé has been quantified as a realist writer at first glace, only because it is the easiest category in which to place him. However, there is much more to his works than what can be seen in a first reading.

> En las novelas y cuentos se traba la experiencia humana mediante la captación del instante y las pulsiones no verbalizadas y, con frecuencia, se consigue fijarlas en el inconsciente del lector gracias a figuraciones que metaforizan la realidad sorteando las limitaciones de su comprensión empírica gracias al acceso intuitivo y polisemántico del símbolo. [In

novels and stories, the human experience is woven by capturing the moment and pulsations not verbalized and, frequently, it is possible to instill them in the reader's unconscious, making use of conceptualizations that become a metaphor for reality, sorting the limitations of its empirical comprehension, and acknowledging the intuitive and poly-semantic access of the symbol.] (59)

The symbol is illustrative of a collective reception of the events being represented and gives way to the inadvertent learning of a socio-historic climate and the stories representative of a collective that has gone silent. While Castro's study analyzes several of Marsé's works, and presents the symbolic representations of concrete remnants of the fascist regime, it is just as important to elucidate how these symbols interact with the detective motif within the context of *El embrujo de Shanghai*. Through the relationship of both aspects of narrative aesthetics—one based on everyday signs and symbols; the other, on a detective novel, also considered an everyday, low-brow genre—this reading presents the development of how the crime depicted in *El embrujo de Shanghai* evolves.

The events and symbols uncovered through reading offer insight into the recuperation of forgotten memories, more so, the recuperation of a crime committed against a society that required a segment to be forced into an inner exile.[9] It is important to note that it was in the early 1990s that the recuperation of the memory of the Spanish Civil War and post-war began to be placed at the forefront. It is thus possible to see this novel as a conversation among writers of contemporary post-war narrative, with the breaking of barriers in the postmodernist era, the boom of globalization and the entrance of foreign cultures into a country once isolated from all exterior influences. On one hand there is a clear indication of inner exile through Daniel's narration and his encounters ambulating with Blay through the streets of Barcelona, attempting to get signatures on a petition that would end the revolting smell that comes from the underground and the toxic fumes coming from the factory chimney. But it is parallel to this plot line that the narration of Nandu Forcat, depicting the adventures of Kim, delineates the experiences of a *maqui* in exile.

Daniel experiences the creation of a false reality that begins with Blay's embodiment of his position as invisible man, an imaginative role needed in order to escape prosecution. This role provides a shared imaginative sphere in which they seek to recuperate a Barcelona that previously existed, one without the putrid smell. As mentioned earlier, Blay represents inner exile, a reality suffered by a section of the Spanish population that was unable to leave Spain during the regime. It is as a result of these circumstances that for almost three years he has been locked up in a small room. As Daniel recounts:

... durante casi tres años el capitán no había caminado cien metros seguidos en línea recta ni había salido de su casa para nada ... Cuando por fin decidió salir a la calle había perdido treinta kilos de peso, una guerra y dos hijos, el respeto de su mujer y según todas las apariencias, buena parte del poco seso que siempre tuvo. [... during nearly three years the captain had not walked one hundred continuous meters in a straight line nor had he left his house for anything ... When he finally decided to go out to the street he had lost thirty pounds of weight, a war and two sons, respect for his wife and according to all appearances, a good part of any brains he ever had.] (30)

Daniel's involvement with Blay is at first as that of a guardian, as Conxa, Blay's wife, asks him to make sure that Blay, the "viejo pirado" (29), old crazy man, not be allowed to speak about politics with strangers and not say anything stupid. It must be noted that Blay always speaks in Castilian, not in Catalan, the language of the region and the one his wife speaks at home, which places the novel at a cultural borderland, inserting it within the parameters of the multicultural detective fiction motif. Gosselin proposes that this occurs when "theorizing from the borderlands" and quoting Anzaldúa he clarifies that "such a process necessitates a multilingual dialogue involving a 'language of borderlands,' a dialogue that occurs at 'junctures of culture [where] languages cross-pollinate and are revitalized' (Anzaldúa, Preface)". In a literal sense Blay presents a borderland of language between Castilian and Catalan. Both, Blay and his wife being from Cataluña have total fluency in the language, but because of an aneurism Blay is said to have forgotten his first language. Nonetheless, within the novel, the bilingual dialogue that is representative of this linguistic borderland also portrays a greater meaning,

—Vols Parlar como Déu mana, brétol? – Dijo la *Betibú*
—Dios ya no manda nada, Conxa. Ahora mandan éstos.

Blay's understanding of the language and the presentation of "estos" being in control—meaning the fascist regime—proves that even within all of the insanity that surrounds Blay there is a level of conscientiousness in his awareness of inner exile. It is the reader that, alongside Daniel, must decipher the truth: is there really a dreadful smell, or is Blay a madman? Daniel also shows uncertainty since at the beginning of the novel he believes all of Blay's stories but assures the reader further on, that "al principio me tragara todas las paridas del capitán, todas sus manías y extravagancias, pero poco a poco fui aprendiendo a lidiar al estrafalario personaje" ("at the beginning I put up with all the captain's stupid remarks, all of his obsessions and extravagances, but little by little I learned how to fight this outlandish character") (30-1). As he begins to appreciate Blay, he is also given a new task by him. This commission is to paint Susana as the infirm child she is with the chimney in the background so that the city heads will take notice of the hazardous living conditions being caused by the factory and the toxic stench coming from Barcelona's underground. This mission allows Daniel to participate in the afternoon gatherings and through those meet Forcat and learn about Kim.

Because of these afternoon visits, there appears the secondary mystery that the reader encounters: the story of exterior exile that is represented by Nandu Forcat, who is also the narrator of the secondary plot: the story of Kim. Forcat is seen by the young boys as a heroic figure "que se jugaba la piel con el revólver en la mano y siempre en compañía del Kim, espalda contra espalda, protegiéndose el uno al otro" ("that he risked his neck with the revolver in hand and always in the company of Kim, back to back, protecting one another") (18). The initial suspense comes from Nandu Forcat's presence in the neighborhood, the heightened interest the adults show for the character and how the putrid smell is now presented to the reader as related to Forcat's homecoming.

> Durante cuatro días, Nandu Forcat no salió a la calle y ni siquiera se asomó al balcón. Frente al portal flotaba noche y día el olor a gas y ahora una sensación doblemente excitante se adueñaba de uno al pasar por allí, como si el gas y el pistolero hubiesen establecido una alianza peligrosa. [During four days Nandu Forcat did not leave the house nor did he even peer out over the balcony. In front of the doorway there floated night and day the smell of gas and now a doubly exciting sensation overtook one upon passing through there, as if the gas and the gunman had formed a dangerous alliance.] (18)

During the time locked in the home, a crew from the city, believed to be undercover police, sets itself up to work outside. The reason for this is unknown, since they only pull up the street and then proceed to do nothing, but they bring more suspense to the narration. Although Forcat once again leaves Barcelona, in his next visit he comes to the home of Susana and Anita where he brings news and letters from Kim requesting asylum and treatment deserving of a family member.

Thus, he establishes himself as a connection for Susana and her father and a distraction for Daniel and the Chacón brothers through the telling of stories about Kim. In the evenings, Forcat recounts stories of her father and his adventures to the children. Transporting them to the foreign land of Shanghai, where Kim himself is the protagonist of a mystery, the children are captivated; thus the title of the novel, *El embrujo de Shanghai* (*The Bewitching of Shanghai*). He becomes the narrator and just as the children believe him, so does the reader. The reality is, however, that for Nandu Forcat the stories he tells the children are a means to escape reality—the reality of his own life—and to bring a new reality to Anita, Daniel, and Susana.

Susana is described by Daniel as having "una disposición natural a la ensoñación, a convocar lo deseable y lo hermoso y lo conveniente" ("a natural disposition to dreaming, to summon the desirable and the beautiful and the convenient") (57). Her life revolves around the memory of her escaped father, Kim, and the only memory of him she holds. However,

> También le gustaba recordar [a Susana] que, siendo muy niña, su padre solía levantarla con un solo brazo hasta casi rozar la fúlgida lámpara del comedor, una lámpara muy Antigua que un día, años después, se desplomó de pronto sin que nadie la tocara y se hizo añicos; y que ella tenía muy viva en la memoria esa escena, tenía muy presente el vigor del brazo de su padre, la tensión amorosa y la seguridad que transmitía allá en lo alto, vino a decirme, y también la cegadora luz de la araña de cristal y el vértigo del descenso y la risa de su madre. Y que todavía hoy, sobre todo en las noches que se sentía muy mal … iluminando súbitamente los recuerdos que guardaba de su padre, sentía a veces en la sangre esa explosión de luz cegadora que ya no estaba en casa y aquel impulso del cariño que la alzaba de nuevo por encima de la fiebre y la soledad, del espanto de los vómitos de sangre y los presagios de muerte. [She [Susana] also liked to remember that, as a young child, her father used to pick her up using only one arm until nearly brushing the shiny dining room lamp, a very old-fashioned lamp, that one day, years later, suddenly collapsed without anyone touching it and shattered to smithereens; she had a very vivid recollection of that scene, the memory of her father's powerful arm, the energy of her father's arm, the loving tension and the security that it transmitted there on high, she came to tell me, and also of the blinding light of the crystal spider and the vertigo of the descent and her mother's laughter. And that still today, especially on the nights that she felt very bad … subtly illuminated, the memories that she kept of her father, she sometimes felt that explosion in her blood of the blinding light that no longer existed in the house and that impulse of the affection that again lifted her above the fever and the loneliness from the horror of coughing up blood and the premonitions of death.] (59)

It is Susana's need to have those memories that allows her to create them, just as Daniel did with his father, believing he was missing at war. However, both children provide the reader with memories that are presented as fact, yet are just illusionary concoctions needed to step out of the reality of the poverty and despair surrounding them. Just as the lamp in the living room falls to its annihilation and darkness so does the situation within Susana's household and the reality of all of the participants in the novel.

Upon the Dennis' arrival, the world the children know, the legends of Kim and the world created by Forcat are destroyed. The mystery has been solved and the reality brought to light. The reader can now regress to the first sentence of Marsé's novel: "Los sueños juveniles se corrompen en boca de los adultos" ("Youthful dreams are corrupted in the mouth of adults") (11), proclaimed by captain Blay as he walks down the street in his role of invisible man: "cabeza vendada, gabardina, guantes de piel y gafas negras, y una gesticulación abrupta y fantasiosa ..." ("bandaged head, trench coat, leather gloves and dark glasses, and an abrupt and imaginative gesticulation ...") (11). His words are a precursor to all the events in Marsé's novel and set the scene for the crime: the murder of the juvenile idealism. It is this crime which is foreseen with the opening poem by Luis Garcia Montero.

La verdadera nostalgia, la más honda, no tiene que ver con el pasado, sino con el futuro. Yo siento con frecuencia la nostalgia del futuro, quiero decir, nostalgia de aquellos días de fiesta, cuando todo merodeaba por delate y el futuro estaba en su sitio. [True nostalgia, the deepest, has nothing to do with the past, but with the future. I frequently feel the nostalgia of the future, I mean, nostalgia of those holidays when everything prowled ahead and the future was in its place.] (9)

The nostalgic yearning for the past to be relived in the future is no longer feasible because of a society whose socio-political circumstances are those of a post-Civil War Spain: where a section of society that did not believe in the regime had all personal freedoms usurped, and were forced to live in a an inner exile, represented by Blay, and where poverty is commonplace.

Although retrospective narration continues to be reiterated through the youthful perspective of Daniel, it underlines the essence of Montero's words throughout the text. The reader is informed that Daniel's awakening lies in the experiences he had while walking around with Blay and during the afternoons spent with Susana—where both children escaped reality—listening to Forcat's tales about Kim. These realizations come as Daniel is reaching maturity. He realizes the stories are false; their world is false. As such, nearing the final pages of the novel, it is Daniel who restates how the past is linked to the future when saying "por mucho que uno mira hacia el futuro, uno crece hacia el pasado, en busca tal vez del primer deslumbramiento" ("regardless of how much one looks towards the future, one grows towards the past in search, perhaps, of the first enlightenment") (244).

Notes

1   It is impossible to know the exact date it was written because of Pardo
    Bazán's multiple republications. It is clearly noted by scholars that
    translations of Sherlock Holmes and other British and American kiosk novels
    made their way to Spain and became quite popular.

2   Joaquín Belda publishes *¿Quién disparó? Husmeos y pesquisas de Gapy
    Bermúdez* (1909) and *Una mancha de sangre* (1915), and Manuel A. Bedoga
    publishes *Aventuras de un millonario detective* (1915) and *Mack-Bill contra
    Nick Carter. Aventuras de un millonario detective* (1916).

3   *La novela policiaca* (1918); *Colección Enigma* (1925); *Grandes Éxitos
    Populares*; *Biblioteca Popular Fama* (1928); *El Club del Crimen* (1929);
    Selección Policiaca (1932), *Detective* (1930) and the translated series *Serie
    Detectivesca* and *Serie Amarilla* (1933). For more information consult *The
    detective Novel in Post-Franco Spain* by Renée W. Craig-Odders (12–13).

4   Craig-Odders notes that some exceptions to this were José Mira, Adolfo
    Ober, Pedro Guirao and Tomás Salvador; however, they were considered
    low-brow literature.

5   Hard-Boiled detection "is accordingly both cynical and sentimental
    according to Grella (105), and quintessentially American in its idealization
    of personal autonomy in the face of shadowy coercive forces, such as
    organized crime, ruthless corporations, wealthy families, and corrupt
    government agencies, including, typically, the regular metropolitan police."
    (Rzepka 181).

6   For a detailed listing of Catalan authors and their novels, see the works
    of Resina, *El cadaver en la cocina*; Craig-Odders *The Detective Novel in
    Post-Franco Spain*; and Patricia Hart's *The Spanish Sleuth: The Detective in
    Spanish Fiction*.

7   Since the beginning of the boom the most noted authors are Montalban and
    Eduardo Mendoza.

8   The term multicultural is utilized because the narrative discourse presents a
    clear line between the Catalan and Castilian dimensions and the exchange
    between them (Blay 35, the change of names of streets pp. 171–3).

9   Paul Ilie creates the term in his book *Literatura y exilio interior* (1981) and
    argues that the experience of exile goes beyond territorial ruptures: "Una vez
    que reconocemos que el exilio es una condición mental más que material, que
    aleja a unas gentes de otras gentes y de su manera de vivir, entonces queda
    definir la naturaleza de esta separación, no como un despegue unilateral, sino
    como algo más profundo. La escisión es una relación reciproca; el separa
    un segmento de la población del resto de ella es también dejar al segmento
    más grande separado del pequeño" ("Once we realize that exile is a mental
    condition more than a material one, which separates one people from another
    and from their way of living, then what's left to define is the nature of that
    separation, not like a unilateral division, but like something deeper. The split
    is a reciprocal relationship; to separate a piece of the population from the

rest of its people is also to leave the larger section separated from the smaller one") (7).

Works cited

Cate-Arries, Francie. "Murderous Impulses and Moral Ambiguity: Emilia Pardo Bazán's Crime Stories." *Romance Quarterly* 39.2 (1992): 205.

Colmeiro, José. *La Novela Policíaca Española: Teoría e Historia Crítica.* Prólogo Manuel Vázquez Montalbán. Madrid: Anthropos, 1994.

Craig-Odders, Renée W. *The Detective Novel in Post-Franco Spain. Democracy, Disillusionment, and Beyond.* New Orleans, University Press of the South, 1999.

Craig-Odders, Renée W., Jacky Collins, and Glen S. Close, (eds). *Hispanic and Luso-Brazilian,* Jefferson, NC: McFarland & Co., 2006.

Detective Fiction. Essays on the "Género Negro" Tradition. Jefferson, NC: McFarland & Co., 2006.

Fischer-Hornung, Dorothea and Monika Mueller. *Sleuthing ethnicity: the detective in multiethnic crime fiction.* London: Associated University Presses, Fairleigh Dickinson University Press, 2003.

Gosselin, Adrienne Johnson. *Multicultural Detective Fiction: Murder from the "Other" Side.* New York: Garland Publishing, 2002.

Hart, Patricia. *The Detective in Spanish Fiction.* Rutherford, NJ: Fairleigh Dickinson University Press, 1987.

—*The Spanish Sleuth. The Detective in Spanish Fiction.* Rutherford, NJ: Fairleigh Dickinson University Press, 1987.

Hühn, Peter. "The Detective as Reader: Narrativity and Reading Concepts in Detective Fiction." *Modern Fiction Studies* 33 (1987): 451–66.

Landeira, Ricardo. *El Género Policiaco En La Literatura Española Del Siglo XIX.* San Vicente del Raspeig, Alicante: Universidad de Alicante, 2001.

Paredes Núñez, Juan, ed. *La Novela Policiaca Española.* Granada: Universidad de Granada, 1989.

Pérez, Genaro J. *Ortodoxia y Heterodoxia De La Novela Policíaca Hispana: Variaciones Sobre El Género Negro.* Hispanic Monographs. Newark, NJ: Juan de la Cuesta, 2002.

Resina, Joan Ramon. *El cadáver en la cocina. La novela criminal en la cultura del desencanto.* Barcelona: Anthropos, 1997.

Rzepka, Charles J. *Detective Fiction.* Cambridge: Polity Press, 2005.

Stavans, Ilan. *Antiheroes. Mexico and Its Detective Novel.* Trans. Jesse H. Lytle and Jennifer A. Mattson. Madison: Fairleigh Dickinson University Press, 1997.

Todorov, Tzvetan. "The Typology of Detective Fiction." In *Modern Criticism and Theory: a Reader.* (eds) David Lodge and Nigel Wood 2nd edn. Essex, UK: Pearson Education Limited, 2000. 137–44.

Valles Calatrava, José R. *La novela criminal española.* Granada: Universidad de Granada, 1991.

Vázquez de Parga, Salvador. *La novela policíaca en España.* Barcelona: Ronsel, 1993.

Zapatero, Javier Sánchez and Àlex Martín Escribà. *Manuscrito Criminal: Reflexiones sobre novela y cine negro*. (I Congreso de Novela y Cine Negro 2005) Salamanca: Librería Cervantes, 2006.

4

Two men walk into a bar

Michelle Robinson

"Suppose you had a million dollars. You could buy a boat, a big car, a house, clothes, food, and many good things. But could you buy a friend? Could you buy a spring morning? Could you buy health? And how could we be happy without friends, health and spring?"

QUESTION FROM FREEDOM SCHOOL CURRICULUM

"The relationship, therefore, of a black boy to a white boy is a very complex thing."

JAMES BALDWIN

Black pretexts and formula fictions

"Consider these items," writes literary critic LeRoy Lad Panek: "there was an Irishman, a kangaroo, and a Rolls Royce locked in a deserted ballroom in Croydon. Two things can be made out of these disparate elements, a joke and a detective story" (14–15). For a hodgepodge of "disparate elements," look no further than John Kennedy Toole's *A Confederacy of Dunces*. It isn't easy to advance beyond the opening credits: first up is

Toole's rapacious, obscenely erudite protagonist Ignatius Reilly, who makes his way about town in a "lumbering, elephantine fashion," dressed in an eccentric green hunting cap and grimy plaids that, at least to Ignatius, "suggested a rich inner life" (Toole 1). He is joined by his mother, Mrs Reilly, a widow afflicted with "arthuritis" of the elbow and perennially doused in cheap muscatel, and the anti-"communiss" enthusiast who will become her geriatric suitor, "grampaw" Claude Robichaux. Then there is Lana Lee, the proprietress of the crummy downtown Night of Joy bar, who operates a pornography ring with a pimply juvenile named George; looks like, in the words of Ignatius, a "Nazi commandant" (23); and periodically snarls out aphoristic gems like "Mothers are full of shit" (24). Her two employees are down-and-out B-girl Darlene, who dreams of life as an exotic dancer with a "socko routine" (104), and the young black janitor Burma Jones, who takes a job at the Night of Joy to avoid arrest for vagrancy. To wrap up this initial line-up, there is Policeman Mancuso, a skinny, affable boy scout of a cop with a "platonically intense" love for his motorcycle (35). Mancuso gets saddled with undercover duty, clad in "ballet tights and a yellow sweater" for his failure to arrest "genuine bona fide suspicious characters" (27). And these comic characters make up only a fraction of Toole's motley crew in a novel so jam-packed with uncommon individuals and peculiar events it seems to spiral out of control.

Michael Kline labels Toole's novel "grotesque" since it is so resistant to the "incongruous mental shift toward resolution in the mind of the reader" (284). In contrast to the average joke, which keeps a narrow set of variables on a tight leash, A Confederacy of Dunces lets loose with its company of screwballs and an episodic bent, fueling an inexhaustible narrative engine that propels the novel toward a "humor of unresolved discontinuity" (284). And yet, Kline admits, Toole's book is a miraculous balancing act, which against all odds manages to "accommodate the stasis of unassimilable grotesque to the telos of narration" (287). A strange pattern of cause and effect emerges, and this "coexistence of the grotesque with sequentiality" keeps the plot from hurling itself into a disastrous collision course and a very messy ending (Kline 290). Certainly, crime runs wild in New Orleans, which Ignatius refers to as the "flagrant vice capital of the civilized world": there are "Antichrists, alcoholics, sodomites, drug addicts, fetishists, onanists, pornographers, frauds, jades, litterbugs, and lesbians, all of whom are only too well protected by graft" (Toole 3). The city streets are barely patrolled by a green cop determined to discover "the forces of evil generated by the hideous—and apparently impossible to uncover—underground of suspicious characters" (35). But they are uncovered, and not primarily by Policeman Mancuso. Instead, it is Burma Jones who assists in the apprehension of Lana Lee's pornography syndicate, and it is Burma Jones's machinations that corral the petty crooks and turn them over to the vice squad.

Urban crime rings, cops and undercover agents who find themselves "stumbling across the related sequences of cause and effect, agents and actions" (Kline 287)—if this is not some kind of practical joke, it is at least a detective story. In spite of the general pandemonium and the cast of loose cannons, there is narrative order at work in *A Confederacy of Dunces*—though there is no disputing that Toole played fast and loose with a familiar formula. But in a 1949 letter to James Sandhoe, Raymond Chandler had observed that "The detective or mystery story as an art form has been so thoroughly explored that the real problem for a writer now is to avoid writing a mystery story while appearing to do so" (48). By the mid-1950s, the American hard-boiled detective seemed to be on his last legs, or at the very least double-parked in a blind alley. What was missing from Mikey Spillane's best-selling detective fiction—"the wisecrack, the wit, the repartee, the rapid action and pace, the inevitable urgency of event, as well as the stylistic grace and gusto of a Chandler or Macdonald"—had been replaced by "dictatorial apologetics" and "advance propaganda for the police state" (Grella 116–17). Of course, detective fiction of the 1950s and 1960s was not limited to Spillane's rough Cold War vigilantism and misogyny, stuff that was "so hard-boiled you could break bricks with it" (Bill Ruehlman qtd. in Horsley 89). Ross Macdonald's poetic, highly stylized renderings of generational tensions and society's psychic maladies applied the formula developed by Dashiell Hammett and Chandler to the post-war scene (Horsley 92). Moreover, the police procedural took on the task of corroborating visible social facts, since, as George Dove points out, it "almost always has two faces, one determined by the demands of the real world and the other by narrative necessity" (Dove, *Police* 4).

Robert Skinner has observed that, "The American detective story is, in its most classical form, a story about an outsider, usually a private eye, rogue cop, or everyman who attempts to correct an injustice that law either causes, or at best can't remedy" (qtd. in Bailey, *Mystery Writers* 200), and it is the American detective novel that takes Toole's text from start to finish. The police procedural contributes the crime story as a quasi-realist articulation of the metropolis, as a delineation of the city's social forces and its assorted inhabitants superimposed on a municipal blueprint. And it is perhaps the police procedural's tendency to prioritize "systemic over emotional realism" (Mittel 137) that takes the criminal and crime-fighting characters in *A Confederacy of Dunces* across town and across the color line. Toole's black sleuth Burma Jones is an outsider and a detective. He may bear some resemblance to the hero of Rudyard Kipling's classic spy novel *Kim*, who "was immensely successful in doing nothing at all; he was a watcher who waited" (Winks 55), but Jones finds himself in a fix rarely faced by the classical detective. Not only is he constrained by the terms of the criminal justice system, where "the solution, no matter how logically or aesthetically satisfying, is of no value unless it will lead to the conviction of

the guilty party" (Dove, *Police* 51), Jones is himself a target for the New
Orleans police, who threaten to jail him for vagrancy. When solid proof
and an opportunity to expose Lana Lee's crime spree arrives, however,
he makes the most of it: "Jones, who brings forth the damning evidence,
comes up from 'slavery' once and for all. He will reap a reward and, more
important, be offered a real job" (Clark 274).

Planting a black detective in a comedy of manners was hardly a novelty.
In 1901 Pauline Hopkins expanded what literary critic Stephen Soitos
calls the "narrow parameters of white-male oriented detective fiction"
in her serialized novel *Hagar's Daughter* by re-imagining detection as a
cooperative venture with an interracial and intergenerational scope (25).
Hopkins's novel featured the intrepid domestic Venus Johnson, as well
as Mr Henry, a veteran of the 54th Massachusetts Volunteer Infantry,
among its primary sleuths. Less than a decade later, the Yoruba detective
of J. E. Bruce's *Black Sleuth* (1907–9) experienced first-hand the evils of
the Jim Crow South. The contiguity of the unseen attendant and professional eavesdropper was evident to Charles Chesnutt, who pointed out
in a 1926 symposium for *The Crisis*, "A Pullman porter who performs
wonderful feats in the detection of crime has great possibilities" (qtd. in
Bailey 119). What makes Toole's work particularly interesting, however, is
that its detective plot is a foil for the dubious practice of activist "ethnojournalism" exemplified by the work of John Howard Griffin's 1961 book
Black Like Me.

"Temporarily darkening his skin with dye, melanin pills and a sun lamp,
Griffin speculated that 'If I could take on the skin of a black man, live
whatever might happen and then share that experience with others, perhaps
at the level of shared human experience, we might come to some understanding that was not possible at the level of pure reason'" (217). While
chronicling his "undercover" experiences for the magazine *Sepia*, a provisionally "black" Griffin encountered the daily degradations of black life in
the South, not the least of which was the humiliating experience of trying
to earn a living. Despite his qualifications, Griffin noted that, "the best jobs
I got were menial—shining shoes, unloading trucks, carrying bags in the
bus station. The most I ever earned in one day was $3.95" (qtd. in Bonazzi
59). Though Griffin aimed to deliver a snapshot of these conditions to his
readers, his project was fundamentally flawed. Gayle Wald points out that
Griffin's approach stems from "a white liberal political discourse that posits
black subjects—here the 'deserving,' ennobled poor—as objects of ethno-
graphic contemplation, a positioning that serves retroactively to justify
the white researcher's presumed prerogative of masterful and disinterested
observation," and the "domesticating gaze" he applies to his subject (170).
In *A Confederacy of Dunces*, Toole replicates the defects of Griffin's activist
project in the person of Ignatius Reilly, who inundates the reader with his
sociopathic self-aggrandizement and insensible paternalism. Meanwhile,

Burma Jones, who cuts a wry figure of reason, provides a possible antidote to Reilly's misguided schemes.

A Confederacy of Dunces is, first and foremost, a comic novel that charts the courses of two characters that have been thrown into the workplace against their will. On the one hand, there is the obnoxious, bloated Ignatius Reilly, whose inauspicious entry into workforce consists of a stint for Levy Pants, where he defaces company records, forges letters in his employer's hand, and encourages a labor revolt by the black factory workers. As Pat Gardner points out, Toole is "having a fine time parodying sixties activism" (88) with Ignatius's revolutionary memos and correspondence from his erstwhile "girlfriend" Myrna Minkoff, who hosts lectures on "Erotic Liberty as a Weapon Against Reactionaries" at the New York City YMCA, promising "more and better sex for all and a crash program for minorities" (Toole 176). By contrast, the janitor Burma Jones—who is generally shrouded in sunglasses and a cloud of cigarette smoke—doubles as an armchair detective, marshalling clues and, in consultation with his friend Watson, plotting to sabotage the schemes of his nefarious employer, Lana Lee. If Reilly is an alarmingly long-winded, self-selected civil rights spokesman who plans to investigate the conditions of black workers, Jones's acts of detection: his surreptitious searches of the workplace and experimental communiqués, are engineered to round up a circle of suspects, criminal accessories and the New Orleans police at the Night of Joy bar where he is virtually held captive. In this way, a detective plot embedded in *A Confederacy of Dunces* detonates the picaresque account of Ignatius Reilly exploits and the ticking time bomb that is Reilly's politics.

The radicals are, in their private lives, such shits

Myrna Minkoff writes a letter to Ignatius Reilly. "This 'automobile accident,'" she warns her former classmate, "is a new crutch to help you make excuses for your meaningless, impotent existence"; his hours would be better spent tackling the "crucial problems of our times" (79). Minkoff, an activist and apparently a freelance Freudian, chides Ignatius for his predictable grievances and his implausible anecdotes—he had announced in his latest hand-written epistle that both of his wrists were broken in a collision of considerable force. Myrna, whom Ignatius describes as a "loud, offensive maiden from the Bronx," is a radical of the first order (124). She is never happier, Ignatius snidely reflects, than in the event of a police dog "sinking its fangs into her black leotards or when she was being dragged feet first down stone steps from a Senate hearing" (125). Myrna's latest project is a "bold and shattering movie" about interracial marriage:

We have found a girl from the streets of Harlem to play the wife. She is such a real, vital person that I have made her my very closest friend. I discuss her racial problems with her constantly, drawing her out even when she doesn't feel like discussing them—and I can tell how fervently she appreciates these dialogues with me. (80)

Myrna's possessive adulation of a "real, vital" Harlemite unites her with that brand of 1960s white college activists who became fixated on the destitution of some black southerners and, accordingly, dedicated a segment of the Freedom School curriculum "to explaining the differences between what were called 'Material Things,' which were associated with whites, and 'Soul Things,' which were associated with blacks" (Russell 386–7). Myrna, we discover, has also spent a summer touring the rural South where she hoped to "teach Negroes folk songs she had learned at the Library of Congress" (126). This was one of many passionate schemes to import her odious "liberal doxy" to the lower states, or as Ignatius observes with unusual insight, "Myrna is very sincere; unfortunately, she is also offensive" (126). Myrna Minkoff's film in the making, which is seemingly "chock-full of disturbing truths and has the most fascinating tonalities and ironies," may be just another expression in a laundry list of white liberal hypocrisies, but her utterly misguided schemes stir Ignatius Reilly to action (80). In his typically deranged way, Ignatius is determined to defeat her on her own turf, to relinquish his voluntary "exile" if only to "make Myrna look like a reactionary in the field of social action" (101).

Yes, the past five years have been devoted to composing his barely-started but "magnificent study in contemporary history," watching adolescent television and consuming his drink of choice, Dr Nut, but this monastic seclusion must be ascribed to a few harrowing encounters with the job market (28). As a college instructor, he refused to grade "illiteracies and misconceptions burbling from the dark minds" of his students, and a "misguided trip" to Baton Rouge to interview for a teaching job culminated in a "mental block against working" after Ignatius suffered various paroxysms and much vomiting aboard a Greyhound scenic cruiser (51, 52). But in *A Confederacy of Dunces*, Ignatius is again thrust in front of the want ads and propelled into the workforce by his mother. Mrs Reilly demands her son seek employment at the advice of Patrolman Mancuso (a man who, Ignatius hypothesizes grimly, thinks that "everything will be all right if everyone works continuously" (48)).

Ignatius manages to secure a place at Levy Pants, a floundering enterprise desperate for office workers and devoid of morale. The company consists of a decrepit brick office building, a district of utter bureaucratic incompetence that the office manager Mr Gonzalez refers to as the "brain center" (82). Its dilapidated appendage is "a barnlike prototype of an airplane hangar" where the pants are manufactured (82). Toole presents the

Levy Pant factory as "two structures fused into one macabre unit," a body with brain and bosom, a palpitating heart and the head of an imbecile (82). When he finally makes his "descent into that particular inferno" where the factory workers are housed, Ignatius pointedly differentiates between "the doldrums of the production line," with its egregiously underpaid and disgruntled workforce, and the "fevered hustle of the office" (101, 124). Nevertheless, the "hissing and roaring" that emerges from the factory and the smokestacks that "discharged occasional smoke of a very sickly shade," bear a remarkable resemblance to the erratic operations of Ignatius's pyloric valve (100, 82).

If Levy Pants exemplifies the malfunctioning, monstrous body of Southern industry, Ignatius Reilly is the schizophrenic asset in which its brains and body collide. Before long, the tempo of white-collar life and the workday are scheduled in keeping with the successive phases of Ignatius's unpredictable digestive tract, with whose intricacies, incidentally, Gonzalez and senile associate Miss Trixie are forcibly regaled. Reilly makes over the workplace in his own misshapen image, embellishing the dilapidated office with potted plants, bringing greasy bologna sandwiches for Miss Trixie, and setting up shop beneath an arduously wrought sign which identifies him as Levy Pant's "DEPARTMENT OF RESEARCH AND REFERENCE//I. J. REILLY, CUSTODIAN" (82). Reilly is, however, less a curator of the Levy estate than an agent of corporate espionage. Ruminating after hours in the confines of his bedroom, he thoughtfully titles his tell-all manuscript, "THE JOURNAL OF A WORKING BOY, OR, UP FROM SLOTH." In this "new, extremely commercial project," Ignatius depicts himself as a bright young thing freshly inducted into the professional-managerial class, and intermittently refers to himself as "Darryl, Your Working Boy" (101) or, in another issue of this eccentric missive, signs off as "Gary, Your Militant Working Boy" (127).

Reilly's "Journal of a Working Boy" is a masterpiece of gung-ho initiative, corporate toadying, suppressed rage and deadpan narcissism that poses as a "contemporary, vital, real document of a young man's problems" (101). It is also brainchild of a thin-skinned psychotic office worker whose self-designated mission is to dispose of the company's records. Ignatius's Jekyll-and-Hyde approach to office life seems to verify his hypothesis that "Being actively engaged in the system which I criticize will be an interesting irony in itself" (52–3). As "an observer and critic in disguise," moreover, his exploits at the office are designed to puncture the morale of that so-called social revolutionary Myrna Minkoff, as a "slashing, vicious attack upon her being and worldview" (74, 101). But while Reilly takes African American destitution as the focal point of his printed harangue, what he hopes to realize is his own notoriety, an ambition that does not necessarily entail and may in fact resist any concerted effort to alter material conditions. When, for instance, black rioters finally demand fair wages and "wreak havoc" on the Levy Pants Office, knocking over potted plants and creating mild confusion, Ignatius turns tantrum on his former apprentices for defiling the order *he* has established—and this in addition to his vocal exasperations with the technical difficulties he encounters filming the event ("The Crusade for Moorish Dignity") for documentary purposes.

"The Journal of a Working Boy" is not the only "vital, real" document Ignatius invents for public view. Nor does his stab at cinema verité round out his play with expressive media. At Levy Pants, his every act is a letter, every ounce theatrics to be broadcast as an affront to that "offensive minx" Minkoff, who has accused him of "failure, as an intellectual and soldier of ideas, to actively participate in critical social movements" (80). Ignatius comes upon another opportunity to publicize his fury when he discovers that Abelman's Dry Goods has received inferior goods from the Levy factory: a shipment of pants only "two feet long in the leg," as the rundown manager reports to Mr Levy (87). On the sly, Ignatius concocts a letter in defense of the substandard product, addressed to "Mr I. Abelman, Mongoloid, Esq." and signed by Gus Levy (88). In this missive, Ignatius maintains that the undersized garments were deliberately delivered to the Dry Goods distributor, whose failure to make the garments "a byword in masculine fashion" revealed a lack of "initiative" and faith (89). He also disparages Abelman for his inability to "assimilate stimulating concepts of commerce into your retarded and blighted worldview"—an accusation which, when paired with his proletarian shtick, suggests that the distance between working-class advocate and corporate sycophant is only as broad as Reilly's ego (89).

Ignatius's hostile letter to Abelman is an assault on office bureaucracy; Ignatius's broader front on the inferior political sensibility of Myrna Minkoff is his Journal, whose exposé of business affairs is comparable to the well-known experiment John Howard Griffin undertook and documented in his best-selling *Black Like Me* (1961). Georgina Kleege points out that Griffin's "highly subjective narrative" puts the work in the category of New Journalism (111), but Hugh Rank contends that Griffin's tactics in and of themselves were analogous to those "of the spy, the prisoner-of-war, or the 'innocent prisoner' plotting alone, in secret, against the evil institution" (816). Though Ignatius Reilly lacks Griffin's cosmetic camouflage, he has an agenda that is in many ways comparable: to investigate the wretched conditions at the Levy Plant factory as an eyewitness, to churn out an affidavit of workers' grievances vouched for by his own eyes.

When he finally makes his way to the physical plant, Ignatius reports that the once-throbbing bosom of the factory has degenerated into an arrhythmic heart of darkness. In this "barn-like structure," Ignatius writes in his Journal, he has discovered a dilapidated sweatshop of such primitive character, and a labor force so brutally treated, that the whole obsolete affair might be exhibited at the Smithsonian Institution, at which point "the visitors to that questionable museum would defecate into their garish tourist outfits" (118). This American miscellany "combines the worst of *Uncle Tom's Cabin* and Fritz Lang's *Metropolis*," leaving Ignatius's social conscience so distressed that, "My valve threw in a hearty response" (118–19). The gut-wrenching scene he describes is one part Stowe, one part Lang (or an intermediate agglomeration worse than the sum of its parts) and called "mechanized Negro slavery." Its euphemistic equivalent is "progress," for which Reilly's lack of affinity is clarified in the following addendum: "(were they in the picking stage of their evolution, they would at least be in the healthful outdoors singing and eating watermelons [as they are, I believe, supposed to do when in group alfresco])" (118–19). The decades spent carousing and cotton picking were, according to this logic, the salad days of American industry, and the factory workers, having abandoned their rural seat but not their congenital roughness, are ill-fitted to the shift from "picking cotton to tailoring it" (119).

Though he protests these developments with gusto, even Ignatius senses some analytic defect in his odious commemoration of plantation life. "Lest some professional civil rights organization be offended," the "Working Boy" apologizes for his tasteless and potentially erroneous evocation of the watermelon-eating coon, adding

> I would imagine that today people grasp for the cotton with one hand while the other hand presses a transistor radio to the sides of their heads so that it can spew bulletins about used cars and Sofstyle Hair Relaxer and Royal Crown Hair Dressing and Gallo wine about their eardrums, a filtered menthol cigarette dangling from their lips and threatening to set the entire cotton field ablaze ..." (119)

Reilly's modern worker is jerry-rigged somewhere between a stooping sharecropper, a citizen-sucker in the consumer's republic, and a derelict hepcat coolly poised to set Tara aflame.

Griffin attempted to personally detect the degradations to which blacks in America were subjected, though he was in fact reiterating observations that had been made for decades by writers like Richard Wright and Ralph Ellison. This is ostensibly the purpose of Reilly's undercover intervention, but Reilly's presumptuous grandstanding draws attention to the fundamental flaws of a project like Griffin's. The popularity of *Black Like Me* was predicated both on the assumption that Griffin "could speak for black people" and "the persistence of white readers in assuming black people incapable of elaborating upon their own experiences" (Gubar 29)—an irony of which Griffin was himself aware. Paradoxically, the veracity of Griffin's report and the genuineness of his mission were validated by his proximity to African Americans and his choice to present *his* undercover experiences as exemplary of "blackness." Availing himself of black "authenticity" while exercising white authority, Griffin cast himself as the protagonist of a community deprived of civil rights and manipulated by violence. At the same time, his journalistic clout depended on the public's faith in "the white researcher's presumed prerogative of masterful and disinterested observation" (Wald 170). As Kate Baldwin explains, Griffin's project was an instance of "'good faith' liberal politics in which the 'black' person possesses the ability to place on the well-meaning 'white' person an 'authentic' antiracist personhood through the very fact of association" (117). Moreover, *Black Like Me* is permeated by Griffin's residual "whiteness." The reader is never not aware that he is not black, and it is precisely the mediated narrativization of each event that neutralizes its content and emphasizes Griffin's role as author.

Toole pokes fun at this kind of rhetorical monopoly and shape-shifting authorial voice through Ignatius's Journal—and Ignatius has the gall to defend the merits of "a social history of the United States from my vantage point," explaining that, "[O]ur nation demands the scrutiny of a completely disengaged observer like your Working Boy" (123). The tone of the Journal modulates with such rapidity it can capture Ignatius's straight-faced bigotry, paranoia and hysterical solipsism—not to mention his delusional condescension and unhinged adoration for the workers—in a few sentences. When, for example, Ignatius senses the employees' irritation with his presence, he wallows in his astute assessment of the circumstances, commenting, "Their huge white eyes were already labeling me a 'Mister Charlie.' I would have to struggle to show them my almost psychotic devotion to helping them" (121). To ingratiate himself with the factory workers, Ignatius takes advantage of the music blaring on the loudspeakers. He explains, "I knew the physical spasm which it was supposed to elicit," from his daily devotions to those "blighted children" on American Bandstand; moreover, he has a rhythmic dexterity inherited from ancestral "jigging on the heath" (121). To persuade the employees that he shares in their "high spirits" and is one of their own, he "shuffled about beneath one of the loudspeakers, twisting and shouting, mumbling insanely, 'Go! Go! Do it, baby, do it! Hear me talkin' to ya. Wow!'" (121).

This and other slanderous expressions of "kinship" with the factory workers are instances of blackface minstrelsy. Ignatius's disquieting attempt at cross-racial identification is at once a gesture of admiration, a tentative appeal to camaraderie and a demeaning brand of impersonation that conveys his own superiority—though when the factory workers point at him and laugh, Reilly considers his exaggerated performance a success. Styling himself as a cultural critic with designs to rile up the ideologically compliant proletariat, Reilly laments, "The Negro terrorizes simply by being himself; I however, must browbeat in order to achieve the same end" (106). This "browbeating" is the cornerstone of Reilly's radicalism: a simplistic adulation of black alterity whose greatest mouthpiece was Norman Mailer's notorious essay "White Negro," an exercise in cultural appropriation whose underside is a sort of plantation nostalgia. In Mailer's account, the Negro is a repository for primitive emotional materials. He who lives by necessity "in the enormous present," who "subsisted for his Saturday-night kicks, relinquishing the pleasures of the mind for the more obligatory pleasures of the body" hoards that elemental physicality the white man has long abandoned, by virtue of which in the "wedding of the white and the black it was the Negro who brought the cultural dowry" (156). Mailer's deliberations were set forth as an atlas of the Negro's psychic terrain; they were, to be more precise, an indication that its author was "in the grip of a bad case of the I've-got-the-pseudo-anglo-saxon-technological-male menopausal-twentieth-century-civilized man's blues" (Michele Wallace qtd. in Gubar 178). Mailer's essay is a scantily veiled expression of cross-racial same-sex desire; his monosyllabic cogitations on the "rage and the infinite variations of joy, lust, languor, growl, cramp, pinch, scream, and despair" of the Negro orgasm grant his subject a tremendous sexuality, if nothing else (Mailer 157). Ignatius Reilly's musings are of a similar vein:

> Perhaps I should have been a Negro. I suspect that I would have been a rather large and terrifying one, continually pressing my ample thigh against the withered thighs of old white ladies in public conveyances a great deal and eliciting more than one shriek of panic. (123)

Reilly's musing is an explicit exercise in cross-racial charades, an earnestly obscene meditation on predatory sexuality and its decrepit, geriatric victims.

Mailer's "White Negro" might soothe his anxieties by turning to a racial Other for prosthetic brawn, but his disposition (what Toole duplicates in Reilly's "psychotic devotion") was not so distant from the outlook of the sober champions of civil rights: white liberals in the mainstream. For example, in a 1964 interview for *The Progressive*, Griffin explained that white liberals "tend to adopt the attitude: 'You bring the whiskey and I'll bring the Negro,' to a party or a meeting" (qtd. in Gubar 188). Unrequited interracial love affair or "intellectual fad"? No matter; each makes "blackness" its commodity. Ignatius gives a good impression of this liberal set in his Journal when he objects to the poor facilities and bad pay at Levy Pants, then speculates that the factory workers have "better things to do than loiter about Levy Pants, such as composing jazz or creating new dances or doing whatever those things are that they do with such facility" (122).

Ignatius's attempts to associate with the Levy Pants factory workers replicate Mailer's determination to make the Negro his bedfellow. His own exile from the mainstream is, Ignatius concedes, completely "voluntary," yet as the expert in this double occupancy, he demands the Negro embrace social exclusion and openly decries those who "wish to become active

members of the American middle class" (122). Reilly forthrightly disparages
the pursuit of any measure of bourgeois equality, hypothetically counseling
his elected cohorts to "studiously avoid sitting the middle class in lunch
counters and public transportation," because contact with this materialist
class would impinge upon the "intrinsic honesty of and grandeur of my
being" (122). What's more, Ignatius surmises that blacks must forcefully
resist the path of upward mobility, and discourages cooperation with
activists who feel otherwise: "Personally, I would agitate quite adamantly
if I suspected that anyone were attempting to help me upward toward the
middle class" (122). Succumb to any such pact with the devil, he explains,
and "they may seal their own doom" (122). Ignatius's disquisition on the
economic habits of black America suggests that one permanent fixture of
the fantasy that unites the white man to his "Negro playmate" is the mental
image of black deprivation and the "exoticization of ghetto dwellings"
which blacks are presumed to inhabit (Savran 120). Ignatius's belief that,
"if I were a Negro, I would not be pressured by my mother to find a good
job, for no good jobs would be available" (123) is simply a vulgar reprise
of Mailer's wistful observation that "The cameos of security for the average
white: mother and the home, job and the family, are not even a mockery
to millions of Negroes; they are impossible" (156). The counterculture
of the 1960s offered a third variation on this valorization of poverty by
temporarily aligning themselves with oppressed blacks, then "asserting an
incommensurability between what they believe to be the black struggle for
the "sick" perquisites of bourgeois culture and the hippie struggle for peace,
love, and enlightenment" (Savran 120).

What might have been an attack on the corporeal and corporate
whiteness of Mr Levy and his business associates in Reilly's Journal is
merely a narcissistic enterprise. Ignatius's depiction of the Negro worker
as the consummate figure of exploitation, a captive of capitalist modernity,
and the repository of some primal nihilism is purely self-serving. Indeed,
Reilly's radical agenda is barely distinguishable from Myrna's free lessons in
black folk music or white student activists "teaching black Mississippians
the value of the ascetic life" (Russell 387). In spite of his anarchic outlook
and handy forgeries, however, the radical event Ignatius hopes for does not
materialize, nor does the "Crusade for Moorish Dignity" amount to much
more than a protest banner that Ignatius has scrawled on his own soiled bed
sheet. In his offensive against office bureaucracy, Reilly designs a workplace
in which data and historical record are best disposed of, contracts are
consciously rendered meaningless, and whatever is "blackness" is misused
as commodity and defined by white activists. Under such circumstances,
how might an African American presence make itself known?

Unregistered offenders

A young black man named Burma Jones listens "in attentive detachment somewhere within his cloud" to the story of the unpleasant confrontation between Patrolman Mancuso and Ignatius Reilly and the ensuing accusations of "cawmniss" leanings that led to Mr Robichaux's arrest (16). Jones's sole commentary on this strange incident is the exclamation "Ooo-wee," a refrain that, as it turns out, is as habitual to Jones as his exhalations of smoke. Toole calls him a "cloud of smoke," he is unseen in the "secrecy of his cloud"; conversely, the "smoke screen" is also the index of Jones's unceasing surveillance. A cloud of smoke is not his only synecdochal by-product. Behind his dark, "space-age sunglasses" (13–14) Jones is "eyeless"; this disposition reflects his visual remoteness to others and alludes perhaps to the kind of impassive, objective eye one associates with the detective, otherwise it is a humorless crack at the black man's dispossession. Though Toole notes that, "through his glasses he [Jones] could hardly see anything at all" (35), this visual impediment hardly impairs the man's cognitive acuity. Jones shrewdly sees through Lana Lee's dubious charitable enterprise and makes a "mental association" at every instance he hears that "fat cat in the green cap"—a sort of corpulent Robin Hood—has been sighted wreaking havoc on the city (34). The smoke, moreover, works to his favor: What stands for also stands between, which is undoubtedly why, when an old white lady regards him with apprehension, Jones finds himself "wishing he could smoke on the bus," presumably to invoke that camouflage which shields him from scrutiny.

In the case of Burma Jones, Toole's use of synecdoche deftly skirts the problem of physical caricature, and in doing so, cannily indicates that a black body appears, even to the novel's author, primarily as a distortion. On the other hand, one could as easily argue that the novel lacks the guile to do anything other than parrot the squeamish white women on the public bus whose chief concern is to "avoid any contact with the anatomy of Jones" (54). The character's envelope of smoke is a partition that endlessly evokes and seemingly perpetuates the regime of segregation that persisted in parts of Louisiana well into the 1960s. And yet Burma Jones hones in on the visible indicators of white supremacist sensibility that persist even (or especially) in the face of desegregation.

> "Look at that old gal," Jones mused to his psyche as the bus bounced and threw him against the woman sitting beside him. "She think cause I color I gonna rape her. She about to throw her grammaw ass out the window. Whoa! I ain gonna rape nobody." (53)

Jones shifts "discreetly away from her, crossing his legs," to assuage her fears of his carnal appetites, it would seem. But he is not merely the recipient of a bigoted gaze. Instead, he carries on an astute inner dialogue about a disagreeable stranger in an integrated public space that has only just begun to exist, and achieves a paradoxical "attentive detachment," especially when he "retreats into his cloud," a sort of extra-diagetical site from which all others are excluded.

With this scene Toole is clearly borrowing from a realm of experience that Griffin describes in *Black Like Me*, though Gayle Wald points out that Griffin "cannot ever resolve the two 'unreconciled strivings' of his fieldwork: the desire to record his observations (to remain in a position of white mastery), and the desire to become a full 'participant' by ditching his notebooks (to relinquish white privilege)" (160). When Griffin rides a New Orleans bus and notices a tired middle-aged white woman standing in the aisle, he is suddenly "tormented" by his "lack of gallantry" and instinctively rises to relinquish his seat (21). He is immediately, acutely aware, however, of the "frowned disapproval" he receives from the Negro passengers for what he refers to as "going against the race"—a remark whose accuracy proves so dubious in this instance that Griffin himself introduces scare quotes at either end (21). A "subtle tug-of-war became instantly clear," he explains—no want of vacant seats keeps white passengers in the aisles, only a stubborn resistance to succumb to the spirit of desegregation—and, "To give them your seat," Griffin reflects grimly, taking the part of the blacks in the interminable face-off, "was to let them win" (21). At the same time, Griffin is demoralized by the stares of black passengers and again parks himself in his seat, "slumped back under the intensity of their stares" (21). Yet Griffin naively imagines he might negotiate a detente, and turns his own just-cowed gaze on the white woman in the aisle.

> For an instant our eyes met. I felt sympathy for her, and thought I detected sympathy in her glance. The exchange blurred the barriers of race (so new to me) long enough for me to smile and vaguely indicate the empty seat beside me, letting her know she was welcome to accept it.
>
> Her blue eyes, so pale before, sharpened and she spat out, "What you looking at me like *that* for?" (21–2)

Griffin's artless double consciousness does not permit him to sit in solidarity with his new "fellows," nor does it prepare him to traverse the color line. By contrast, Jones's more discerning gaze appraises race relations with relative ease.

It is one thing to call Jones a cultural critic and quite another to present him as a detective, even a "faux ethnic" detective who, in the tradition of Charlie Chan, is a custom-made exotic (Earl Derr Bigger's Chan was best known for "his flowery, Confucian aphorisms, his lapses into pidgin English, his patience, his attention to detail," and so forth (Macdonald and Macdonald 60)). Jones's outrageous and marvelous attacks on Lana Lee, the crooked proprietor of the Night of Joy, are a welcome disturbance—and when are his remarks anything other than interruption? He can only talk out of turn since it is never his turn to speak; however, there is little prestige in the part of comic relief. What distinguishes Jones from many of the other characters in the novel is his refusal to affect a proairetic sensibility: his repudiation, for example, of Patrolman Mancuso's single-minded capitulation to the tasks assigned by his police superiors, which rules out any chance Mancuso will make sense out of a series of seemingly haphazard events and leaves him (Mancuso) ever unmindful of their eventualities. By contrast, Jones very deliberately and explicitly "connects the dots" between the irregular pandemonium Ignatius Reilly sets off about the city, the suspect business dealings between Lana Lee and her tight-jeaned adolescent associate George, and the pathetic failures of Patrolman Mancuso, now an eccentric "undercover" agent.

In this sense, Jones constitutes an "interpretive community" of one (or, we might say, embodies an interpretive strategy typical of the *reader* of detective fiction) by taking initiative as a *writer* of texts, one who is responsible for "constituting their properties and assigning their intentions" rather than simply reading them (Stanley Fish qtd. in Dove, "Detection Formula" 28). Jones undertakes an investigative line of attack whose end is to incriminate Lana Lee. Peter Hühn reminds us that, at its most basic level, "the detective novel hinges on the social effects that the concealment and the 'publication' of a particular story, namely that of the crime, will have" (Hühn 451), and Jones's cautious audit of Lana Lee's "charitable" activities presume no other end. "Now I jus waitin to get some kinda evidence," Jones explains, "When I do, I really gonna flap my mouth at the precinct" (71). Jones's ambition to substantiate that "the Night of Joy a glorify cathouse" demonstrates his grasp of the "social dimensions of narrativity" (Hühn 451) as well as his evidentiary criteria for a legitimate narrative.

That Burma Jones's investigative work has as its antithesis Ignatius Reilly's vicious but wholesome report "The Journal of a Working Boy, or, Up from Sloth" is a detail in his favor; that Reilly's labor politics are brilliantly erroneous, even offensive to a fault, is another. Jones is the recipient of rumors and anecdotal evidence that almost always come to him second hand, and so easily takes the part of a long-distance "armchair detective" rather than a sleuth on the prowl—though the story of his arrest outside of a Woolworth's implies, at least in Toole's tongue-in-cheek fashion, that this character is not entitled to a seat. But he is neither a passive observer nor a helpless target. When Lana Lee barks, "why don't you try keeping your mouth shut, boy?" Jones retorts, "Say, who you callin boy?" and snaps, "You ain Scarla O'Horror" (75).

Lee's name is undoubtedly a cross between Hollywood's notorious "Nightclub Queen" Lana Turner and Vivian Leigh, the face of Margaret Mitchell's *Gone With the Wind*, and she rules the seedy Night of Joy bar with a fist fit for an overseer. Jones admits to Darlene, his B-girl co-worker, that Lee "ain exactly *hire* me. She kinda buyin me off a auction block" (34). His assessment of the Night of Joy bar as a remnant of antebellum atrocities may seem far-fetched, but Lee's arrangement with Burma Jones does in fact deliver the non-offending delinquent over to indentured servitude. As a janitor, Jones finds himself in a bind: "Hey! I'm workin in modren slavery. If I quit, I get report for bein vagran. If I stay, I'm gainfully employ on a salary ain even startin to be a minimal wage" (131). Jones's stack of auxiliary verbs, specifically his "ain even startin to be" with regards to basic compensation, speak to an era of legal protection and fair compensation that has yet to be inaugurated. But Lana Lee appreciates that civil stasis is fast disappearing, and that getting her hooks into Jones is a serendipitous event and "something of a deal, like a discount price," as "in my line of business, you gotta keep your eye peeled for a bargain" (107).

Jones menaces Lana Lee with talk of civil rights, yet he has already discovered that to become "gainfully employ" and "a member of the community" is an ugly prospect: "Yeah, I got me a nigger job and nigger pay. Now I really a member of the community. Now I a real nigger. No vagran. Just nigger" (53). The disagreeable truth is that the "auction block" is his only invitation to society, predicated on the difficult irony that ceasing to be dispossessed requires a black man to relinquish bodily freedom. So long as Lana Lee is determined to control his fate, to foist on him the role of "old-timey nigger" (or if not, to pack him off to the police as a two-time offender), Burma Jones's prospects for change depend on his capacity to stage a civil rights spectacle, and the fall of the Night of Joy is a drama he arranges personally.

When Jones "connects the dots," he is not simply unearthing a web of pre-existing, inter-reliant intrigue (or reading for the plot, as Peter Brooks would put it). Instead, he is enlisting apparently discontinuous narrative fragments in a single storyline. Lana Lee's shifty dealings with the "United Orphan Fun"; the repeated assaults on Patrolman Mancuso (including a well-deserved bruising by a triad of violent dykes named "Frieda Club, Betty Bumper, and Liz Steele" (104)); the mystifying exploits of the "fat mother got him the green cap" (89)—all these events are purposefully assembled so that, in its outward appearance "the unreconstructed incongruousness of the grotesque situation or description joins the dynamism of the metonymically motivated causal sequences of plot" (Kline 288). The aim of these circumspect maneuvers is no secret to the reader. As he informs his friend Watson, Jones fully intends to recruit that "fat freak" Ignatius Reilly, and to "drop him in the Night of Joy like a nuclar bum" (241). Jones envisions the Cold War as a subsidiary of the Civil War; in a sort of impromptu echo of General Sherman, he declares that "The cotton fiel be burn to the groun before I'm through" (241), though his tactics are as grim as Dr Strangelove's.

An experimental communiqué proves Burma Jones's best means of tracking Lana Lee's crimes and unseating her repressive regime. "An address on a package wrapped in plain brown paper," Burma Jones muses, is "as damaging as a fingerprint on a gun" (224). This piece of writing takes anonymity and stamps it with an irrefutable identifying mark: a place of origin. According to this logic, a package with a return address is tale bearing, and if it is cast out aimlessly, a desperate plea for rescue like "a note in a bottle," its end, whatever its itinerary, must be its starting point. In order to escape the notice of Lana Lee's "hawk eyes and bloodhound nose," however, Jones can only trace the address in pencil as "minutely as possible." Nevertheless, he imagines his writing will catch the eye of a "professional saboteur" who would fix on this irregularity: the "something that shouldn't be there" (224): a barely visible indication of propriety on a parcel which, by its plain brown wrapping, broadcasts its illicit content while insisting that neither its recipient nor its distributor can be traced. As an effort to corral a saboteur (Ignatius Reilly) and a police officer (Mancuso) to wrap up the case of the "United Orphan Fun," this act signals his determination to play the detective by "reconnecting the fragmented signifying strings to design that makes sense, even if the sense is often 'nonsense'" (Kline 287).

Jones's experimental dispatch has massive consequences for the many characters in *A Confederacy of Dunces*. To begin with, it rounds up suspicious persons and lures them to the Night of Joy bar to finally reveal the emperor undressed; that is, not only will Jones ensure Lana Lee's pornographic photos are laid before the police at (of all times) the debut of Darlene's striptease show, but by apprehending the pornographers, Jones will bare himself of the structural arrangements that prescribe his own servitude. A return address is an attempt to secure recognition, of course, and it turns the tables on Lana Lee by rounding up the police and putting them on track to arrest her. But this episode is perhaps most eventful because of what it discloses: "Jones knelt down and, for the first time in the Night of Joy, took off his sunglasses" (224), fully exposing the private eye in an act of "sabotage that could finish Lana Lee forever" (223).

Burma Jones has launched an investigative project whose success hinges on his grasp of images and appearances and will end in newspaper coverage of a "Wild Incident on Bourbon Street." Jones tracks Ignatius Reilly, whose bombastic discourse reverberates through the city, and easily monitors Patrolman Mancuso, who is a sore thumb and sorrier cop, but these measures are implemented as part of an investigation that tosses Lana Lee in jail. In doing so, Jones retaliates against the standard assault on blacks' sexual propriety: he exposes images of his unclothed employer posing as an unusually depraved teacher, photos that are peddled to high school students as "school supplies."

A letter (or two, or three) arrives at its destination

Ignatius snatches a paper-wrapped package out of the hands of Lana Lee's distributor George, tears it open and discovers an exquisite pornographic print: "A nude woman was sitting on the edge of a desk next to a globe of the world. The suggested onanism with the piece of chalk intrigued Ignatius. Her face was hidden behind a large book" (288). A scribbled address takes him to the Night of Joy bar where a poster hawks the premiere of "*Harlett O'Hara, the Virgin-ny Belle* (and pet!)," and Burma Jones finds it all too easy to persuade Ignatius that this is the Boethius-reading beauty, held hostage by the bar's "Nazi proprietress." Jones assures Ignatius that "Harla talkin" is a harmless misrepresentation of Darlene's mangled striptease dialogue, but Ignatius pounces on the prospect, imagining "some incisive commentary which no one in her audience could fully comprehend" (297). Jones, thrilled at the success of his scheme, reflects, "The sabotage was working too perfectly. The fat mother really wanted to come to the Night of Joy" (297). But what is the pornographic picture if Ignatius's own literary productions returned to him in their true awfulness: An onanistic pedagogue, face swapped for *De Consolatio Philosophiae*, towering over the globe? His narcissistic ideal and none other than Lana Lee, the "Nazi proprietress," resident overseer, she who could administer those lashes Ignatius frequently orders?

It might seem more accurate to say that Ignatius was Jones's true premeditated missive, a missile he purposefully deposited in the Night of Joy bar since, as he reports to Watson in the aftermath of this explosive affair, "That fat freak a guarantee one hunner percent nucular bum. Shit. Drop him on somebody, everybody gettin caught in the fallout, gettin their ass blowed up" (350). But it is the parcel of pornography that assembles a network of unrelated parties by virtue of their interest in its perverse promise. To Lana Lee and George it denotes profits, to Ignatius it signifies an object of intimate and intellectual communion (and thus "a lance" he might "hurl right between Myrna's offensive eye" (327)), for Mancuso it portends a possible promotion, and for Jones it might provide escape from the prison of the "minimal wage." As "an object that circulates among the subjects and, by its very circulation, makes out of them a closed intersubjective community" the package of pornographic photos takes on something of the role of "the letter" (Žižek 18), which is to say that it gives shape "to the constitutive inconsistency of the symbolic order" as a latent effect whose motion propels the narrative but whose arrival would utterly compromise whatever order exists, like the three wishes that brought the fisherman more ill than good.

Jones determines the path of this "letter" and welcomes whatever upheaval it may bring by inscribing an address upon it, just as Jones entices Ignatius

into the Night of Joy bar and delivers Lana Lee, the subject of the incrimi-
nating photos, over to the police. But Ignatius is the self-elected addressee of
that remarkable print; he happens to be its intended recipient at the moment
he snatches a photo from George's stack and gloats, "This one is *mine*" (289).
When Ignatius skims through the article detailing the catastrophic events, his
eyes alight on a triptych of newspaper snapshots: Darlene, the B-girl turned
Bourbon Street starlet; Mancuso shoving Lana Lee into a police patrol car,
and "In the center the doped Negro was grinning at what looked like a
dead cow lying in the street" (337). Jones is the maker of a media spectacle
that Ignatius, for all his attempts, never achieved. Moreover, the newspaper
image reverses the patterns of political distortion Reilly has rehearsed again
and again. In the picture, Ignatius is merely a white stain, a bloated and inert
bulk sprawled in the road that Jones surveys. In short, Jones comes out on
top: his manipulations obliterate the particular institution that held him
captive; and his image is distinct from the law on his right and sensual enter-
tainments on his left. In spite of his successful detecting, Jones is not much
better off financially than where he started, and remarks to Watson, "Now I
sabotage myself right back to bin a vagran" (349).

And yet there is another piece of unfinished business: counterfeit correspondence with the owner of Abelman's Dry Goods, in which Ignatius,
posing as Gus Levy, described the vendor and his affiliates as a "faithless
people" who spout "incomprehensible babble" for daring to make inquiries
regarding a shipment of substandard pants (89). This particular letter seems
almost indefinitely to hang in the wings, but ultimately descends with a
vengeance. Abelman serves Gus Levy a $500,000 lawsuit for libel. Gus
Levy goes on the prowl for the author of this damaging note, whose culprit
could only be a member of the Levy Pants's staff: Doddering Miss Trixie is
only too happy to cast herself as a saboteur and finally get the sack, if only
to escape the clutches of the meddlesome Mrs Levy. Gus Levy, having hit
upon a self-elected scapegoat and foiled his spouse, feels finally disburdened
of his father's legacy. Inspired by the abbreviated garments that triggered
this string of events, Levy resolves to euthanize Levy Pants and breathe
life into a new and more profitable venture, Levy Shorts, and to bestow
an award in honor of his father, Leon Levy, for "meritorious service and
bravery" (375) to the hero of that "Wild Incident on Bourbon Street."

> Whoever Burma Jones was, he deserved a generous award … or reward.
> Offering him a job at the new Levy Shorts would be even better for
> public relations. An award and a job. With some good newspaper
> publicity to tie in with the opening of Levy Shorts. Was that a gimmick
> or wasn't it? (377)

Is it a gimmick or isn't it? Yes, it must be a gimmick if Jones ascends to
the place of an honest-to-god wage earner with decent career prospects on

the turn of a dime, or if a pornography bust and the arrival of Ignatius Reilly, the "nuclear bum," solve the economic problems of a black man in New Orleans. But Burma Jones does overcome the perverse stereotypes that govern his civic life and curb economic opportunities, and the detective plot is the route Toole takes to transform the social arrangement to Jones's advantage. The detective novel attempts to organize the world; it restores order at the moment when narrative seems to have failed, when it seems that there is only "mystery, of obscure origin, of obscure nature, of obscure purpose, hidden, secret" (Winks 44), and Jones's triumph is a utopian gesture on Toole's part. Generally speaking, detective novels end with the discreet withdrawal of the detective, though Toole ends by expunging Ignatius and a brand of activism that "frames" his sleuth in a world of distortion. Jones, who above all lacked recognition, is finally a "face" on the front page. If this is not an effect of detection it is at least a good joke.

Works cited

Bailey, Frankie Y. *Out of the Woodpile: Black Characters in Crime and Detective Fiction*. New York: Greenwood Press, 1991.

—*African American Mystery Writers: A Historical and Thematic Study*. Jefferson, North Carolina: McFarland and Company, Inc., 2008.

Baldwin, Kate. "Black Like Who? Cross-Testing the 'Real' Lines of John Howard Griffin's 'Black Like Me'." *Cultural Critique*. No. 40, The Futures of American Studies (Autumn, 1998): 103–43.

Bonazzi, Robert. *Man in the Mirror: John Howard Griffin and the Story of BLACK LIKE ME*. Maryknoll, New York: Orbis Books, 1997.

Chandler, Raymond, Dorothy Gardiner, and Kathrine Sorley Walker. *Raymond Chandler Speaking*. Boston: Houghton Mifflin, 1962.

Clark, William Bedford. "All Toole's Children: A Reading of *A Confederacy of Dunces*." *Essays in Literature* 14:2 (1987): 269–80.

Dove, George N. *The Police Procedural*. Bowling Green, Ohio: Bowling Green University Popular Press, 1982.

—"The Detection Formula and the Act of Reading." *The Cunning Craft: Original Essays on Detective Fiction and Contemporary Literary Theory*. Ed. Ronald G. Walker and June M. Frazer. Macomb, Illinois: Western Illinois University Press, 1990. 25–37.

Gardner, Pat. "Midst Great Laughter." *The Southern Quarterly* 34.2 (1996): 87–90.

Grella, George. "Murder and the Mean Streets: The Hard Boiled Detective Novel." In *Detective Fiction: A Collection of Critical Essays*. Ed. Robin W. Winks. Englewood Cliffs, NJ: Prentice-Hall, 1980. 103–20.

Griffin, John Howard. *Black Like Me: The Definitive Griffin Estate Edition*. San Antonio, Texas: Wings Press, 2004.

Gubar, Susan. *Racechanges: White Skin, Black Face in American Culture*. New York: Oxford University Press, 1997.

Hopkins, Pauline E. *The Magazine Novels of Pauline Hopkins*. New York: Oxford University Press, 1988.

Horsley, Lee. *Twentieth-century Crime Fiction*. New York: Oxford University Press, 2005.

Hühn, Peter. "The Detective as Reader: Narrativity and Reading Concepts in Detective Fiction." *Modern Fiction Studies* 33 (1987): 451–66.

Kleege, Georgina. "The Strange Life and Times of John Howard Griffin." *Raritan* 26.4 (Spring 2007): 96–112.

Kline, Michael. "Narrating the Grotesque: The Rhetoric of Humor in John Kennedy Toole's *A Confederacy of Dunces*." *The Southern Quarterly* 37.3-4 (1999): 283–91.

Macdonald, Gina and Andrew Macdonald. "Ethnic Detectives in Popular Fiction: New Directions for an America Genre." In *Diversity and Detective Fiction*. Ed. Kathleen Gregory Klein. Bowling Green, Ohio: Bowling Green State University Popular Press, 1988. 60–113.

Mailer, Norman. *The White Negro*. San Francisco: City Lights Books, 1957.

Mittel, Jason. *Genre and Television: From Cop Shows to Cartoons*. New York: Routledge, 2004.

Panek, LeRoy. *Watteau's Shepherds: The Detective Novel in Britain, 1914–1940*. Bowling Green, Ohio: Bowling Green University Popular Press, 1979.

Rank, Hugh. "The Rhetorical Effectiveness of *Black Like Me*." *The English Journal* 57.6 (1968): 813–17.

Russell, Thaddeus. "Citizenship and the Problem of Desire in the Postwar Labor and Civil Rights Movements." In *The Columbia History of Post-World War II America*. Ed. Mark C. Carnes. New York: Columbia, 2007. 366–401.

Savran, David. *Taking it Like a Man: White Masculinity, Masochism, and Contemporary American Culture*. Princeton, NJ: Princeton University Press, 1998.

Toole, John Kennedy. *A Confederacy of Dunces*. New York: Grove Press, 1980.

Wald, Gayle. "'A Most Disagreeable Mirror': Reflections on White Identity in *Black Like Me*." In *Passing and the Fictions of Identity*. Ed. Elaine K. Ginsberg. Durham: Duke University Press, 1996. 151–77.

Winks, Robin W. *Modus Operandi: An Excursion in to Detective Fiction*. Boston: David R. Godine, 1982.

Žižek, Slavoj. *Enjoy Your Symptom: Jacques Lacan in Hollywood and Out*. New York: Routledge, 2001.

5

Espionage and the war on secrecy and terror in Graham Greene and beyond

Sofia Ahlberg

Between March 1952 and June 1955, Graham Greene wrote a novel which unveils the intricate links between politics, the status of the personal, the social and the ethical in times of war. More poignantly, it is also a novel about desire and encounters with the other. *The Quiet American* was written before the Americans got into Vietnam properly, yet the author manages to capture the dangerous paradoxes that made it such a disaster. Greene's novel is not only a masterful window into American foreign policy of the 1950s and 1960s, but the blurring of fiction, narrative, structure, and the world outside the text also resonates to readers of post-9/11 fiction. As a journalist narrator, Fowler is in Vietnam to report on the war in Vietnam. Unlike a foreign editor, he has no opinions, writes no columns, takes up no position. Fowler renders reality in print, objectively and without sentimentality. The narrative frame of the novel includes the interrogation of Fowler by the French inspector Vigot, who suspects that Fowler might be involved in Pyle's (the quiet American of the title) death. Fowler ridicules the investigation of Pyle's death by suggesting that Vigot recover Pyle's black dog and "'analyse the earth on its paws'" (28), highlighting the fact that the scrutiny of a detective has no place in the battlefield, where one dead body is simply one of many.

It is certainly not a coincidence that a similarly mocking tone is used in a later novel, otherwise of quite a different narrative structure, by the same author. *Our Man in Havana: An Entertainment* (1958) is set in Cuba during the Fulgencio Batista regime. As the subtitle indicates, Greene has attempted to belittle any parallels between the novel and the real world (this in spite of the fact that aspects of the plot that involve secret military instructions uncannily anticipate the Cuban Missile Crisis of 1962). A British Secret Service agent offers James Wormold, a vacuum cleaner retailer, the job to collect information and establish a network of informancy in Havana. At loss with what is expected of him, Wormold fabricates his reports by using a fictitious group of agents that not only bears witness to a singularly creative mind, but also to the absurdity of the secret service. Hawthorne, the agent who signs Wormold up, suspects his liberal use of the imagination (that includes the sketching of a blown-up vacuum cleaner to approximate unidentified weapons, such as in recent times would be described as weapons of mass destruction). However, he is naturally reluctant to inform on his own recruit and thereby reveal his own poor lack of judgment. Both Wormold and Secret Agent Hawthorne separate the real world from the world of make-believe. Greene might have had the American author Nathaniel Hawthorne in mind when he gave his secret agent his name. Hawthorne famously claimed not to write novels as such, but romances removed from "the possible or probable course of ordinary experience" (Porte 95).

I shall pursue this idea of the romantic housing extraordinary experience in the following pages and argue that information and intelligence are subject to the same narrative design as romance. By looking in the broadest sense at the centrality of romance to the transferral of knowledge in *The Quiet American* as well as, to a lesser extent, *Our Man in Havana*, this chapter looks closely at detection as a means of uncovering the truth. Greene's novels come very close to describing reality, or a soon-to-become reality in Vietnam and Cuba respectively. Present-day reality, by comparison, is governed by rules of fiction as facts are disclosed to the public through information stunts authorized by WikiLeaks, following a narrative scheme that includes conflict, climax and dénouement. Faced with a fantasy of reportage and espionage that resonates with reality, and a present-day reality that appears all the more fantastic in its peculiar and sometimes theatrical disclosure of facts, it can be concluded that truth arises from the way it is shared and not strictly from its content. With this in mind, I will demonstrate how detection pushes contemporary fiction toward a literature of social administration along the lines of the massive revolt against the conspiracy of silence recently witnessed through the actions of Julian Assange, founder of WikiLeaks. These examples from both the literary and the real world confirm the role of romance and the imagination in the age of terrorism today.

Indeed, the development of so-called "sock puppets" is well and truly underway as a means of overseeing U.S. armed operations in the Middle East and central Asia (Fielding 9). By allowing a single U.S. serviceman or woman to control ten online personas all over the world, the "war against terror" links with the war against communism as played out in Greene's novel *Our Man in Havana* in which Wormold constructs fake agents in an approximation of what is expected of a secret agent. It must also be added that to some twenty-first-century readers, Wormold's absurd drawings of a gigantic vacuum cleaner that miraculously escapes expert scrutiny are really no more or less absurd than anything else that passes for nuclear weapons these days. Unlike the means through which the transaction of knowledge takes place (postal, digital?), imagination is timeless. Detection often bridges the world of yesterday with that of tomorrow. The satirical tone found in *The Quiet American* is matched if not word for word then certainly skepticism for skepticism in *Our Man in Havana*. When it dawns on him what exactly it is Hawthorne wants him to do, Wormold queries:

"Do you expect me to analyse the fluff [in the vacuum cleaner]?"

"It may seem a joke to you, old man, but the main source of the French intelligence at the time of Dreyfus was a charwoman who collected the scraps out of the waste-paper baskets at the German Embassy." (29)

The imaginary in Greene's novels teeters on the brink of absurdity in the minds of his world-weary characters with whom his equally world-weary readers identify. It is by granting equal narrative attention to the imagination and reality, romance and the atrocious, innocence and corruption, that Greene's literary world of the 1950s and 1960s meets the world of today. More so perhaps than in *Our Man in Havana*, the characters in *The Quiet American* reflect a somber world view due to the presence of war. When Fowler mockingly suggests that Detective Vigot investigate the paws of the deceased's dog, the latter shows no offense and readily admits that "'I'm not Lecoq, or even Maigret, and there's a war on'" (28). War is to blame for Fowler's catatonic, opium-induced state of passivity, his having "no real opinions about anything" (72), as well as for Vigot's shortcomings as a detective. Greene knows that on the battlefield, neither the soldier nor the reporter relies on psychology and perspicacity for survival and that detachment is indeed preferable.

All the same, the role of detection appears as a persistent motif in the relationship between the American Pyle, the Vietnamese Phuong, the Englishman Fowler and the Frenchman Vigot in a paranoid battle for epistemological control that foreshadows the "War on Terror" post-9/11.

During interrogations, inspector Vigot comes close to uncovering Fowler's involvement in the murder of his rival Pyle, but decides to take Fowler's word in good faith. Wormold in *Our Man in Havana* finds himself in the odd situation of escaping detection when embellishing his lies about the existence of a network of agents. This is not dissimilar to the principle of information overload used by WikiLeaks, according to one of Assange's former collaborators, Daniel Domscheit-Berg:

> To create the impression of unassailability to the outside world, you only had to make the context as complicated and confusing as possible. To that end, I would make my explanation of technical issues to journalists as complex as I could. It was the same principle used by terrorists and bureaucrats. (45)

In the attempt to avoid detection, subjects produce a fiction that ironically works as social critique in a way more powerful, certainly, than the sanctioned reporting of actual events in the hands of reporters, as Fowler and the whistleblowers of WikiLeaks demonstrate. Indeed, in Greene's spectacular drama of sexual competition against the backdrop of a violent struggle for military control in Vietnam in *The Quiet American*, investigative journalism links author with reader in an ethically corrosive exchange across multiple political situations.

On the surface, *The Quiet American* follows a standard detective fiction set-up, featuring a cast of people assembled in an isolated place and the discovery that one amongst them has been murdered. Pyle and Fowler are the two anglophones in the novel, competing for the companionship of the beautiful, but distant Vietnamese woman Phuong. The novel opens with the confirmation that Pyle has been murdered, according to Fowler's plan to prevent further corruption from the Americans and perhaps also to eliminate the competition for Phuong who has deserted Fowler for the younger Pyle. True to its genre, the eccentric detective (Vigot) arrives to review the evidence, question the suspects and name the culprit, propelling the narrative from disclosure to closure. However, Greene's novel also departs from these generic conventions in several dramatic ways, not least in being placed in a war-torn Vietnam rather than the typically dormant English county. Interestingly, however, the turmoil of Vietnam at the time of violence and chaos, is presented in a calm and controlled manner. As a novel of detection, war and chaos are normalized through narrative, much in the same way Greene's entertaining novel about Cuba might be perceived to trivialize the terror of Batista's rule at the time. Indeed, all narratives risk a similar charge when they depict or allude to real atrocities. Though that may or may not be the case with Greene's novels, both *Our Man in Havana* and *The Quiet American* make up for it by poignantly criticizing the arrogant belief held by authorities such as the British Secret Service and other custodians of classified information that they are beyond ridicule and exposure.

Fowler's reconstruction of the events leading up to Pyle's murder and other sporadic divulgences, erotic and philosophical, is part of a narrative strategy to gain the trust of the reader and satisfy his or her desire for closure, while representing disorder. By gaining knowledge of Pyle through a series of discerning conversations in life-threatening moments, Fowler broadens the reader's understanding of the quiet American, but his detection of the man transcends into something beyond the subject, an exponential growth of knowledge threatening to expose Fowler instead.[1] Greene's novels, so often set in exotic locations, capture an age when information became a most valuable currency. As revealed in these pre-Cold War espionage novels, detection constitutes the archives of knowledge, demonstrating its enormous potential to narrators and statesmen alike. Greene captures a time that appears both prophetic and quaint to the contemporary reader, his novels revealing a sometimes naive sense of what is appropriate conduct with regards to knowledge transferral. After Wormold's deceit has been discovered in *Our Man in Havana*, he is castigated by the British Ambassador: "The whole subject is distasteful to me, Wormold. I can't tell you how distasteful it is. The correct sources for information abroad are the embassies. We have our attachés for that purpose" (207). Annoyed with the promiscuity of knowledge flow, the British Ambassador in *Our Man in Havana* laments that "this so-called secret information is a trouble to every ambassador" (207). Indeed.

Importantly, Greene's novels emphasize the unpredictability of knowledge, subject as it is to the human factor. This is certainly the case in *Our Man in Havana* in which Wormold is enslaved to his daughter's extravagant tastes and thus receptive to the secret service's attempt to recruit. It is also true in *The Quiet American*, where the occupied territory of Vietnam subordinates mind to body in the case of Fowler. Since the mind cannot be trusted and is subject to corruption in times of war and occupation, Fowler surrenders to the physical enjoyment he has during nights spent with Phuong and, of course, smoking his daily opium pipe which Phuong prepares with loving care. Whereas Fowler prefers the eroticism of the body to the frenzy of politics, Pyle believes the bodily experience inferior to the intellect. After Pyle's murder, Fowler rummages through his bookcase where there is no reading for pleasure short of a book titled *The Physiology of Marriage*, which leads Fowler to ponder whether Pyle "was studying sex, as he had studied the East, on paper" (29). Wedded to an alternative vision of society, Pyle is an idealist to whom sexual love comes secondary to the struggle to save Vietnam from communist China. The battle between the hedonics of the body and the ascetics of the soul is dramatized through the awkward friendship between Fowler and Pyle, and partially resolved through the element of narrative detection where pleasure naturally comingles with games of power. As any fan of the genre will confess, the contest for episte-mological certainty is part of its attraction.

The appeal of detection lies in its perceived ability to restore order to a world of chaos and confusion. As such, it competes with religion as the sole power to exonerate and expiate. The detective novel as that which offers a solution, an end to speculation and self-doubt, a place of confession? Certainly in Greene's *The Quiet American*, set in what was to become the political minefield of the twentieth century, faith gives way to detection and the priest has traded in his collar for a magnifying glass. As emblematic of the modern condition, detection is now the basis of ethical hope in a world that has become increasingly threatening and incomprehensible. When guilt is passed on to one individual, as is generally the case in the detective novel, the expulsion of that criminal has a cathartic effect on society as a whole (Grella 32). This chapter will demonstrate, more generally, how the rise of detection in contemporary fiction has led to the eclipse of faith as a promise of justice yet to come. In writing the detective novel manqué that is *The Quiet American*, Greene foreshadows a world in which detection is ubiquitous in the art of narration as a way of grappling with questions of commitment, judgment, and belief.

As Fowler reconstructs the events leading up to Pyle's murder, self-detecting as it were, he returns to the past to expose the true nature of Pyle's mission in Vietnam and find atonement for orchestrating his murder. His story is one of detection and duplicity, a narrative that evades respon-sibility, or rather shifts it from author to reader, who has learned to remain skeptical against seductive narratives. A short detour to Walter Benjamin will illustrate the extent to which Greene's espionage novels both commis-erate and celebrate the art of narrative. In this passage that mourns the end of ideals, authority and experience, Benjamin diagnoses the end of story-telling with the end of the First World War:

> In every case the storyteller is a man who has counsel for his readers. But if today "having counsel" is beginning to have an old-fashioned ring, this is because the communicability of experience is decreasing. In conse-quence we have no counsel either for ourselves or for others. After all, counsel is less an answer to a question than a proposal concerning the continuation of a story which is just unfolding. To seek this counsel one would first have to be able to tell the story. (Quite apart from the fact that a man is receptive to counsel only to the extent that he allows his situation to speak.) Counsel woven into the fabric of real life is wisdom. The art of storytelling is reaching its end because the epic side of truth, wisdom, is dying out. (3)

Through recourse to recent narrative theory located at the intersection between authorial design and reader response theory in works by James

Phelan, especially, it is possible to salvage Benjamin's art of storytelling. Specifically, through an intensified engagement with the weary contemporary reader, "the epic side of truth" is replaced through a more explorative path to knowledge. While reading is essentially a transparent activity, espionage novels assume that information can be inadvertently or incompetently misread. At the very least, they make the process of reading a not-so-innocent act, even if by emphasizing the act of deliberate fictionalizing as in *Our Man in Havana* in which Wormold constructs a make-believe world of secret agents and weapons of unprecedented scale. Detection in contemporary literature reminds the reader that what he or she reads could be located neither inside the book, nor inside the author, but somewhere between or somewhere outside altogether. Today in the age of whistle-blowing, we think of truth along the lines of *how* we become aware of it, not necessarily by what it is. Rather than disclosing any one particular truth, individuals such as Assange for example, expose custodians of classified information to the general public. Secrets made open through detection have the potential to compel the public to act in a way that ordinary reading does not.

Its strong emphasis on action notwithstanding, it is necessary to start thinking about the structure of this exposure as heavily shaped by narratology. Contemporary fiction that includes elements of detection is helpful in this regard because it collapses the boundaries between narrativized plot and real events that inform the author's literary landscape (such as the war in Vietnam and the Batista dictatorship in Cuba in the case of Greene). As Benjamin notes, it can no longer be said that counsel is found in literature, and consequently, the narrator is not an exclusive source of knowledge. To say that the narrator is no longer an oracle, however, is not to dismiss the powers of narration or its role in and out of fiction. Narrativity encourages two main activities: observing and judging (Phelan 323). It is the act of judging, especially, that has the potential to make the reader more complicit with what is on the page and thus encouraging political action. By emphasizing his role "to expose and record" (88) as an investigative journalist, Fowler reminds the reader of the interpretive dimensions of his narrative. Phelan envisages that this technique encourages the reader to "reconstruct the ethical principles upon which [a] narrative is built" (325), rather than apply a pre-existing ethical system to the narrative. In other words, the reader remains open to the text and allows for the possibility that the experience of reading might change his or her world view.

Phelan does not mention the role of the detective, but when reducing a narrator to the functions of "reporting, interpreting, and evaluating" (326) as he does, then it must be conjectured that he is the figure that most strictly fits this mould. An overwhelming number of contemporary novels borrows elements of detection from the detective novel genre. One explanation for the ubiquitous presence of detection in contemporary fiction is that modern life cannot be explained even by the most gifted minds. The detective novel, while not being able to deliver either "counsel" or "the epic side of truth," is nonetheless able to reduce even the most irrational and perplexing chain of events into something plausible and logical (Grella 47). Walter Benjamin suggests that whereas intelligence (either spatial from foreign countries or temporal in the form of tradition) possesses a certain authority, information "lays claim to prompt verifiability" (4). Intelligence, Benjamin argues, breeds storytelling, whereas the modern equivalent, information, must above all "sound plausible" and what sounds plausible is often far removed from the mythical aspects of storytelling (4). I do not wish to argue with Benjamin's suggestion that the dissemination of information has undermined the art of storytelling. Indeed, one might only turn to present day "infotainment" to see precisely how enmeshed the two have become, arguably to the detriment of each. However, detection in contemporary novels does bind the reader to the author through, specifically, the transfer of information. In other words, detection renews the power of storytelling in the modern world, while at the same time making the reader aware that all knowledge arrives at its destination battered by narratology.

For far too long, critics have been dismissive of the detective genre. George Grella dismisses the power of the detective novel to engage the reader: "the reader does not share the detective's ability, rather he marvels at it" (32). It is testimony to Greene's remarkable ability to tell a story, that Fowler's powers of perception and reconstruction of the events leading up to Pyle's death in *The Quiet American* do not disappoint even towards the end when it is revealed that he has orchestrated the murder. Fowler does not attempt to persuade the reader. Indeed, his narrative voice is remarkably neutral, almost emotionally chilling, leaving most if not all to the imagination of the reader. Grella has argued that the distant narrative usually found in detective fiction prevents the reader from engaging with the text: "With the intellectualization of potentially sensational matters, without any direct involvement, knowledge of the murderer's character, or sense of doom, the reader neither experiences complicity nor requires catharsis" (33). This is a common prejudice against the detective novel genre, preventing it from becoming anything more than genre fiction. Elements of detection, however, do not obfuscate the reader's involvement. On the contrary, as Phelan's narrative theory demonstrates, such "restricted narration" (326) has the potential to engage the reader more than a narrative that purports to go under the skin of its characters, since it opens up point of view. It is the way the reader is invited to participate in the process of detection that sets *The Quiet American*, especially, apart from other novels.

Fowler's narrative in *The Quiet American* transcends the personal in the way it sets up complex encounters with the other and entangles the social and the political through the body of a woman. Phuong's predicament reflects the Vietnamese situation more generally. She is represented as being subordinate to whichever power happens to be the stronger. Just like it matters little to the Vietnamese people whether it is French or American forces that conquer them, Phuong does not appear to care which of the two men she resides with. Either way she submits, to her old sister who acts as her marriage broker, and to the power of the white male. The enigma of Phuong is the enigma of the Vietnamese people in the eyes of their conquerors. Fowler is different to the other expatriates in Vietnam in that he does not pretend to understand the Vietnamese, or superimpose his own value system onto them.[2] There are divisions of knowledge—some accessible to foreigners living in Vietnam, but most not. The detective is a useful figure in capturing the complexity of the world of information into which the twenty-first-century reader has already been seduced, but which would have appeared foreign and off-limits to the 1950s reader. As much as detection in the contemporary novel is a narrative technique for solving a mystery through amassing information and knowledge, it also acknowledges that not all can be revealed, and by doing so, preserves some of the mystery of storytelling.

Our Man in Havana shows this paradox to humorous effects when Wormold's drawings of new "weapons" of fearful proportions created by Engineer Cifuentes (one of Wormold's fictional secret agents) cannot be verified by the headquarters in London because the extraordinariness of the findings would be undermined by the fastidiousness of the bureaucrats in London: "'You know what those fellows are like. They'll criticize points of detail, say the whole thing is unreliable, that the tube is out of proportion or points the wrong way'" (78). The desire to believe in the implausible is sometimes stronger than the faith in science and empirical facts. Wormold's friend Dr Hasselbacher, whose initial suggestion it is to invent the secret agents, intuits that compulsive desire for the romantic and the extraordinary:

> "Medicine is my experience, Mr Wormold. Have you never read the advertisement for secret remedies? A hair tonic confided by the dying Chief of a Red Indian tribe. With a secret remedy you don't have to print the formula. And this is something about a secret which makes people believe ... perhaps a relic of magic." (58)

Dr Hasselbacher is right on the money when he alludes to the magic of secrecy, and by extension, the way in which detection works as a conduit for this magic. He also reminds the reader that Benjamin's lament over the end of storytelling can be backdated a century or so to coincide with when science replaced primitive magic in the Western world.

Where Walter Benjamin's concerns dovetail with narrative and detection is in the realm of belief and faith. Graham Greene is of course well known for his struggles with religious faith as evident in numerous novels, including

The End of the Affair (1951) in which the power of narrative is significantly interlocked with the narrators' belief systems. In *The Quiet American*, by comparison, Fowler finds himself in a meditative space halfway through the novel, which is the omphalos of confusion and doubt. Fowler's interview with the Pope's deputy discloses nothing of significance. Indeed, religion is here portrayed as the height of hypocrisy in its claim of absolutes and God's love of truth (85). Seeking shelter from the fierce sunlight, Fowler escapes into the cathedral in Tanyin, home of the Caodaists who at the time are at war with the Hoa-Haos. In the nave of the cathedral, Fowler observes what it means to be living with faith in a world of doubt and injustice, as evident in Fowler's examination of his own reasons for not believing:

> But I had never desired faith. The job of a reporter is to expose and record. I had never in my career discovered the inexplicable. The Pope worked his prophecies with a pencil in a movable lid and the people believed. In any vision somewhere you could find the planchette. I had no visions or miracles in my repertoire of memory. (88)

To admit to never having encountered that which cannot be rationally explained is a symptom of either profound apathy or blindness to the extraordinary and the romantic along the lines of another Greene hero, the indifferent Querry from *A Burnt-Out Case* (1960). All the same, *The Quiet American* resolves the anxieties of this malaise through its belief in discourse and detection. Indeed, Fowler's narrative encourages the reader to gather evidence through close reading and by so doing, he suggests how detection may fulfill the role of religion during highly skeptical, pessimistic times. Detection, in other words, becomes the means by which the reader becomes engrossed in the narrative and helps produce more varied and critical spaces for audience identification. Even so, it would be far too simplistic to assume that the detective novel relies on the work of an informant in lieu of a miracle worker. Suffice it to say that detection as a narrative technique attempts to eradicate hypocrisy, blind acceptance of any fact, and absolute tenets of belief immune to intellectual scrutiny.

Unlike works by authors who aim to impose a particular world view on their readers—Greene's novels do not profess or aim to instruct. In a discussion in 1948 with Elizabeth Bowen and V. S. Pritchett on the role of the writer (fragments of which later informed the lecture "The Virtue of Disloyalty" from 1969), Greene considers his role as writing "from the point of view of the black square as well as of the white: doubt and even denial must be given their chance of self-expression" (*A Life in Letters* 152). "Literature," writes Greene, "has nothing to do with edification" (*A Life in Letters* 151). This becomes quite clear in Greene's own fiction. Whether due to insubordination, an overheated imagination, or the war, people are not what they appear to be in *The Quiet American*. The innocent are able to commit genocide for a so-called good cause, the unengaged murder, and actual detectives are camouflaged priests. For all that, however, or perhaps rather *because* of that, the reader becomes hopelessly attached to these terribly flawed characters. Far from alienating the reader from fictional characters, detection brings him or her closer by identifying with a varied cast of characters through manipulating and challenging perceived behavioral patterns.

If one accepts the author's freedom to write as she/he sees fit, even if it means to be equivocal, contradictory, and elusive, one must also accept that the act of reading presents similar proclivities towards the "unfaithful." The subject of one of the longest and most ambitious of four stories in Greene's collection *A Sense of Reality*, "Under the Garden" is also recalcitrance. In this story a man diagnosed with cancer returns to his childhood home and recalls there an odd and complex dream. The central figure of the dream is an obscene monarch of an underground world in a cave formed by the enormous roots of an ancient tree. Reminiscent of Lewis Carroll, "deeper here than any grave was ever dug to bury secrets in" (34), the foul-mouthed monarch instructs the protagonist:

> "Be disloyal. It's your duty to the human race. The human race needs to survive and it's the loyal man who dies first from anxiety or a bullet or overwork. If you have to earn a living, boy, and the price they make you pay is loyalty, be a double agent – and never let either of the two sides know your real name." (48)

In a letter to V. S. Pritchett dated 1948, Greene elaborates on his notion of interrogation and disloyalty. "Loyalty," he writes, "confines us to accepted opinions: loyalty forbids us to comprehend sympathetically our dissident fellows; but disloyalty encourages us to roam experimentally through any human mind: it gives to the novelist the extra dimension of sympathy" (*A Life in Letters* 155). Through engaging in a process of detection, one risks being charged with the offense of disloyalty (by contrast, not to question or detect is a sign of devotion). Greene overturns this dictum in life and fiction. The virtues of disloyalty, according to Greene, are numerous. I quote Greene once again from his letter to Pritchett:

> If we can awaken sympathetic comprehension in our readers, not only for our most evil characters (that is easy: there is a cord there fastened to all hearts that we can twitch at will), but of our smug, complacent, successful characters, we have surely succeeded in making the work of the State a degree more difficult – and that is a genuine duty we owe society, to be a piece of grit in the State machinery. (155)

Wormold in *Our Man in Havana* becomes that "piece of grit in the State machinery" by inventing a network of spies. Though discovered at the end of the novel, he interestingly escapes punishment. After all, Wormold "had invented secrets, he hadn't given them away [thus] they could hardly charge him under the Official Secrets Act" (213). As in the story "Under the Garden," knowledge suppurates in the damp and dark earth, in the recesses of the mind. Elsewhere, Greene described this as anterior wisdom, that which through cunning detection is extracted out of automatic, reactive information.[3] Greene placed enormous faith in the power of detection to bring the erudite to the surface.

Unlike the so-called cypherpunks of the information age, Greene was an author of fiction, to whom the imagination lends the reader the freedom to seek truths that are likely to defy received wisdom. Where Benjamin laments the end of storytelling because wisdom is threatened, I celebrate detection as that which braves (if not always resurrects) "the epic side of truth" through continuous questioning even at the risk of appearing disloyal. In the passage above in which Greene describes how fictional knowledge disrupts a world view, he appears more interested in explaining the process by which the imagination evokes recognizant knowledge in those who already possess it, rather than how it might ignite it in those who may not. Insofar as Assange and other whistle-blowers wish to convert the unbelievers by indiscriminately gathering and spreading information, they represent the vacuum cleaner effect to knowledge acquisition. Wormold in *Our Man in Havana*, it must be recalled, abandons the vacuum cleaner retail business in favor of a more considered, discerning assembling of information. The fact that it happens to be fictitious is not important. What is important is that his form of acquiring and giving information is ordered and categorized. The process of detecting, unlike vacuuming, is reliant on the imagination because it requires interpretation. The vacuum cleaner does not discriminate between the insignificant fluff and the clues that might provide evidence or support a particular hypothesis—a detective does.

There is something fundamentally human about detection, challenging perceived wisdom, questioning cultural narratives and other interpretive work. In the first few pages of *The Experience of Nothingness*, Michael Novak reminds the reader that everything is open for detection or subject to inquiry:

> Whatever the presuppositions of a culture or a way of life, questions can be addressed against them and other alternatives can be imagined. Whatever the massive solidity of institutions, cultural forms, or basic symbols, accurately placed questions can shatter their claims upon us. The drive to ask questions is the most persistent and basic drive of human consciousness ... Without this drive, cultural change would not be possible. (12)

In the act of challenging the status quo and querying the foundations of society (including its "cultural forms" and "basic symbols" as Novak posits above), there is no doubt that detection moves beyond genre literature and begins to confront moral, social and cosmological questions. A passage towards the end of *The Quiet American* illustrates this shift. Towards the end of the novel, Vigot requests another conversation with Fowler. It is Fowler, however, who interrogates the detective:

> "What made you into a policeman, Vigot?"
> "There were a number of factors. The need to earn a living, a curiosity about people, and – yes, even that, a love of Gaboriau."
> "Perhaps you ought to have been a priest."
> "I didn't read the right authors for that – in those days." (139)

In Greene's world, the roles played by detectives and priests are interchangeable. In a dialogue from *The Heart of the Matter* (1948), police officer Scobie tells Father Rank that he "ought to have been a policeman" (68). Both detectives and priests extract confessions from those who have erred through a process of detection that reveals the unreliability of "text," on the one hand, and the power of the word, on the other. The dialogue above between Fowler and Vigot suggests that reading is both a source of instability as well as a powerful agent of change. The nineteenth-century French writer Émile Gaboriau, father of modern detective fiction, was an inspiration for Vigot to become a policeman. Had he, however, read religious novels, the implication is that he would have become a priest. A passage from the end of *The Quiet American* will suffice to show how detection in the contemporary novel may throw light on the ethos of moral judgment:

> It was strange how disturbed I had been by Vigot's visit. It was as though a poet had brought me his work to criticize and through some careless action I had destroyed it. I was a man without a vocation—one cannot seriously consider journalism as a vocation, but I could recognize a vocation in another. Now that Vigot was gone to close his uncompleted file, I wished I had the courage to call him back and say, "You are right. I did see Pyle the night he died." (171)

Fowler is humbled by the poetics of detection, in particular its perceived higher purpose, as distinct from the hack work of journalism. Unlike the reporter, the detective is inspired. In this last scene of interrogation between Vigot and Fowler, the former succumbs to a "force immobile and profound. For all I knew, he might have been praying" (170). The priest cum detective creates, whereas the journalist merely reports. By not confessing his stake in Pyle's murder and through his refusal to comply, Fowler destroys and disrupts the case that Vigot presents him with. By not playing his part,

Vigot's file will remain incomplete, unfinished, a work in progress. What Fowler's self-detection has revealed to himself and his readers is both his involvement in Pyle's murder as well as his inability, despite all claims to the contrary, to remain neutral and uninvolved. In other words, detection exposes him as an impostor, an alazon who pretends to be something more than he is (Grella 43). Fowler's justification for being in Vietnam as a foreigner has been his self-proclaimed neutrality, his not getting involved. Towards the end of this narrative, Vigot's as well as Fowler's (self-) detection exposes the latter's weakness, but also his humanity, his being caught in "some moment of emotion" (168). Fowler is one of those people who because they cannot make art in life, make their lives into works of art.

Having been given instructions by the Chinese Mr Heng to construct a fictitious appointment with Pyle on the evening of his murder, Fowler wishes to leave it open to destiny. Despite his atheism, he handed the decision back "to that Somebody in whom I didn't believe: You can intervene if You want to: a telegram on his desk: a message from the Minister. You cannot exist unless you have the power to alter the future" (180). Detection shows once again that it is not just what characters do that determines what happens to them, but also what they know or what they are prepared to admit to knowing. Intelligence, in other words, becomes a contemporary version of Benjamin's "wisdom." In her discussion about freedom, Svetlana Boym argues that intelligence is "a torturous but honest road between imagination and lived experience, between contemplation and action" (6). Detection is the means towards intelligence, a gathering of information that bridges the invisible with the visible, the hypothetical with the actual, *vita contemplativa* with *vita activa*, the unthinkable with the well-thought-through. Fowler's attempt to bargain with God is but one example of this.

With inside knowledge of the plot to kill Pyle, Fowler's existence has renewed purpose, allowing him to become, as Grella notes with regards to the detective figure generally speaking, "the tricky slave, the benevolent elf, or the Prospero of a particular world" (45). Fowler is all of those things in his relationship to Phuong, particularly when he is at risk of losing her to Pyle. He interrogates her as would a detective a suspect. The possibility of her infidelity causes him to lose all self-control. Many of Greene's novels are about infidelity—*The Quiet American*, *The End of the Affair*, *The Heart of the Matter* to mention a few. Unlike faithlessness and insubordination against God and other powers of authority, these sexual affairs are accompanied with a profound loss of self. In the event of suspected sexual infidelity, detection becomes a means of relieving a suspicious mind. Fowler's desire to gather as much information as he can about Phuong's movements in his absence is an attempt to regain control through detection (140). In a discussion about the jealous subject, Malcolm Bowie argues that jealousy may be acted out and experienced in the mode of the empirical scientist who has embarked on an endless search for mastery of the facts, someone who "relives in the solitude of his own body, the general human quest for knowledge" (50).

To Bowie, there is a connection between the quest and sexual jealousy. If this is the case, Fowler is surely the embodiment of that link, obsessing over Phuong's attraction to Pyle as well as his attempts to confess to someone or something his precise involvement in the murder of Pyle. The question of whether or not the culprit shall be caught turns detection into a narrative technique of infinite deferral when the detective is also the murderer. As simultaneously the detective and the culprit, he is driven by the illusory lure of closure and finality in a narrative that is based on the promise of forgiveness from the reader, and perhaps, most poignantly, from the victim. The murdered victim haunts the pages of any detective novel and it is the detective's success that lays him or her to rest, that brings closure to the narrative of his or her life. Certainly, the muted presence of the (already) quiet American functions as a specter of conscience in Fowler's narrative. Fowler's self-detection is an attempt to reassemble the fragments of an obscure life, an attempt to re-member the fractured body of the quiet American. After Pyle's death, Fowler becomes what Grella ambitiously notes is a common characteristic of all great detectives: an "engineer of destiny, with the power to recreate a new society from the ruins of the old" (45).

Auden suggests that the fantasy indulged by the detective novel reader is the fantasy of returning to a state of innocence (158). When detection occurs in a narrative that takes place against the backdrop of complicated foreign policy and turbulent dark times, to what does a state of innocence refer? Certainly, there is no suggestion in *The Quiet American* that with the elimination of Pyle, the Americans will change strategy in Vietnam. On the contrary, Pyle, it becomes obvious, is merely the prototype for the many young, enthusiastic, engaged Americans who hope to save the world from communism in times to come. It cannot be said from reading *The Quiet American*, that detection takes either the reader or the detective to the Garden of Eden. Indeed, the only certainty to arise out of *The Quiet American* is that the war will go on, the occupation will continue. Although Novak celebrates the process of questioning in *The Experience of Nothingness* as that which elevates the human race and has the potential to create progress, he also cautions against interrogation and the search for meaning:

The experience of nothingness is a mode of human consciousness; it occurs in human beings, not in cats or trees. It is, often, a kind of exhaustion of spirit that comes from seeking 'meaning' too long and too ardently. It is accompanied by terror. It seems like a kind of death, an inertness, a paralysis. Meanwhile, the dark impulses of destruction find only thin resistance, they beat upon the doors for instantaneous release. (9)

The detective, in other words, embodies the terror and the experience of nothingness that are the result of the search for meaning "too long and too ardently." While satisfying the reader's need for closure, the detective figure represents disorder. The terror that Novak notes is felt by Greene's characters as well, especially when overwhelmed by those with more power than themselves. In a scene of astounding insight, Wormold in *Our Man in Havana* reflects on what it means to be questioned by the law as he "began to realize what the criminal class knows so well, the impossibility of explaining anything to a man with power" (66). In this passage, Wormold is subjected to the reverse of the dictum "innocent until proven guilty"; it is an experience he shares with the majority of the world's powerless and disenfranchised human beings. In his discussion on property and individualism, Pierre-Joseph Proudhon argues that a select few become powerful by deluding themselves of the invincibility of their reason and will:

But man becomes skilful only by observation and experiment. He reflects, then, because to observe and experiment is to reflect; he reasons, because he cannot help reasoning, and in reflecting, he becomes deluded; in reasoning, he errs and yet, thinking himself right, persists in his error. He trusts his opinions, esteems himself, and despises others. Thus he isolates himself, for he could not submit to the majority without renouncing his will and his reason, that is, without denying himself, which is impossible. (190–1)

Greene's novel *The Quiet American* prompts comparisons between the war in Vietnam and the current difficulties surrounding Afghanistan. The Vietnamese were never supported by the Chinese, as the Americans feared after China became communist in 1949. Similarly, there were never any weapons of mass destruction and the American invasion of Iraq was based on spurious information. Yet, the war on terror will seek new victims as time goes on, and an increasingly severe form of interrogation has become legitimate in everyday encounters with the stranger. Proudhon attributes disorder and terror to the egotism of reason: "The mother of poverty, crime, revolts, and war was inequality of condition, which was the daughter of property, which was born of selfishness, which was created by private opinion, which descended in a direct line from the autocracy of reason" (191). Greene's espionage novels signal the threat of individual despondency and terror that come with pure reason, detection without a heart. At the same time, they also reveal kinship and collectivity as that which takes the process of detection beyond its potential "inertness" and "paralysis".

Detection manages to eschew the desire for self-knowledge in contemporary fiction. At stake in both *The Quiet American* and *Our Man in Havana*, is that which passes for the truth. Unlike a crime or an offense, reality or truth cannot be revealed or unlocked, shrouded as it is in representations that are themselves always approximations and transcriptions of the real. In lieu of an epiphany, the reader of contemporary fiction must make do with what Josh Toth calls "a state of 'indecision,' a state in which the decision process ... is animated by *both* the impossibility of the certainly right decision, or representation, *and* the promise of pure indecision" (121). Detection maintains this state of procrastination and prolonging, and some would say, makes the moment of indecision pleasurable because it sustains hope. A reliance on reason alone risks bringing with it the experience of nothingness, inertia and paralysis. Detection must not be divorced from essential humanity, which is often that which escapes detection, that which cannot be articulated within the process of detection. Roland Barthes comes close to describing the remains of detection in his work of rereading Sarrasine in *S/Z*. In this passage he refers to the "pensive text" to distinguish between the inexpressible and the unexpressed:

> ... replete with meaning ... it still seems to be keeping in reserve some ultimate meaning, one it does not express but whose place it keeps free and signifying; this zero degree of meaning (which is not its annulment, but on the contrary its recognition), this supplementary, unexpected meaning which is the theatrical sign of the implicit, its pensiveness: the pensive (in faces, in texts) is the signifier of the inexpressible, not of the unexpressed. (216)

In a world of investigation and detection, the signifier of the inexpressible is also a repository for the vestiges of humanity in an increasingly impervious world. The point of differentiation lies in the way the truth becomes known or information passed on. Exposure is different from disclosure, the former being undifferentiated, unmediated and indiscriminate, once again, like the vacuum cleaner effect. The lesson to be learned from *The Quiet American*, specifically, is that disclosure always occurs from a point of view, or "in a borrowed light," as Emmanuel Levinas calls it in an essay on discourse in *Totality and Infinity*. Levinas' work on truth and objectivity gives an interesting perspective on the foreign correspondent as the impartial reporter. Scrutinizing claims of objectivity, Levinas argues that "Though objective knowledge remain disinterested, it is nevertheless marked by the way the knowing being has approached the Real" (64). The real, as Levinas points out, is marked by temporality and thus "to know objectively is to know the historical, the *fact*, the *already happened*, the already passed by" (65). The foreign correspondent relies on detection and intelligence as much as the detective. Both bear witness to, decipher, and deduce. As recently argued by Timothy Garton Ash in an article in *The Guardian* on the declining status of the foreign correspondent, the amateur eyewitness reports that rely on digital cameras, blogs and audio clips bring foreign news closer to home in often evocative ways. With regards to the deciphering and the interpreting, local sources have been found to be more reliable, especially as they speak the local language and are familiar with their customs (22). In other words, when in a gesture of disclosure and not exposure, detection is able to bridge knowing with reality.

The knowledge derived from Fowler's interrogation of self is that he is far from uninvolved and neutral. In his use of detection as a narrative technique, Greene addresses both the end of storytelling as diagnosed by Benjamin, as well as the role of the ineffectual so-called objective reporter in a complex world of conflict. Unlike reporters such as Fowler, the detective is always engaged in a moral judgment. This ethical dimension also separates disclosure from exposure. In the end, Greene's detective has overshadowed the reporter. The detective reconstructs the past from the fragments of evidence that lay scattered around him or her. Each of these fragments leads the detective to the present moment. To Fowler, they lead him to a moment of despair and regret: "Everything had gone right with me since he had died, but how I wished there existed someone to whom I could say that I was sorry" (189). As an atheist, Fowler is unable to ask for and receive forgiveness from a higher being. As a reporter, he has broken the rules of objectivity and become *engagé* against his will. As a detective, however, his destiny reinforces the norm of acceptable behavior. True, Fowler is not convicted (although Vigot highly suspects his involvement) for his crime, but the narrative he leaves the reader with makes public what has hitherto been undisclosed. The reader is left to prosecute as he or she sees fit.

Graham Greene is of course correct when he suggests that the only prosecution that matters is the internal one. Whether there is a God or not, there is always an Other, a reader in this case, to whom the offender must be seen to be doing a certain amount of soul-searching in order to be included in society. Perhaps that reader is one's own conscience, the victim, or perhaps it is "the strangeness of the interlocutors, the revelation of the other to me" (Levinas 73). Whichever it is, Fowler's public self-interrogation must satisfy the reader's wish for redemption. Importantly, Fowler's reconstruction of the past leads him to the point of moral retribution. Although not convicted for his part of the murder of Pyle, Fowler's freedom is severely limited by his own sense of justice that he has developed in the process of self-detection. To emphasize the liminality of liberty and containment, Graham Greene leaves the reader caught in a *mise en abyme* that resonates with today's complex world in which citizens are caught between detection and duplicity. Vigot's suspicion that Fowler might be involved in Pyle's murder is confirmed by doing precisely what Fowler mockingly suggested he do at the beginning of the novel, namely analyze the paws of Pyle's dog. By so doing, Vigot finds evidence that severely casts doubt on Fowler's proclaimed innocence. Vigot finds cement in the dog's paws, which proves that Pyle must have been to see Fowler on the night he was murdered since builders are at work on the ground floor of Fowler's apartment (170).

Greene's novel encourages the reader to look for that which lies in between: a series of mirrors that first appear duplicitous, but through detection, become clues. The author suggests that it is all there, between the first and final encounter with Pyle, Fowler's dismissive description of Pyle as "quiet" and the actual silencing of Pyle through death, as well as the tongue-in-cheek suggestion that Vigot investigate the paws of Pyle's dog and Vigot's actual detection of Pyle's dog. Detection bridges the gap between the hypothetical and the real, the possible and the actual. *The Quiet American* anticipates a world in which the borderline between fiction and reality has become more shady, a world in which anything, provided that readers are willing to imagine it, can exist. Such a world is potentially dangerous, a world of terror and chaos. While detection cannot prevent this, it gives readers the means by which they may recognize the role of the imagination in the realm of the political, the social and the ethical in times of war. As a disclosure of heart and mind, detection both transcends and elevates narrative.

Notes

1   Incidentally, this notion of detection as exponential growth of knowledge, threatening to consume the individual, is what the public has witnessed in recent months in relation to Assange of WikiLeaks, now subject to investigation in Sweden for sexual misconduct.

2   In describing a neighborhood, Fowler says: "This was the level of life where everything was known, but you couldn't step down to that level as you could step into the street" (144).

3   You cannot talk of the Karamazovs in terms of class, and if you speak with hatred of the kulak doesn't the rich humorous memory of the hero of Dead Souls come back to kill your hatred? Sooner or later the strenuous note of social responsibility, of Marxism, of the greatest material good of the greatest number must die in the ear, and then perhaps certain memories will come back, of long purposeless discussions in the moonlight about life and art, the click of a billiard ball, the sunny afternoons of that month in the country, the blows of an axe that has only just begun to fell the cherry trees. (*A Life in Letters* 156)

Works cited

Ash, Timothy Garton. "Foreign Reporting Needs New Strategies." *The Guardian Weekly*. December 17–30, 2010: 22.

Auden, W. H. "The Guilty Vicarage." In *The Dyer's Hand and Other Essays*. New York: Random House, 1962. 146–58.

Barthes, Roland. *S/Z: An Essay*. Trans. Richard Miller. New York: Hill and Wang, 1974.

Benjamin, Walter. "The Storyteller: Reflections on the Works of Nikolai Leskov." In *Illuminations*. Trans. Harry Zohn. Ed. Hannah Arendt. New York: Schocken Books, 1969. 1–14.

Bowie, Malcolm. *Freud, Proust and Lacan: Theory as Fiction*. Cambridge: Cambridge University Press, 1987.

Boym, Svetlana. *Another Freedom: The Alternative History of an Idea*. Chicago & London: The University of Chicago Press, 2010.

Domscheit-Berg, Daniel and Tina Klopp. *Inside WikiLeaks: My Time with Julian Assange at the World's Most Dangerous Website*. London: Jonathan Cape, 2011.

Fielding, Nick, Ian Cobain, and Dominic Rushe. "US Military Taps 'Sock Puppets'." *The Guardian Weekly*. March 25, 2011: 9.

Greene, Graham. *The End of the Affair*. New York: Viking Press, 1951.

—*Our Man in Havana: An Entertainment*. Middlesex: Penguin, 1962.

—*The Quiet American*. London: Penguin Books, 1973.

—*The Heart of the Matter*. Middlesex: Penguin Books, 1974.

—*A Burnt-Out Case*. Harmondsworth: Penguin, 1975.

—"Under the Garden." In *A Sense of Reality*. Middlesex: Penguin Books, 1981. 9–64.

—*A Life in Letters*. Ed. Richard Greene. London: Little, Brown, 2007.

Grella, George. "Murder and Manners: The Formal Detective Novel." *NOVEL: A Forum on Fiction* 4.1 (1970): 30–48.

Levinas, Emmanuel. *Totality and Infinity: An Essay on Exteriority*. Trans. Alphonso Lingis. Pittsburgh, PA: Duquesne University Press, 1969.

Manne, Robert. "Robert Manne on Julian Assange." *The Monthly*. March 2011: 16–35.

Novak, Michael. *The Experience of Nothingness*. New Brunswick & London: Transaction Publishers, 1998.

Phelan, James. "Narrative Judgments and the Rhetorical Theory of Narrative: Ian McEwan's *Atonement*." In *A Companion to Narrative Theory*. James Phelan and Peter J. Rabinowitz (eds) Malden & Oxford: Blackwell Publishing, 2005. 322–36.

Porte, Joel. *The Romance in America: Studies in Cooper, Poe, Hawthorne, Melville, and James*. Middletown, CT: Wesleyan University Press, 1969.

Proudhon, Pierre-Joseph. *What is Property?* Trans. Donald R. Kelley and Bonnie G. Smith. Cambridge: Cambridge University Press, 1994.

Toth, Josh. *The Passing of Postmodernism: A Spectroanalysis of the Contemporary*. Albany: State University of New York Press, 2010.

6

The stories we all tell: the function of language and knowledge in Julia Kristeva's novel *Possessions*

Rossitsa Terzieva-Artemis

At this point the story grows obscure. The information has run out, and the events that follow this last sentence will never be known. It would be foolish even to hazard a guess.

PAUL AUSTER, *CITY OF GLASS*

For more than 40 years now Julia Kristeva's continuous search in philosophy, psychoanalysis, linguistics, literature, and art history has produced a body of complex scholarly work. It does not come as a surprise to those acquainted with Kristeva's academic agenda that she is immersed in the study of art, since in her view psychoanalysis and art share two important characteristic features which are the focus of her own theoretical work: both examine questions of subjectivity and sexual differences, and attest to the operation of the unconscious. Besides an academic and an analyst, Kristeva is also an accomplished fiction writer, debuting in 1993 with the intellectual "picaresque" novel *The Samurai* followed by the trilogy of detective novels *The Old Man and the Wolves* (1994), *Possessions* (1998), and *Murder in Byzantium* (2006). It is interesting to pose the question what need does fiction-writing satisfy in the prolific career of a scholar like Kristeva? And also, in what ways do literature—fiction-writing in particular—and psychoanalysis tackle the problems of subjectivity and sexuality, and what discourse do they share according to Kristeva?

In Kristeva's view literature is a strong material testimony for the existence of transgressions made aesthetically visible by means of poetic language. This in itself is a significant move to divest such transgressions of the false secrecy and prejudice with which very often they are approached by society. In a recent interview she muses on the specificity of literature and points out that,

> ... writing and literature are ways whereupon thought can emerge. For the subjects that interest me – that is, subjectivity; the position of the individual in the world; crisis; revolt – for these subjects exactly, those thoughts, thoughts in the special medium of art, are most suitable ... When an artist expresses herself, when an author expresses herself, the language is transformed. It becomes sensuous, filled with feeling, and that means the speaker is not neutral. She carries herself into the language. (2006 167)

It seems that Kristeva pinpoints here a special common feature between psychoanalysis and literature: both probe the existential difficulties entailed by the function of the subject in modernity. Unambiguously for those who have followed closely her writing through the years, this kind of research in subjectivity for Kristeva is embedded into another important discourse—the discourse of love. If in her early work *Revolution in Poetic Language* (1974) Kristeva analyzes the linguistic aspect of human interaction, her books in the 1980s, *Powers of Horror* (1980), *Tales of Love* (1983), and *Black Sun* (1987), turn to the affective aspects of human existence. Kristeva recaptures in later theoretical texts, but equally so in her detective novels, this double bind of language and affect that structures the process of subject formation. Such a double bind becomes more and more conspicuous in her own writing style over the years, as she herself is aware that,

... a formal change has occurred. For instance, my French was more abstract, more technical in the earlier books. Then, in the books on psychoanalysis, the language became more physical, more complete. Because I believe that one through psychoanalysis acquires a language – and French was, at any rate, a foreign language to me – that you can enter the childhood with, enter the body with. I also think that I have extended my everyday and sensuous language through writing novels. (2006 166–7)

Love, psychoanalysis, and literature are intricately connected in her work since in Kristeva's view these three discourses can provide effective ways of dealing with the unsymbolizable chaos of the Real, with the entrapments hidden in the Imaginary and, paradoxically, with the oppressive limits set by the Symbolic if we refer to the Lacanian psychic domains. The latter paradox, for instance, is based on the fact that language as a structure belongs to the Symbolic, yet in the practices of literature, psychoanalysis, and love it bends exactly the limits of the law through the unveiling of the unconscious. In other words, in the center of Kristeva's research and literary practice we can find "the crises in meaning, value, and authority" that are embodied in language or else arrested in silence, and emphatically re-surface in the practices of psychoanalysis and postmodern literature. (Beardsworth 2004, 13)

It is not surprising then that Kristeva approaches a much revered, well-established literary genre in her own "escapes" into literature. That there are indisputable affinities between detection and psychoanalysis is a well established fact in literary theory, as De Nooy points out, for example:

Historically, the two practices flourished at around the same time ... Both psychoanalysis and detective fiction promote an interpretative practice that is attentive to clues, to the uncanny, and to the pathological. Both seek truth through the rehearsal of past events. And both are concerned with cases. (2003 114)

However, instead of such an obvious affinity, when asked about her own inspiration to write fiction, Kristeva states that the idea to write a detective novel crossed her mind for the first time in 1989, after the loss of her father who, in her opinion, was earlier treated with criminal negligence in a hospital in Bulgaria. This is how the first book in her trilogy of detective novels, *The Old Man and the Wolves*, comes to life. It is a novel that tries to surmount, not simply to transgress, the genre of the detective novel by applying dense intertextuality to a medium which from its classical inception in Poe and Doyle relies on logic, deduction and a clear denouement, just as much as it relies on a wide reading audience. Some readers, however, are easily put off by the novel exactly because of the imposing intertextual rigor which variously refers them to literary sources in Latin, to artworks, and historical events which might seem superfluous in the plot. The text offers more than the usual stumbling blocks on the way to comprehension; it is rather a well-thought and measured exercise in what will become a Kristevan signature—a highly allegorical detective novel, surely "thick" with crime as it is thick with allusions and references.

Kristeva further explains her motivation to write *The Old Man and the Wolves* in the following way:

> That is when I felt the urge to write a novel. To endure the grief. It was a kind of grief therapy. And the form that stood out as the natural choice was the crime genre ... This I believe to a large extent mirrors what we experience in the modern world. There are many crimes, and we can't find the perpetrators. Hypotheses are being put forward, but one is never certain. In the end, some are found out, because we do have trials, but we still know that there is more to the case than what is revealed. Things are often much more complex than our understanding of them. (2006 172)

While the idea of writing as a kind of "grief therapy" hardly needs justification, the key word here is "natural" in relation to the choice of genre. For, as many would agree, the detective genre is one which ultimately pits reason against a form of physical and moral excess, while grief, as understood in psychoanalysis, is always a negation of logic. A legitimate question could be posed then: how is Kristeva's specific understanding of "grief" and "reason" exercised in what will turn out to be a continuous interest in the form of the detective novel for her? More importantly, is there in Kristeva an "abundance" of truth, knowledge and justice, if these belong to the stock material of any respectable detective novel? The superficial answer to these questions will be probably "No," if we follow a view which bluntly states that, "Kristeva's excursions into the genre of the thriller is not terribly thrilling" (Kingcaid 1998, 252). "Thrilling" in this case refers to the popular demands of movement, advancement and resolution which the conventional detective novel readily provides. In other words, the detective novel addresses the need in the reader for solutions to disruptive, unsettling enigmas. As Belsey defines the genre embodied in the traditional Sherlock Holmes stories, for example, the ideological purpose is clearly

> ... to dispel magic and mystery, to make everything explicit, accountable, subject to scientific analysis ... The stories begin in enigma, mystery, the impossible, and conclude with an explanation which makes it clear that logical deduction and scientific method render all mysteries accountable to reason ... (1985 59)

It is obvious from the above brief definition that the conventional detective novel is trying to strike a balance of humanistically understood *justice* in a world of discordance via appeal to reason, both the reader's and the detective's, where "transgression is provoked, measured and perhaps betrayed by the mess it makes" (Trotter 1991, 70). If there is a "method in the madness" that motivates the mess made by the murderer, it is more than necessary for the detective to display equally awesome method in the detection of the perpetrator on the pages of a fast-paced thriller. In other words, "the conventional detective, of course, always solves the crime, restoring order through ratiocination ... The detective novel, by the close of its pages, must leave no room for mystery" (Swope 1998, 207). For many readers of Kristeva's highly referential, intertextually complex novels, though, the experience of finding that deduction and conclusive explanations are scarce and hardly leave all mysteries attended is what makes her books more appealing and, arguably perhaps, true-to-life in the long run.

It will be a risky leap of faith, yet one worth taking, to discuss Kristeva's detective novels, and especially her second one, *Possessions*, as belonging to postmodern literature, aspiring to a model recognized as that of the metaphysical detective novel. However, I propose to follow the relevant argument that, "Like much of postmodern fiction, metaphysical detective novels appropriate and parody narratives of the literary past, in this case the conventional detective story" (Swope 1998, 207). If we are to read *Possessions* as such a metaphysical detective novel rather than as a classical detective work, we are probably going to have fewer difficulties in defining the novel, difficulties evident in Knapp's book review in which she asks,

> Is it, perchance, a parody, a satire, a burlesque of this [detective] genre, garnished with what the author could have considered insightful, comic, and ironic overtones? Written in Kristeva's habitual crisp, objective, and virtually scientific style, the work opens with the arresting image of a decapitated red-haired, satin-skinned woman who, judging from the rest of her body, was still beautiful. (1997 349)

Far from claiming to be cognizant of Kristeva's "master plan," I would argue that *Possessions* could be read as a parody or, even better, a re-writing of the traditional *whodunit* which illuminates a rather unexpected "who": that of the detective *in combination with* the criminal(s) and the rest of the characters. Together with the motivating "whys" and the very memorable "hows" in the murder of Gloria Harrison, the novel explores an ambiguous human universe of drives and desires experienced only too well in the psychoanalytic setting. That is why the writer's choice of genre is not totally disparate, since as Davis acutely observes,

For Kristeva, on the contrary, the detective novel represents the immersion in desires that can no longer be identified with any particular subject. Like the psychoanalytic encounter, the novel does not offer innocence; instead as it tracks the emergence of a story out of the troubled material of the mind, it points toward the possibility of meaning, and a kind of forgiveness. (2002 295)

Thus in the place of ultimate knowledge and balance of powers struck between good and evil in the style of the traditional detective novel, Kristeva proposes in *Possessions* a mosaic of insights into the workings of desire and language, of desire in language, of desires in the silences between language and speech. To summarize the plot of *Possessions* is a difficult task namely for this reason: a brief summary will inevitably hinge on the visible linguistic signs and will circumscribe the vast silences that the writer masterfully explores. A horrible murder has been committed in a land which is used to the horrific and the criminal: in Santa Varvara life goes on as it usually does, yet life has no value. Having arrived to investigate a series of shady mafia-style dealings at various political levels, the protagonist of the novel, Stéphanie Delacour, unexpectedly finds herself investigating the murder of her friend, Gloria Harrison, who dies in what turns to be a chain of poisoning, strangulation, stabbing and decapitation thus unequivocally suggesting the hand of a psychopath. In the opening paragraph Delacour visualizes for the reader the crime scene and muses on the unhappy lot of the victim,

Gloria was lying in a pool of blood with her head cut off. The ivory satin evening dress, the rounded arms, the long manicured hands, the Cartier watch, the diamond on the ring finger of the left hand, the sun-tanned legs, the shoes matching the dress—no doubt about it, that was Gloria. There was nothing missing except the head. "My sexual organ," as she laughingly used to call it, referring to the cerebral pleasure she got out of her work as a translator and the equally intense pain she suffered from her headaches. Sometimes she'd amend the description and call her head "the tool of her trade." And now here she was, bereft of her organ or tool, and so made almost anonymous. But only almost. For, head or no head, Gloria Harrison was easily recognizable. True, her auburn hair and sea-green eyes were no longer there to prove who she was, but the strong fingers, the shapely gymnast's thighs, the slim ankles, and above all the arrogant breasts that she flaunted so openly, even if they had started to sag these last few years, were evidence enough that it was she. And that unmistakable bosom was encased, perfectly as usual, in the bodice of an ivory satin evening dress, on the left side of which spread a crimson stain. It looked like a knife wound. (1998 3)[1]

The body in its present gruesome abjectness and former beauty is a focal point in the crime scene and it also generates a chain of disturbing findings that the police and Delacour sometimes choose to share. Through a series of reconstructive interpretations, it becomes obvious what is at stake in the investigation of the murder of this prominent and pretty much troubled woman. A number of people are questioned: a crowd of people who hardly loved Gloria, but basked in her presence, claim to "have known" her and readily pin the crime on an escaped mental patient. A few of the people close to Gloria—her deaf son, Jerry, and his caregiver, Pauline, and Stéphanie Delacour, of course—do not share such a view or, at least, they do not speak of it as a plausible scenario. In fact, Jerry hardly ever speaks, period; but he endlessly draws and learns to communicate with Pauline who is a speech therapist, herself a foreigner in Santa Varvara. So, in the process of a year-long investigation one perpetrator is found who is *not* the escaped mental patient, but Gloria's former playboy-husband. Still there is the haunting sense that there is something more hiding at the bottom of the case, that there is somebody else lurking in the shades of the enigma.

In the place of the traditional detective, Kristeva creates a questionable protagonist, thrice removed from the "golden standard" for a detective set as early as the nineteenth century by the forerunners Poe and Doyle. Stéphanie Delacour is a woman, an investigative journalist, and a foreigner: any one of these aspects of her identity is a disadvantage for her in the fictional country of Santa Varvara; any one of these aspects gives her certain advantages in France of today; the combination of the three, however, make Stéphanie at the same time an outsider and insider in what is seen by Kristeva as a bigger, more encompassing realm—the realm of language.

Stéphanie is versed—in "possession" of—more than one language: for once, professionally, she knows the language of the media, while intimately she speaks the French of logic and reason and the Santavarvarian of her childhood:

> No way of escaping the barrage of Santavarvaran. So I dive into it, immerse myself in it, get drunk on it ... For it's a language that, like American, gesticulates from the throat and the guts, excluding the respiratory system ... But all that's no longer familiar to me, I've got ties elsewhere, I've adopted the high-pitched delivery, the clipped and prettily mannered tones of French. (19–20)

But at the same time Stéphanie is possessed by at least one more "language," the equally important language of art. What some critics find irritatingly distracting in the texture of *Possessions* are

> ... sequences of asides and ideas that float around here and there, all mar the flow of what could have been an interesting detective story. The

plethora of excursuses referring to decollations in mythology, literature, and art ultimately reach the point of dulling the reader's interest in learning about the facts of the murder. (Knapp 1997, 349)

The obvious regret expressed here is in the proliferation of ideas which distract the reader from their voyeuristic participation in the unraveling of the gory murder case in which Stéphanie is yet again entangled. The linear, or even the "parallel," advancement towards the solution of the puzzle embodied in Stéphanie's and inspector Rilsky's investigations is slowed down by numerous references to music, literature, and fine art. Kristeva's purpose here, I would argue, is to give access to other forms of expression of desires in language: Rilsky's favorite language is that of classical music as an alternative to the bureaucratic, scarring language of the (missing) Law in Santa Varvara; for Stéphanie, evidently, it is the language of literature and fine art, for as she argues,

I admit my pictorial reminiscences might strike some readers as literary and irrelevant, perhaps to the point of obscenity. But what use is art if it can't help us look death in the face? My purpose in remembering museum encounters with painters and sculptors is to be able to draw on them when I'm confronted with macabre experiences. Such ordeals aren't all that rare in Santa Varvara, and here more than anywhere I need art to help me see my way, to retain my common sense, and, if you'll forgive the expression, to keep my head. (9)

Thus, instead of the classical detective, an "instrument of pure logic," the detective in *Possessions* belongs to the language of sense and sensual experiences. (Holquist 1971, 141). The narrative voices in the novel— alternating between the first person of Stéphanie's voice and the voice of the omniscient but very reticent third person narrator—manage to touch upon luminal experiences which otherwise would have remained unsymbolizable, amalgamated in the horror of the murder and its consequent abject encounter. Interpreted in such a way, if the narration does not provide a kind of expected, linear arrangements of *bouts* of detection, the epistemological outcome is questioned and substituted by what Swope calls "ontological shift" which is at the heart of the metaphysical detective novel so that, "the metaphysical detective no longer achieves resolution; the questions of existence remain questions, as even the metaphysical detective himself becomes vulnerable to losing his way in the postmodern labyrinth" (1998 211).

If Stéphanie is interpreted as such a metaphysical detective threatening to lose *her* way in the postmodern political labyrinth of Santa Varvara, "losing her head" in the investigation of the murder case of her friend Gloria could be prevented by recourses to the various forms of language she possesses and is possessed by. In an interesting parallel with Gloria, who is a translator, an unlikely social outcast and a "foreigner" in her native Santa Varvara, Stéphanie learns to read and translate the hidden and the obvious traces of the abject abundant in the case. Yet the effect of such ongoing reading/ translation/investigation hardly produces a truth, Truth, or epistemological certainty. Quite on the contrary: it is, after all, the ontological status of Stéphanie that is continuously brought into question. Dubiously "at home" and "abject" in Santa Varvara, at home in Paris, but yearning to go back to Santa Varvara, "at home" in the dynamics of the investigation, yet even more so in the glass cocoon of Bob's borrowed studio. Stéphanie's forays in language are as much an attempt to formulate abject experiences as they are attempts to formulate a self, even more so towards the end of the novel.

If in psychoanalysis the unconscious is seen as the knot between the Real, the Symbolic, and the Imaginary, Kristeva sees a productive reconfiguration of the subject possible via a return to the semiotic origins. Those semiotic origins are to be found scattered, not centered, in language and its "margins": into the rhythm, the repetition, the displacement, the substitution, the elision where the unconscious is embedded. Language and its obverse, or marginalized, are the two aspects that merge into the semiotic and disrupt the symbolic status quo. This inherent duplicity of language is something advantageous rather than detrimental in subject formation, for it produces possibilities to criss-cross between the Symbolic and the semiotic, and captures instances of the unconscious that make the other, "shadowy" aspect of the subject visible. That is why in her theoretical work Kristeva is preoccupied by what she calls "the heteronomy of our psyche" made flesh in language; as she states,

I am interested in language [*langage*], and in the other side of language which is filtered inevitably by language and yet is not language. I have named that heterogeneity variously. I have sought it out in the experience of love, of abjection, of horror. I have called it the semiotic in relation to the symbolic. (1998 8)

But language is a symbolic practice, not simply a theory; therefore, it has to do with the poetics of process and becoming, of building up a communicative system and sharing it with others. Having memories, histories and stories, speaking about oneself, to someone, are the ways to heal what Kristeva calls a "shattered narcissism" or, a shattered sense of self (1998 11). This shattered self is displayed ever so well in an analytic situation, but equally strongly in *Possessions* too: the novel suggests a gap in the very subject that needs the reader's attention more than epistemological certainty. As Stéphanie admits,

Again that feeling, dating back to my youth, that everything is appearance, delusion, hallucination. Not that there ever *was* any certainty somewhere governing the inessential and eventually justifying it. On the contrary, the semblance that stealthily surrounds us, that is constantly creating us, may well be mere foam on the surface of something that seems threatening but turns out to be serene; the fallout of a vast, hidden, advancing spirit, separate forever from appearances. (209)

While there is no "solution" to the subject's lack, in this case Stéphanie's lack, she works in the direction of a return to the semiotic and the opening up of the discourse of love as ways to embrace subjectivity to say simply, "But as I don't like giving in, I analyze" (209). A social conundrum more than a murder case, whether complicated or not, is what Kristeva analyzes in her psychoanalytic cases but also offers to the reader of this unlikely detective novel,

> The modern Narcissus, encountered in the therapeutic setting, reveals that modern Western cultures lack the kinds of discourses of love, loss, and separateness that are necessary for symbolic life, connections with others, and the social bond. (Beardsworth 2004, 12)

Paradoxically, lacking a discourse of love, Gloria's *love* for her deaf son Jerry is disfigured into a passion to foreshadow her murder. Despite her rigorous translations from Russian and English of writers like Shakespeare, Faulkner and Roth, strangely lacking reference outside her relationship with her son, Gloria is totally obliterated well before her health:

> Gloria didn't panic. She clung on to poor little Jerry. A love. Her love. The only one. The only one that was certain. That was forever. People say babies cling to their mothers as monkeys do. Not true. It's the opposite. If Gloria hadn't had Jerry to cling to she wouldn't have survived. Survived what? Life, Santa Varvara, childhood memories, all the things that are really unimportant. (47)

The narcissistic bind, where the ego is unproductively centered on itself, supports essentially a strict subject/object opposition which upholds one's self at the expense of another as Gloria's case is depicted in the novel. Unlike Freud, for example, who has paired love and hypnosis in his *Group Psychology and the Analysis of the Ego* (1921), for Kristeva the way out is through a production of a new discourse of love which can reposition the subject vis-à-vis the other players on the social scene.

Being human is speaking about love and simply loving, but both literature and psychoanalysis testify that neither of these is easy in the context of modernity, probably to the surprise of all who see an excessive proliferation of pseudo-amorous images and symbols in the media. Through an effective return to the semiotic language and the embracing of the unconscious rather than a mystification of it, the discourse of love makes the precipitation of the subject possible. For Stéphanie, the discourse of love is embodied in her new attitude towards Jerry which is suggested at the end of the novel. Coming to terms with aspects of the motive which leads Pauline to participate in the murder of Gloria—in fact, to decapitate hence to symbolically obliterate the threatening mythic mother—Stéphanie concludes,

> What's blindingly obvious is the power of usefulness: Pauline is indispensable. And she knows it. I know she knows it, but there's nothing I can do about either her knowledge or mine. Whatever she's done, whatever she might have done, whatever I think she's done, whatever she certainly did do, this now allows life to go on after death. Her life, of course, for I am sure she is free now, emptied of the hatred that once built up under her synthetic image. But even more the life of Jerry, whom I too am beginning to love (wonders will never cease!). (208)

An acceptance of the aftermaths, if not a total understanding of the murder, has been achieved and here Kristeva once more chooses to diverge from the traditional detective story. The moral issues of repentance, punishment, and distribution of justice are circumscribed not at the expense of a new-found cynicism in Stéphanie, but through a very measured approach. So, it seems at the end that "Stéphanie wouldn't tell Rilsky anything anyway. Was it up to a journalist, a young woman from Paris, to imagine us, to plunge again into the quagmire that was Santa Varvara? All in all, Rilsky was right, and there simply wasn't anything to be said." (211) *Naturally*, could one trust a woman, a foreigner, a journalist? However, as Kristeva insightfully explores the "difficulty of being a woman, in *Possessions*," the novel accentuates more than the issue of murder and perpetrator. Likewise, her last book in the detective trilogy, *Murder in Byzantium*, will highlight "the difficulty of being a stranger," a philosophical problem inherent in a plot replete with murder, crime and excess. (2006 166) The detective in all three novels, Stéphanie Delacour, faces up to not only the scourge of the abject only too visible in the murderous human impulses and the bodies relinquished to death in Santa Varvara, but she has to face also her own humanity: her body and her impulses, her conscious self and its unconscious enigmatic other. Delacour turns out to be as willing and capable an investigator in all criminal cases as she is a subject of her own investigation, quite aware of this double positioning as evident in the introspective "asides" on the way.

Although Kristeva persistently relates the concept of "woman" and "nature," thus opening herself to criticism on the grounds of essentialism and imperative heterosexuality, in fact she supports a broader view of woman, in abjection, in the paradoxical poverty of social discourses.

Kristeva approaches the notions of sexuality and subjectivity via language or, as Ainley summarizes the position of Kristeva,

> If the structuration of identity is at the level of language, but this process is constantly invaded by the 'language' of the other [semiotic] realm, then its stability is called into question. Perhaps by insisting upon the disruptive rather than the constitutive elements of language, a sufficiently transgressive notion of the subject can be produced to allow it to reformulate itself, 'more or less' masculine or feminine? (1994 419)

Kristeva also argues in favor of such a connection between the unconscious and sexuality, ever since her earlier works "Stabat Mater" (1977), *Tales of Love* (1987), *Black Sun* (1989) among others. There is, however, an important difference in Kristeva's terms: the unconscious surely is undermining the subject's position, but at the same time, through linguistic regressions to the semiotic, it permits repositioning of the subject in a revolutionary way. It seems to me, that here Kristeva touches upon yet another concept that she analyzes extensively in her most recent theoretical books, namely the concept of "revolt." In her view, the possibility to rethink the mental disposition that makes us carry on with our lives, yet which is not a cliché, but an active re-examination of our interior life is a form of revolt.

It is interesting to see the connection between love and revolt which Kristeva makes here. There is an accent on hope and recuperation rather than on impossibility, and this makes love a valuable source in the study of the subject, not of the subject's deterioration. Naturally, as a practicing psychoanalyst and a scholar, Kristeva cannot endorse a solely optimistic script that will lead one to the easy path of subject formation as her most recent works *The Sense and Non-Sense of Revolt* (2000) and *Intimate Revolt* (2002) have shown. Even more so, her detective novels, and especially the character of the protagonist Stéphanie Delacour, negate, partially or thoroughly, any epistemic security and promote that ontological questioning which further renders problematic the very idea of one solid subjectivity. What remains sure, again in the words of Kristeva, is that "At the moment, I am thinking a lot about a forthcoming novel that will be a detective novel as well, but also will concern itself with time. But I won't say more at the moment ..." (2006 176).

Note

1   All references to the text of *Possessions* will be from the 1998 edition, translated from the French by Barbara Bray, hereafter given in page numbers after the text.

Works cited

Ainley, Alison. "French Feminist Philosophy: De Beauvoir, Kristeva, Irigaray, Le Doeuff, Cixous." In *Twentieth-Century Continental Philosophy*. Vol. VIII. Ed. Richard Kearney. London: Routledge, 1994. 409–40.

Beardsworth, Sara. *Julia Kristeva: Psychoanalysis and Modernity*. Albany: SUNY Press, 2004.

Belsey, Catherine. "Constructing the Subject: Deconstructing the Text." In *Feminist Criticism and Social Change: Sex, Class and Race in Literature and Culture*. Ed. Judith Newton and Deborah Rosenfelt. New York: Methuen, 1985. 45–64.

Davis, Colin. "Psychoanalysis, Detection and Fiction: Julia Kristeva's Detective Novels." *Sites, the Journal of 20th century/Contemporary French Studies* 2.2 (2002): 294–305.

De Nooy, Juliana. "How to Keep Your Head When All about You Are Losing Theirs: Translating Possessions into Revolt in Kristeva." In *The Kristeva Critical Reader*. Ed. John Lechte and Mary Zournazi. Edinburgh: Edinburgh University Press, 2003. 113–29.

Holquist, Michael. "Whodunit and Other Questions: Metaphysical Detective Stories in Post-War Fiction." *New Literary History*. No. 3 (1971–2): 135–56.

Kingcaid, Renee. Book Review of Julia Kristeva. *Possessions*. *Review of Contemporary Fiction* 18.3 (Fall 1998): 252–3.

Knapp, Bettina L. Book Review of Julia Kristeva. *Possessions*. *World Literature Today* 71.2 (Spring 1997): 349–50.

Kristeva, J. "Crossing the Borders: an Interview with Birgitte Huitfeldt Midttun." *Hypatia* 21.4 (Fall 2006): 164–77.

—*Possessions*. Trans. Barbara Bray. New York: Columbia University Press, 1998.

—"Psychoanalysis and the Imaginary." In *Cultural Semiosis: Tracing the Signifier*. Ed. Hugh Silverman. New York: Routledge, 1998. 181–95.

Swope, Richard. "Approaching the Threshold(s) in Postmodern Detective Fiction: Hawthorne's "Wakefield" and Other Missing Persons." *Critique* 39.3 (Spring 1998): 207–27.

Trotter, David. "Theory and Detective Fiction." *Critical Quarterly* 33.2 (Summer 1991): 66–77.

7

Zen Keytsch: mystery handymen with dragon tattoos

Sheng-mei Ma

"You *are* handy!" commends Trinity, pleasantly surprised when the Keymaker produces from his huge loop of keys the exact one to start her getaway motorcycle in *The Matrix Reloaded* (2003). The Keymaker's function does not end there: he crouches behind Trinity in the following highway chase scene; his safe portage provides the raison d'être for the high-octane car crashes and gun fights. In the subsequent, contrapuntal "pregnant moment" of stillness, the Keymaker in a somber tone enlightens rebels on how to infiltrate the Matrix mainframe. The Keymaker is the well-nigh Oracle, prophesying the showdown between Neo and the Architect, the Maker of the Matrix. The Keymaker inhabits the ambivalence between the Mother, rebel-nurturing Oracle, and the Father, rebel-crushing Maker. The Keymaker's very existence is mentioned almost in passing as the Oracle takes leave of Neo; his name restores him, though, as a "chip off the old block" of the Matrix Maker. Given birth by the Oracle's incidental words, he up and dies while shielding Neo and Morpheus from agents' bullets. To readers from the outer space who have not yet watched *The Matrix* trilogy, I hasten to add the obvious, the visually self-explanatory minor point, namely, the Keymaker is Asian-looking, played by Korean American Randall Duk Kim. That minor point, however, arrives with a battery of racial and ethnic givens and stereotypes, deployed for a complicit public and with utter impunity. The Keymaker is presented as a serf held in the Frenchman Merovingian's dungeon, where Neo and company must rescue him, for the Keymaker holds or, more precisely, *is* the Key to the Matrix. With his slight physique and lined face, Charlie Chan mincing gait, and dirty coolie fingernails, such a pathetic squirt is alchemized into the Hitchcockian MacGuffin,[1] the nominal treasure and the empty sign that drives thrillers. The Keymaker's imprisonment heralds the face-off between indestructible agents and heroic rebels; the handyman, so dwarfed by giants vying over him as to appear handicapped, initiates the archetypal duel of good and evil of *The Matrix Reloaded*.

The handicapped handyman proffers white heroes the key to the mystery. Déjà vu, all over again, Hollywood's addiction to facile, although self-contradictory, formulas has regaled us with a string of Chinaman Handyman, a.k.a., Zen master-cum-yellow slave suspended between the paradox of enlightenment and servitude: Kwai Chen Cain's blind Shaolin *shifu* in the TV series *Kung Fu* (1972–5); the jujitsu warrior Bruce Lee who doubles as the chauffeur and house boy in *The Green Hornet* (1966–7); Luke Skywalker's midget teacher Yoda whose mumblings smack of Japanese-inversion syntax in *Star Wars* (1980, 1983); the tyrannical, abusive kung fu master poisoned by his favorite fish head in *Kill Bill I* and *II* (2003, 2004). The list of minority actors playing minor roles is inexhaustible, easily forgotten once they serve the function of unlocking Orientalist and sci-fi fantasies. On the one hand, they are nonessential extras providing services and comic relief. On the other, they are essential in bringing about the apocalyptic dawning, often through their tragic deaths. If not for their cameo appearances and predictable "exeunt," Western readers and dreamers would be denied access to this alien and exotic construct, which largely exteriorizes the West's own psyche. No doubt "a cliché" as Charles J. Rzepka observes in "Race, Region, Rule," this "othering of foreign, colonized, and resident alien races" consolidates "a dominant European American group identity" (1463). Mystery handymen are thus the key to Orientalist kitsch, or tropes of, as Matei Calinescu notes in *Five Faces of Modernity* (1987), "repetition, banality, triteness" (226); they comprise Zen keytsch, for they are popular culture's wishful duplications of what alleges to be the transcendental from Eastern mysticism.

Depicted by Calinescu, kitsch is one manifestation of modernity. Modernity's radical break with the traditional, at least in theory, is subconsciously compensated by the kitschy and sentimental in pop culture. Post-Enlightenment reason and logic characterizes the modern era to such an extent that human affect, including the intuitive, is displaced onto the non-West. Ergo, the Keymaker and the horde of mystery handymen. More a figure of speech than literal, these keys can be construed as Oriental-sounding titles and/or epigraphs which supposedly orient the following narrative but oftentimes bear tangentially on the Western content. Even if readers remember the title, such as Charles Frazier's *Cold Mountain* (1997) that borrows its title and epigraph from the Tang dynasty monk-poet Han Shan (literally, cold mountain) to open an American Civil War romance, this kind of literary indebtedness creates no more than an ambience of chilliness and desolation for the story. Even Ruth Rendell's *The Speaker of Mandarin* (1983) proceeds as a typical detective novel, after the tease of the title. Readers partake in the novelist's willful amnesia over the namesake. As such, the novel, which constitutes Ferdinand de Saussure's sign, is split between the signifier and the signified, the name/title and the named/narrative.[2] Filmically, literary epigraphs morph into the intertitles or establishing shots. Charlie Chaplin's *A Countess from Hong Kong* (1967), for instance, opens with epigraphic, high-angle shots of a bustling Hong Kong street scene, almost a bird's-eye view overlooking ant-like, coolie-looking dockhands, which immediately, inexorably moves to studio sets of a transoceanic liner, occupied exclusively by whites, bound for Hawaii. Hong Kong or the East is the prison-house from which the Russian Countess flees. The title and the high-angle shots are haphazardly, cavalierly executed; however, they embody the hazard facing the stowaway Countess. Likewise, the Keymaker personifies the key to freedom as well as the reality of enslavement. Put another way, the Keymaker is the keyhole, the tantalizing fissure through which imagination takes flight from the human condition.

Part of ancient Eastern wisdom, Zen has been aged just about right for our New Age, one shot through with science and technology, hence yearning for what lies beyond, namely, conceptual and spiritual transcendence. The ego reaches out to the cosmos, the small I to the big I. A kind of romantic melancholia,[3] this quest conceives of our skin as staking out two infinities, radiating in opposite directions, one into the outer space and the other the inner space. Or perhaps it is but one infinity, refracted through a thin membrane, a stained glass, a mere hindrance and discoloration to the oneness of things, a miniscule cut in the cosmos that quickly heals as the body crumbles. Surely, the miracle of the human body and mind counts far more than a hindrance and discoloration, yet we seem to be born, kept, and die in captivity, in this controlled environment of a zoo of humanity, this "world ... pulled over your eyes," as Morpheus puts it in *The Matrix* (1999), without ever having so much as a glimpse of the unveiled self, the architect of the cage. This line of thinking denies us of that rarest of diamonds in *The Diamond Sutra*, the heart so crystalline clear that nothing inhabits there, yet invincible, receiving and giving light as it comes and goes. What we have are refractions, external stimuli and internal reactions as well as internal stimuli and external reactions, passing in and out of our skin. One such refraction is the trope of Zen Cops in detective fiction and film, with narrative clues keying into the mystery, the denouement arriving only when a Zenified sudden illumination strikes.

The denouement is in relation to what Rzepka calls "the puzzle element" that moves detective fiction into detection (*Detective Fiction* 12), yet the quintessentially Orientalist mystique rubbing off on Zen Cops seems to escape Rzepka here and elsewhere in his magisterial book. Within the genre of detective fiction, Rzepka astutely analyzes the twin "locked rooms" of the physical universe and the human mind as well as their "keys" in Enlightenment's metonymic induction and Romanticism's metaphoric intuition (32–49). But the reluctance to think beyond the Western paradigm, particularly when detectives hail from what is assumed to be the Other, severely circumscribes the finding. A case in point: inferences or reading of clues often give way to feeling or illogical leaps of inspiration in Zen Cops against the genre and reader expectation. Granted that Zen lies beyond words and must be intuited, any description of Zen is bound to be false. Rather than religious transcendence, Zen, as deployed in popular culture, indicates a radical break like a leap of faith beyond metonymy into metaphor and symbols; the switch from the more literal frame of reference to the more figurative one suggests a cognitive elevation. All good detectives are perhaps prone to such strokes of genius, exemplified by Sherlock Holmes' sudden illumination after a night on "a sort of Eastern divan" in "The Man with the Twisted Lip," yet Zen-like trance and awakening multiply amongst literary and filmic mystery handymen from the East. To borrow from Homi Bhabha's concept of the "mimic man," these handymen are not quite themselves, their uncanny power coming from somewhere other than the head, a kind of heedless headlessness characteristic of non-Western aliens in the colonial mindset. Zen Cops, of course, can be a policeman, private eye, journalist, computer hacker, and the like, so long as they all, pardon the racist expression, "look alike" in having been "blessed" with the mystique from the East, be it the Charlie Squad's fortune cookie aphorism; Judge Dee's serendipitous scheming; or Stieg Larsson's alien girl from east of Sweden lightly traced, so to speak, with Slavic dracul/dragon, but markedly tattooed with one by the English translator, publisher, and filmmakers.

Since their respective golden age of the 1960s and of the 1920s to 1930s, the Zen cult and mystery reading vent pressure from modernity's vise, a quintessential Huck Finn impulse to "light out for the territory," culminating in the deus ex machina of either the Zen master or the master detective. Given that the U.S. has run out of territory on the Californian shore, West Coast noir of Dashiell Hammett and Raymond Chandler in novels and John Huston, Howard Hawks, and Orson Welles in films leaps across the ocean for, to rephrase Welles's *A Touch of Evil* (1959), a touch of yellow.[4] Given that the Christian West is troubled by some measure of guilt and self-doubt, it casts its gaze eastward for inspiration or ornamentation, hence the antinomy of the title's Zen and the subtitle's handymen. Detectives of mysterious crimes and gurus of the mysterious mind prosecute parallel hunts,[5] following the scent of culprits outward or tearing internal veils over the true self. In secular, pseudoscientific terms, these gurus take on the mantle of psychiatrists after "the primal wound"; shrinks who burrow into patients' subconsciousness reincarnate pre-modern spiritual quests.

Accordingly, contemporary pop culture informed by pop psychology features Zen masters and handymen as close of kin. Both seem to bypass the brain's protracted logical thinking in favor of a direct, spontaneous grasp of the nature of things. Both are doers, not thinkers, one good with hands, the other advocating the emptying of the mind. It is not surprising that they merge in kung fu choreography in global cinema: the crash course of Neo's enlightenment consists of downloads of martial arts programs, a hand-to-hand combat with Morpheus, and a novice's mind-bending advice that "there is no spoon ... only yourself." Thinking becomes a handicap to Zen's sudden illumination of emptiness that shatters all delusions. An awakening tantamount to Christian epiphany, Zen is "value-added" in that it not only claims to be transcendental but does so from outside the Western system. However, the West in late capitalism merely displaces its own repressed desire for mystery onto Zen, a wish fulfillment in the name of the other. This comes through conspicuously in a long view of East and West.

When Zen becomes fashionable in the 1960s counterculture movement, it belongs in part to the long pendulum history of Western exoticism, Orientalism included, swinging from the positive, near-idolatrous extreme to the negative, near-paranoiac opposite and back. The West has always hedged between countless pairs of trite representation, for instance, the mystical and desirable Orient of Marco Polo's Cathay versus the evil, barbaric twin of Genghis Khan the yellow peril. Yet the twins are not so much symmetrical as revolving, reversible. This conceptual and representational indeterminacy motivates all the creators of Zen Cops. Earl Derr Biggers' Charlie Chan novels since 1925, John P. Marquand's Mr Moto series since 1936, and Robert Hans van Gulik's Judge Dee mysteries since 1958,[6] as well as subsequent Hollywood adaptations. All these narratives thrive on Zen master detectives, who are also deflated as yellowface puppets, if only subconsciously. While applauding Eastern perspicacity and probity embodied in these characters, the West upholds its own superiority over Chan's and Moto's clownishness and atrocious English as well as over Judge Dee's stylistic incongruities—narrative rigidity juxtaposed with illustrated laxity. Admiration for Zen Cops' mental, almost preternatural, acuity fizzles out amidst patronizing condescension over pidgin, weird mannerism and concepts, and alien culture. That the representations of mystery handymen or Zen keytsch shuttle between positions higher and lower than, superior and inferior to, Western viewers in effect situates the West in the heart of humanity, blessed and guarded by the anagram of God and dog, by the loyal omnipotent servants.

To call these Oriental detectives in operation from the turn of the last century to the 1960s—the clown Charlie Chan, the ever-morphing Mr Moto, and the formal, almost deadpan, Judge Dee—"Zen masters" may seem retroactive, anachronistic, but what better term is there to denote their direct, intuitive grasp of the crime, the culmination of supreme intelligence, rational and methodical investigation, and primal and serendipitous instinct? The solving of "Whodunit" resembles the enlightenment induced by a koan ("public/official case") seemingly inexplicable to Zen disciples. Theoretically, only when the disciple moves out of the system—civilization's trappings—can he (rarely a "she" in classic Zen) perceive thingness, hence achieving illumination. That the three Orientals are discursively removed from the Western detective tradition endows them with more mystic Zengeist or power. On the other hand, that intuitive grasp would appear to cynics to be utterly nonsensical and kitschy, cheap and bad art. Instead of Zen master detectives, they are mere pawns in the game played by Biggers and others. In lay terms or, rather, in a tongue-in-cheek manner, Zen master simply means *master* of masters, one who triumphs over all contests and transcends all boundaries, namely, the detective who apprehends the murderer. The "gotcha" moment, akin to a mini-epiphany, formulaically comes as the denouement to provide a narrative closure, which paradoxically whets the reader's appetite for the next serving of mystery.

Philosophically, detectives battle not only messengers of death but Death itself. Detective stories routinely open, in medias res, with a corpse, after the crime has been committed. As such, death is the beginning rather than the end of the life of discourse. The investigation then unfolds in time as well as flashbacks to the cause and execution of crime, thus denying the very essence of Death—its irreversibility. These detectives manifest universal human longing for immortality despite their Oriental disguise. Indeed, yellowface signifies mask or performativity of the non-self. The duality of "yellow" puppet/eer manifests itself as we parse the irony of stereotypical, Orientalist puppets of Chan, Moto, and Dee who are made to orchestrate the investigation, on the one hand, and, on the other, the master puppeteers of Biggers, Marquand, and van Gulik blind to the racial and sexual injustice in their narrative pursuit of justice. That yellow puppet/eer lives on well into the new millennial globalization is only too clear from the surge of Orientalist mysteries, from William Gibson's cyberpunk and Marc Horne's *Tokyo Zero* (2004) to John Burdett's camp detective series set in Bangkok.

The Charlie Squad

The Charlie Squad follows the prototype of Charlie Chan, but the term also puns with "squat," for they as a group crouch subserviently in the shadow of Western imaginary. Whenever commenting on the detective genre, Western critics, such as J. Randolf Cox in "The Detective Novel," mention Chan and Moto as de rigueur of the discipline, without elaborating on their marginal and yet potentially pivotal role. Some extreme cases, though, do not even refer to the Charlie Squad, evidenced in Adrienne Johnson Gosselin's *Multicultural Detective Fiction* (1999) on African American, Native American, Hispanic, Jewish American, and queer detectives. In their respective debut in the 1920s and 1930s, Chan and Moto are comic sidekicks to New England blue blood protagonists, despite being the namesakes for the detective stories. They gradually move into center stage, coming into their own, never quite allowed, however, to lose their laughable house boy identity. Biggers has initiated the obsession with Zen keytsch in Charlie Chan's "grand entry" in *The House Without a Key* (1925), followed by *Keeper of the Keys* (1932). The former title does not refer to a specific locked house; rather, readers infer that it is a difficult murder investigation with few clues, involving a long-buried crime. After summing up the case, a task far beyond Chan's mangled English, the prosecutor commends Chan, reminiscent of Trinity's praise: "A great idea, Charlie, ... the Oriental mind ... Rather subtle, isn't it?" (146). There is nothing subtle about the pat, formulaic Zen keytsch, which Chan's refrains throughout the corpus seek to confirm: "Chinese most psychic people." The sixth sense inherent in a race comes with that race's "speech defect," which epitomizes, as Yunte Huang puts it, "a racist conception of the Chinese language and its speakers" (118); the Zen extrasensory perception debunks itself in malapropism, convoluted syntax, and a grammar so outlandish that it comprises, to rephrase George Orwell, Chanspeak, stretching all the way back to nineteenth-century missionary writings and early twentieth-century comics. Were Charlie Chan a newborn in *The House Without a Key*, his first cry goes "No knife are present in neighborhood of crime" (40). Note that Chanspeak never means to confuse native speakers of English, only to entertain, as the errors of the plural verb, the word choice of "neighborhood," and the overall stiltedness are easily detected and corrected. The linguistic deficit undercuts Chan's intelligence, giving readers an upper hand in amending, as it were, the investigation.

Focusing primarily on *The House Without a Key*, Rzepka in "Race, Region, Rule" salvages Biggers from Asian Americanist criticism of racism. Rzepka's defense pivots on generic "rule subversion" and the regionalism of Hawaii. Comparing Chan's debut to Miss Jane Marple's in Agatha Christie's *The Body in the Library* (1941), Rzepka draws attention to how "stereotypical [racial] markers" are invoked precisely in order to be overwritten by that of detection" (1467). In other words, against characters' demurral over a Chinese or spinster detective, either Hawaii's old-timer (*kama'aina*) or London's insider offers whole-hearted endorsement. In Chan's case, a Hawaiian old-timer comments: "I'm glad they brought him [Charlie Chan]. He's the best detective on the force" (*House* 37). However, it is not so much "overwritten" as "underwritten" by yet another racial marker—the Zen handyman intuiting and doing in the criminal.

Some seven years later, *Keeper of the Keys* features a Chinese pair, Chan and Ah Sing, the eponymous keeper of the keys for his white master who has committed a crime of passion. Ah Sing is so loyal that he is willing to be the scapegoat, if not for Chan's perceptive intervention. Chan and Ah Sing are doppelgangers, or different stages of evolution, as Chan muses: "[T]hough among Caucasians many more years than I, [Ah Sing] still remains Chinese. As Chinese to-day as in the first moon of his existence. While I—I bear the brand—the label—Americanized" (634). Being Chinese is equated with self-sacrifice and servitude, as opposed to fact-finding and truth-unraveling intrinsic to Americanization. Chanspeak retains Oriental-sounding fabrication, such as "the first moon of his existence." Any native speaker of Chinese would be hard pressed regarding its meaning: is it the first night, first month, or first year of Ah Sing's life? Most likely, it alludes to *manyue* (full moon) for the first month celebration of a newborn. *Yue* in Chinese signals both moon and month, and a native speaker would no doubt choose "month" because of contextual logic. Opting for the former over the latter against the grain, as it were, creates a quaint and poetic Orient. That Biggers' phrasing smacks of Orientalism exposes the discourse as Biggersspeak. Chan's rumination also evokes the metaphor of masquerade. If Americanization is "the brand," "the label" Chan bears/ wears, then Chineseness lurks beneath the New World costume and English words. Ah Sing becomes both Chan's avatar and the undying core of his existence, the "perennial alien" in Asian American studies parlance. In fact, Chanspeak has improved dramatically over the course of seven years. Even in *Keeper* itself, Chinglish is dropped halfway through, allowing Chan to speak in complete sentences, joking, prodding, and insinuating at times. In part, this language proficiency is necessitated by the fact that the Hawaiian detective is *the* detective in charge, who must conduct interviews and recap the sequence of events himself.

John P. Marquand has tapped into the rise of Japan in the mid- to late 1930s to publish his Mr Moto series. That Japan invaded and colonized Korea and China only aroused the reading public's interest in a capable yet comical Japanese detective, until the Pearl Harbor attack cut short Mr Moto's career. In Moto, Marquand may have subconsciously mirrored the United States' own antinomies, contradictions such as the American ideal of freedom and democracy versus the American empire that expands. Similar to Charlie Chan's maturation, Moto figures as a minor character in his debut, *Thank You, Mr. Moto* (1936), but increasingly takes control of subsequent stories. While Moto always accompanies a white protagonist, the first-person narrative of *Thank You* from a New England upper-class character has shifted to a third-person narrative in *Think Fast, Mr. Moto* (1938). Somewhat reflecting Japan's power of the 1930s, Mr. Moto is tougher and more forthright than Charlie Chan, although so polite as to be forever apologizing. The mantra of "very, very sorry" is an irredeemable, boring stereotype. So is the suicide-prone, death-embracing samurai image perpetuated by Moto himself. One of Moto's mottos is "All men must die" (*Think Fast* 215). Orientals are distorted as sublimating Freudian eros within thanatos. Such an Oriental thanatos infects Chinese as well, evidenced in a decapitation, almost obligatory in Oriental savagery. "He appeared to share with all his countrymen the idea that his death was logical. Certainly no one in the room thought otherwise," observes the white protagonist. "'Bend your head,' [the executioner] said. And the old man bent his head. I was afflicted with a momentary nausea and dizziness" (*Thank You* 93). White humanity is highlighted against Chinese apathy, including the one about to be beheaded. That dis-ease of "nausea and dizziness" denotes human emotions not yet dulled. Marquand continues to deploy tired clichés of polarization between Chinese domestics and mandarins, Chinese abjection and aesthetics, evil aliens and Oriental integrity. Mr. Moto the dedicated detective contends with the archvillain Wu Lo Feng, the strange-sounding, incomprehensible name suggesting the darkness within the character and echoing all the fictitious Fu Manchus.

Judging Dee

Quite different from Biggers's and Marquand's cavalier dabbling in things "Chinee," Robert Hans van Gulik is an Old China Hand. An accomplished linguist with estimable Chinese handwriting for a nonnative speaker, the Dutch diplomat-scholar van Gulik began with the translation of classical Chinese crime narratives in the late 1940s and wrote 17 Judge Dee crime mysteries until his death in 1967. These mysteries fall squarely in Zen keytsch in their formulaic, repetitious narrative of interwoven murder cases, usually three in each mystery, solved by the eponymous, near-clairvoyant protagonist. The series is kept in circulation in recent decades by the prestigious University of Chicago Press as well as by commercial presses such as HarperCollins. Judge Dee is modeled after, as van Gulik's postscript to every mystery expounds, the historical figure of Di Renje (A.D. 630–700), a Tang dynasty magistrate and "master-detective" of such upstanding character that he has turned into a legend of justice and probity in Chinese popular imagination. As reported by Janwillem van de Wetering, Judge Dee is Gulik's thinly-veiled alter ego, sharing many of Gulik's obsessions—crime and detection, Chinese lutes (*qin*), gibbons (*yuan*), and, more implicitly, Oriental erotica.[7] In addition to crime mysteries, van Gulik published sinological monographs and translations on these very subjects, such as *The Lore of the Chinese Lute* (1940) and *The Gibbon in*

China (1967). Van Gulik manages to work his hobbies into his mysteries, exemplified by the gibbon that helps solve the crime in *The Monkey and the Tiger* (1965). Ultimately, China *is* van Gulik's hobby. As A. F. P. Hulsewé notes in "Nécrologie," van Gulik conducts, despite his far-ranging output, "an enquiry ... of the old Chinese scholar-official class" (118).

Likewise, van Gulik's interest in Ming dynasty erotica permeates Judge Dee mysteries and scholarly endeavors. Evolving away from his early faithful translation of *Dee Goong An* (*The Cases of Judge Dee* 1949) and *T'ang-yin pi-shih* (*Parallel Cases from under the Pear Tree* 1956), a thirteenth-century legal manual, van Gulik yokes in Judge Dee Western detective mysteries and Oriental erotica. Any cursory observer of van Gulik's mysteries would see that they are strewn with gratuitous erotica, crystallized in the author's own cartoonish, amateurish illustrations allegedly in the Chinese style, of naked "wenches," an archaic usage for a young woman or prostitute. Frequently, illustrated nudes are far more revealing than the text. In *The Red Pavilion* (1964), a description such as "her oval face with the finely chiseled nose and the large expressive eyes were most attractive, and the wet gauze clinging to her bare body revealed its smooth whiteness and its sensuous curves with discerning clarity" (7) transforms itself two pages later into frontal nudity, where "oval face," "nose," and "expressive eyes" are overshadowed by the striptease pose of raised arms, bare breasts, hourglass body, and curvaceous thighs. The postscript to *The Chinese Gold Murders* (1959) even concludes on the sexual taboo over women's feet, which prompts van Gulik to conceal them in two illustrations of nudes. One wonders whether van Gulik follows Chinese taboos or reveals his own eccentricities here, particularly when the first nude is a Korean prostitute unlikely to have bound feet. Van Gulik's liberties are taken in the name of Chinese sexual mores. The willful fable-like narrative structure and the erotic chinoiserie "doodling" cross children's story with male fantasy, naiveté with soft porn. In addition, van Gulik published the respectable *Sexual Life in Ancient China: A Preliminary Study of Chinese Sex and Society from ca. 1500 B.C. till 1644 A.D.* (1961). The scholarly pedantry contrasts sharply with the mysteries' artistic license in violation of plot coherence and character development.

Herein lies the ultimate irony of narrative mastery and cowardly duplicity. The "yellow" master-detective is but the white man's puppet/ handyman, who is presented as stoic, ascetic, and immune to sexual temptation. Rising above corruption and lechery, Judge Dee, nonetheless, exhibits close proximity and even kinship to evil, which gives him the upper hand in fighting crimes. After all, he is tied to the underworld in that his trusted investigators include Ma Joong, Chiao Tai, and Tao Gan. The former two hail from the "green woods" or criminals' shady hideout, supplying the brawn in action sequences that punctuate any investigation; the last is a con man whose machinations mirror Judge Dee the trickster's own endless deceptions and intrigues. So rife with conspiracy as to appear paranoiac, Judge Dee mysteries emplot endless disguises, smokescreens to conceal the truth and to be dispelled by reason and intuition. Duplicities are surely evil as barriers to the oneness of things, such as cause and effect, and crime and punishment; however, they turn good in the right hand as a tool to truth. Of course, any claim of the ideal oneness is subject to interpretation: believers view it as a transcendent vision to be achieved in the future; skeptics view it as a regression to infantile, fetal wholeness. From the latter perspective, van Gulik's narratives invariably gravitate to violence and his illustrations to sex, both to be resolved by the deus ex machina of Judge Dee. The downward double helix can be seen as the DNA of Zen keytsch in general and, in this case, as the "Fantasizing Dutchman" letting go of his darker impulses repressed by his diplomatic and scholarly pursuits. To the extent that he is an Old China Hand, the propensity to project repressions onto the old China seems particularly egregious.

Wedding yellowface detectives—Charlie Chan and Mr. Moto—with exotic settings—Agatha Christie's Oriental mysteries, Raymond Chandler's "yellow peril" detective stories, and "a touch of yellow" in film noir from *The Lady from Shanghai* (1948) to *Chinatown* (1974), van Gulik creates a near *total* fictitious construct of Chinese otherness, which is probably why Hollywood has never taken to this particular member of the Charlie Squad. The Oriental universe betrays itself, however, in the use of racist and sexist stereotypes and in such incongruous elements as Christian "Amen!" and pidgin-like "noon-rice," "morning-rice," and "evening-rice," all interjected mindlessly into the seventh-century China. In this new millennium, half a century after van Gulik's Dee came into being, it is time to reopen the case of Judge Dee both as a yellowface puppet under authorial control and as a clue to the puppeteer van Gulik's own "yellowness." Stripped of racism and taken in a strictly descriptive sense like "white" and "black," yellowness acknowledges van Gulik's empathy for, even identification with, Chinese culture. Taken pejoratively, though, yellowness suggests his two-faced, even cowardly, dissembling. Empathy turns unwittingly into a narratological domination in manifesting and disguising van Gulik's own Orientalism. Van Gulik might as well be critiquing himself when Judge Dee in *The Willow Pattern* (1965) exposes the guilt of a puppeteer: "Being a puppeteer, you imagined that human beings can be manipulated in the same way as your marionettes" (127).

Zen keytsch surfaces in the early titles: all of them include the racial marker of "Chinese" to anchor exotic imaginary. Surrounding the titles of, for example, *The Chinese Gold Murders* (1958) and *The Chinese Bell Murders* (1959), the cover designs are collages of stereotypical images entirely irrelevant to the Tang dynasty, as several old fading photographs from the turn of the last century are randomly put together to stand in for an olden time, each book cover framed by chinoiserie, lattice-shaped book edges. Even in later works published primarily by the University of

Chicago Press, the absence of the word "Chinese" in the title is more than made up by the cover's chinoiserie icons, with a Judge Dee insert and "A Judge Dee Mystery" gracing the bottom. According to the narratologist Gérard Genette, the book cover belongs to what he calls the "paratext," the "threshold" to a text, "an 'undefined zone' between the inside and the outside" (*Paratexts* 1–2). Seemingly as marginal as the Keymaker, the paratext grows in stature when Genette quickly cites Philippe Lejeune in *Le Pacte Autobiographie*: "a fringe of the printed text which in reality controls one's whole reading of the text" (45). Genette refrains from taking up the cover design other than the verbal aspect, perhaps because images fall outside the purview of his book. However, the paratextual cover design with its split between a Tang dynasty personage and Western representations heralds the internal, textual fissures to come, blatantly so between words and illustrations. In effect, van Gulik acknowledges a certain anachronism in his Ming-style nudity illustrating Tang dynasty tales six centuries prior. Readers must suspend their disbelief before entering into this make-believe Orient unmoored from time and space.

In comparison to Biggers and Marquand, van Gulik draws from specific historical sources for Judge Dee's ingenious methods of investigation, King Solomon-style outwitting of criminals. He also learned well from translating *Parallel Cases from under the Pear Tree* and other Chinese classics in the overall symmetrical structure of his mystery. Each chapter is headed by what appears to be a two-line couplet divided by a semicolon, each line on one thematic strand of that chapter. No doubt betokening the scales of justice, one that neutralizes crime with punishment, the parallel heading signals as well the officialdom juxtaposed with the underworld. Between the two, much trafficking is taking place, given corrupt officials and highwaymen-turned-Dee's assistants. Furthermore, the symbiotic relationship exists in the high vis-à-vis low society as well as in the human yang realm vis-à-vis the supernatural yin realm. Although an avowed Confucianist, Judge Dee is disturbed by a ghost and weretiger in the debut of *The Chinese Gold Murders*. Although almost all intrigues are tied to Buddhist monks, temples, and practices, supernatural beings shunned by Confucianism evidently fascinate van Gulik to the extent that *Gold* ends with a cliffhanger validation of the existence of ghost seeking revenge. In the subsequent *The Chinese Bell Murders*, the mystery deepens in the epigraphic opening of sorts when a first-person narrator at a curio shop in the Ming dynasty puts on Judge Dee's black gauze cap from six centuries ago and is stricken by visions that comprise the three murders in the book. Such extrasensory perception continues unabated, much of which revolves around Judge Dee's uncanny instinct to sniff out crimes.

Similar to all his famous colleagues in the West, Judge Dee uses logic and reasoning power to apprehend the culprit. As Donald F. Lach remarks, "while the judge himself was thought to recognize guilt or innocence intuitively and immediately, he was required to prove his case in public and had to force a confession from the accused" (8). Jurisprudence procedure notwithstanding, Judge Dee is rather given to losing himself to momentary trances when he "had not been listening" to his subordinates (*Gold* 124, 137) or "he looked out at the monotonous landscape with unseeing eyes" (*Bell* 78). Routinely, the narrative seizes as Judge Dee experiences epiphanies: "I had thought that—", cut short by orchestral music at a theater (*Gold* 172), soon followed by an agitated Judge Dee who "jumped up and started pacing the floor ... at last he stood still and said, 'That is it! It all fits!'" (174). True to form, the revelation does not complete itself in order to ratchet up suspense, waiting for Judge Dee's final recap of what exactly fits. In denial of the immediacy of the here and now, which segments the flow of time into a series of presents, such possessed states or dream visions unexpectedly connect the internal and the external, the waking hours and the dream world, whereby a mystical illumination annihilates all obstruction, unraveling the foul deeds under investigation. This wedding of one's thoughts and events is so cataclysmic that it obliterates quotidian concerns, consistent with the romantic striving for oneness at the heart of any Zen keytsch. That oneness is oftentimes cast in the trope of trances, moments when one is both awake and asleep, dreaming with eyes wide open, or retaining dreams in their entirety upon waking up. Reminiscent of the Wordsworthian paradox, these "spots of time" are placed outside of time, as consciousness merges with subconsciousness, Self with Other. The mental process of such theoretical transcendence resembles poetic, metaphoric association far more than prosaic, metonymic induction. Chancing upon theater performances in *Gold*, Judge Dee links the apparently unrelated onstage actions with three murder cases. The frequency with which Judge Dee seems inspired by these chance encounters with the stage, with a gibbon, and with a multitude of happenstance puts him, to rephrase William Blake's assessment of Milton, in the mystery handyman's league without van Gulik's knowing it. Indeed, Judge Dee may come across as a superlative handyman in service of the "August Sovereign" from the Netherlands.

Zen keytsch and mystery handymen appear to belong, exclusively, to Western, Orientalist imaginary. However, the East itself is not immune to such pseudo-transcendent religiosity and paradoxical awakening and servitude. Tsui Hark's Hong Kong action film *Detective Dee and the Mystery of the Phantom Flame* (2010) rejuvenates his career over three decades, uniting Sammo Hung's martial arts choreography with his own trademark Gothic atmospherics, although not as macabre as his flop of *Seven Swords* (2005). In addition, the choice of Detective Dee can be traced back to other national heroes, such as kung fu master Huang Feihong in Tsui's *Once Upon a Time in China* series. The making of Tsui's *Detective Dee* coincides with China's recent craze over the historical figure Di Renjie, who is the lead in several Chinese television series, including *Detective Di Renjie Prequel* (44 episodes in 2010) and the four-part *Detective Di Renjie* (30 episodes in 2006, 40 in 2006, 48 in 2008, and 44 in 2010). In China's meteoric ascent in the new millennium, the internal unease over the gap between rich and poor, urban and rural, coastal and hinterland finds expression in the traditional One Just Man. Almost single-handedly, Di Renjie crushes evil forces, assuaging the public's fear of unrest, maintaining the status quo. Di embodies the working out of Chinese viewers' conflicting neurosis of desiring and dreading change.

This paradoxical effect turns the fright of utter subjugation into a Zen flight, by way of a good old kung fu fistfight. In lieu of the relatively dry and squarish Judge Dee in van Gulik, Hong Kong pop star Andy Lau plays the dynamic lead character. In comparison to Jet Li's role of Huang Feihong, Lau's lack of kung fu training is compensated by film editing and special effects, much of which are computer-generated images from South Korea's AZ Works. There is no more of van Gulik's pretense of courtroom drama, only breathlessly non-stop action sequences of ever more incredulous stunts. A cog in the gigantic Confucianist bureaucracy, Tsui's Detective Dee nonetheless channels what *The Confucian Analects* has long discredited as the "non-rationalist" sentiments and events of *guaililuanshen* ("the strange, the violent, the chaotic/transgressive, and the supernatural") into Buddhism, Taoism, and polytheistic local beliefs. Accordingly in Tsui Hark, the conspiracy of assassinating Empress Wu Zetian, the only woman in Chinese history who ascended the throne and reigned from A.D. 690 to 705, hinges on the collapse of a Buddhist Fanyanna pillar propping up the Empress's statue modeled after *Guanyin* (Buddhist and folk goddess of mercy). In turn, the Empress consolidates her hold on power by the ploy of an Imperial Chaplain complete with Taoist trappings. While both Buddhist and Taoist practices veil characters' murderous intent, Dee is not exactly above such chicanery. His investigation takes him to the phantom bazaar, the old Han city sunken below the current capital Luoyang, literally in the bowels of the earth in an architectural palimpsest, where freaks and monstrosities dwell in shadows.

Tsui Hark's signature Gothic plots repeatedly deliver sensationalist over-stimulations for the global cinema market long inured to violence and sex, or *guaililuanshen*. The Hong Kong veteran filmmaker outdoes van Gulik-esque parallelism in counterpointing the yang world and the yin underworld, favoring perhaps the latter. *Detective Dee* thus unfolds largely in dimly-lit interior studio sets, except when four characters, exposed to sunlight, burst into flames as if in gruesome self-immolation/self-combustion and in confirmation of stereotypical death-prone, suicidal, revenge-crazed Orientals. They have been infected by *chiyan jingguei*,[8] a beetle called fire turtles introduced from *xiyu* or Western Territories of Xinjiang and Central Asia. The one-armed antagonist Shatou also commands a dark-skinned,

Central Asian-looking lieutenant. Akin to the West's mythologizing of the Other, Tsui Hark attributes evil to non-Han races and cultures as well. The genre of *wuxia* (swordplay) films has consistently sought to valorize masculinity at the expense of not only males of other races but also of women. This results in the ambiguous albino-looking character Pei Donglai in the employ of the Supreme Court (*Dali si*, a cross between the Investigative Bureau and the Secret Police). At the outset, his harsh behavior and ghostly pale make-up and hair render him near-diabolical. Yet his queer, almost feminine "sunbonnet" associates him with eunuchs, traditionally construed as perverse and malevolent in Chinese history and, specifically, in *wuxia* films ever since King Hu's *Xianu* (*A Touch of Zen* 1971). Subsequently though, Pei Donglai becomes an endearing, devoted comrade-in-arms.

Likewise, female characters hover between masculine aggression and feminine tenderness. Empress Wu alternates between the imperial robe and woman's costume, even in full armor astride a horse on the parade ground. Her legendary strong-arm tactic to consolidate her rule puts her on a par with any emperor; however, the film concludes with Detective Dee saving Empress Wu and counseling the throne be restored to its rightful owner, i.e., male heirs of the Tang dynasty. By the same patriarchy-affirming logic, the Empress's confidant Shangguan Jing'er cross-dresses and masquerades as the Imperial Chaplain, resorting to techniques of transfiguration and ventriloquism. All the power Jing'er has wielded in disguise evaporates once she falls in love with Dee and dies in his stead. Consistent with his fellow snoops in the West, Tsui Hark's Dee instinctively grasps any dissimulation, in control of his fate even as a shackled prisoner burning memorials at the palace incinerator. The utterly abject slave, no better than the kept Keymaker, foresees and masters his own destiny and the nation's. This reversal of fortune and rebound from the nadir lies at the heart of any drama, specifically action thriller. In the context of Zen keytsch, Detective Dee exhibits the magical sleight of hand of all the handicapped handymen. Similar to van Gulik's Judge Dee in trance, one who "had not been listening" and not quite himself, Tsui's Dee undergoes a drugged state in his confrontation with Jing'er within a hypnotizing vortex of Taoist *baguazhen* (eight trigrams formation). Barely able to defend himself in his deliriousness, Dee nevertheless shields her from a ricocheting knife with his own body, a move reminiscent of the Keymaker's. This surrender of oneself for romantic love leads to Jing'er's and Pei Donglai's tear-jerking sacrifices.

Dragon tattoos

Since his trilogy *The Girl with the Dragon Tattoo* (henceforth *Dragon*, 2005), *The Girl Who Played with Fire* (henceforth *Fire* 2006), and *The Girl Who Kicked the Hornet's Nest* (henceforth *Hornet's Nest* 2007) contains not a single Asian character, except the mixed race Miriam Wu, definitely neither a Charlie Chan nor a Judge Dee, is Stieg Larsson then the weakest link in this argument on Zen Cops? On the contrary, it is the strongest proof yet of Zen keytsch, now that mystery handymen have shed their yellowface masks to reveal white faces. Given that the Charlie Squad has been a trope all along, the veiled alien Lisbeth Salander turns out to be apparently white, after all. The conundrum that is Salander propels an unknown Swedish journalist's mystery to a global phenomenon, occupying the *New York Times* best-seller list for months. A tantalizing puzzle throughout, Salander resembles a cyborg without the need of mechanical body parts. Her photographic memory and computer hacker devilry demonstrate an eerie bonding with machines. She is omniscient and, indeed, God-like on the computer, meting out justice after breaking into crooks' hard drives and secrets. In addition, she lacks emotional connectedness due to a suspected Asperger's Syndrome, one characterized by affective alienation from the world, by excellent "rote memory" (Asperger 75), and by "psychopathic clarity of vision" (74). Declared incompetent and violent by the Swedish Security in order to shield her abusive, murderous father Alexander Zalachenko, a Soviet defector with intelligence of high value, Salander is in fact a victim of the State. Pitted against the state apparatus of police, mental institution, and prison since early teens, Salander seems strangely untroubled, her robotic "unfeelingness" shutting out the world, a virtual uberman with no fear and debilitating self-pity. Of Swedish and Russian, West and East European, parentage, of human and nonhuman quality, Salander announces her difference from the world by sporting a T-shirt with the words "I AM ALSO AN ALIEN" (*Dragon* 51–2).

Beneath her counterculture punk rock outfit, Salander wears tattoos that point to the ambivalence of white wasp and foreign dragon identity. While the dragon tattoo recurs as a reference in the trilogy, the English title of the first installment and all three Swedish films highlight it by inscribing the entire length of the inimitable actress Noomi Rapace's bare back with a coiling dragon. Anorexic-looking at 4 ft 11 in. but with a ruthless killer's precision and drive, this scrawny "girl" in her mid-twenties comes to be endowed with the symbol of dubious power.[9] The state of vulnerable nakedness happens to reveal the source of her strength.

> [Lisbeth Salander] had a wasp tattoo about an inch long on her neck, a tattooed loop around the biceps of her left arm and another around her left ankle. A dragon tattoo on her left shoulder blade. She had a wide mouth, a small nose, and high cheekbones that gave her an almost Asian look. (*Dragon* 41)

Needless to say, her whiteness is visibly displayed like the wasp on her neck. Although she has the tattoo surgically removed in *Fire*, her Web username remains Wasp. By contrast, a tattoo on the shoulder blade in Larsson grows to envelop an entire back. The exotic tattoo culminates in the hint of "an almost Asian look." Perhaps a tease out of Larsson's subconsciousness, Salander's alienness/Asianness derives from her Eastern/Russian descent, inducing stereotypical Asian expressionlessness and emotionlessness.

Tattoos are writings on the body for self-identity, but they are oftentimes veiled from the public. Tattoos both reveal and conceal their wearer. Within the body politic of the West, the Charlie Squad squats like barely unnoticeable yet conspiratorially lurking dragon tattoos, ever ready to be summoned to play mystery handymen for the erect, phallic masters. Normally located in hidden places on the torso or limbs, first-world late-capitalist tattoos are not designed to challenge the integrity and sanctity of the face, the epitome of human identity. Whereas facial tattoos are associated with indigenous scarification and erstwhile criminals, mystery handymen have their Orientalness carved on their faces and bodies. Put another way, Orientals are tattoos on the West's body politic, to be flaunted whenever necessary, otherwise to be suppressed. As any other alien epigraph, the dragon tattoo supplies Larsson's mystery a darkly menacing aura, shrouding the narratives in a looming shadow. Dragons have long been a symbol of evil in the West, from the fire-spewing monster threatening Beowulf and medieval knights to Bram Stoker's blood-sucking Dracula (son of Dragon) from "the East" across "the most Western of splendid bridges over the Danube" (*Dracula* 1). Yet this stand-in for the yellow peril comes attenuated in modern times when dragons are imperial and divine icons from Chinese and East Asian cultures. Indeed, even the color yellow used to be the imperial province as a result of trivial and capricious happenstance which has been calcified into conventions and norms. To be specific, *huang* is a homophone for both yellow and royal in Mandarin. Even in post-dynastic, postmodern China, the color yellow continues to evoke positive associations, its contemporary insinuation of pornography notwithstanding. By the same token, the notorious bat or vampire in the West is used as a symbol of bliss in China. Once again, *fu* is the homonym for bat and blessedness.

The East–West, good–bad montage gives rise to the synthetic paradox of Lisbeth Salander, the spelling of her last name and the choice of her tattoo betraying her membership in the Zalachenko family. The reason for getting such an extensive and no doubt painful procedure remains unknown, as Salander rejects outright a friendly surgeon's query in *Hornet's Nest*. But she soon relents: as if in apology for her abrupt dismissal, she disrobes to show him the tattoo in its entirety. Given that her revenge against the guardian Bjurman who rapes her consists of tattooing on his abdomen the phrase "I AM A SADISTIC PIG, A PERVERT, AND A RAPIST" (*Dragon* 288), her own tattoo may well be a sadomasochistic act punishing the Zalachenko bloodline within herself, while claiming ownership of the evil forces. This confessional self-splitting is reprised in the family, so to speak: Salander cannot, allegedly, feel emotional pain and her half-brother Niedermann cannot feel physical pain due to congenital analgesia. Both psychological and medical conditions are "inherited genetic defect[s]" (*Fire* 576). Whatever the psychological motive for the dragon tattoo, this kinship with the Eastern symbol enables her to outmaneuver and slay the dragon.

Larsson's West European mystery exhibits a paranoiac and conspiratory mindset typical of the genre, one forever fraught with secrecy and disinformation. Suspense even comes from Larsson withholding certain characters' identities, such as Niedermann's in *Fire*, and deferring denouement until the very end, such as the face-to-face meeting of the one-time lovers Salander and Bloomkvist on the last page of *Fire*. To work backwards in order to emplot the trilogy, the story begins when Sweden's Sapo or Security Services becomes "infected," led astray by a Russian spy Zalachenko, whose testimonies drive the fanatic group's "internal personnel control" or hunt for communists in their midst. Zalachenko from the East is thus the veiled mover of the trilogy. In the wake of the collapse of the Soviet Union of the late 1980s and the creation of the European Union in 1993, Western Europe attributes to Eastern Europe and the Slavic an Orientalist split that reflects Western Europe's own schizophrenia. The polarized pendulum comprises bad, victimizer East of Zalachenko, his Nazi-looking Golem son Ronald Niedermann, the Serbian Nikolich brothers dispatched for assassinations and human trafficking, the pedophiliac psychiatrist with the Armenian-sounding name of Dr Teleborian, and a shadowy figure Clinton à la the U.S. president, at one extreme, and, at the other, good, victimized East of East European prostitutes raped and mutilated, a Kurdish janitor, Salander's lesbian partner Miriam Wu, Salander's ex-employer Dragan Armansky of Armenian Jewish and Bosnian Muslim Greek extraction, and the Jewish police detective Bulanski.

Between the Good and Evil Other resides Sweden's liberal journalist Mikael Bloomkvist and his magazine *Millennium* fighting corrupt officials and bureaucrats. Given the psychic projection inherent in the genre of crime novels, a self-reflexive and pseudo-incestuous stirring runs through the trilogy. *Dragon* opens with a freezing, snow-bound Northern Sweden where the Vanger family commits unspeakable crimes of murders, incest, and parricide. The core puzzle involves the Nazi, anti-semitic Vanger males mutilating women with "traditional Jewish names" in accordance to what they believe to be scriptures from the book of Leviticus (*Dragon* 417). Asiatic Jews play the role of demons in the delusion of the Vanger males. The horror of incest occurs when Harriet Vanger was forced into sex by her father, a transgression taken over by Harriet's brother after she drowned the drunken rapist. Bloomkvist solves the mystery by means of a series of epiphanies, narrated in words reminiscent of mental blockages followed by Zen enlightenment, as in "I saw *something* [in the Vanger family album]. I don't know what it was yet. It was something that almost became an idea, but I missed it" (316) followed by "the insight struck him like a thunderbold out of a clear sky" (323) and "an intuitive leap" (348). In the film, celluloid magic renders that *"something"* into consecutive location shots from newspaper archives strung into a slide show of sorts that eventually reveals the satanic serial killer and perpetrator of incest.

This "family business" of self-directed violence continues into *Fire* when Salander tracks down Zalachenko with the intention of completing the parricide that has failed over a decade ago. Her father muses with a leer after she is subdued by her half-brother: "Maybe I should ask Niedermann to screw you. You look as if you need it." Venom out of Zalachenko's innermost darkness, such violation of human taboos should have incensed and horrified Salander. Yet her riposte showing little emotion seeks to provoke and unsettle Zalachenko: "Then maybe you should screw me" (601). As Dr Teleborian aptly remarks in the film version of *Hornet's Nest*, the family bloodbath bears a certain resemblance to Greek tragedy with archetypal Oedipal and Electral drives. Although devoid of this apposite reference, the novel *Hornet's Nest* elaborates with great intensity Zalachenko and Salander's duel inside a Swedish hospital, having both sustained massive injuries at the other's hand. Drama and mythology in general and mystery thrillers in particular have long exploited the reversibility of slavery and mastery, of debilitation and divinity, of handicap and handyman: the wish-granting genie trapped in the magic lantern; the traumata institutionalized as Christian iconography; the shaved, denuded, and energy-generating Neo unplugged to become the One. Surviving three bullets, including one lodged in the brain, and a burial, Salander avenges her mother and herself. In her precarious condition after emergency surgery, she proceeds to make use of the palm computer Bloomkvist has smuggled into her ward. She hacks into her opponents' computer hard drives to make possible courtroom revelations that close the trilogy with a bang. Along the way, on no more than "[j]ust a hunch," she identifies the cyberstalker haunting *Millennium* ex-editor Erika Berger, who is one of Bloomkvist's many lovers (387). Her sixth sense falls in line with not only the investigative journalist's instinct but all the other yellowface Keymakers' oracular properties.

Similar to the dichotomy attributed to the Eastern Other, the liberal journalist-novelist Larsson may have done the same in terms of gender and sexuality, suspended between the extremes of dehumanizing sadomasochism and free love. On the outcome of the former extreme, *The New York Times* film critics A. O. Scott and Manohla Dargis muse whether this trend of gun-toting female avengers led by Lisbeth Salander signals "empowerment or exploitation," "[f]eminism or fetishism" (8). Indeed, as reprehensible as sadism and torture are, Larsson's text dwells on these fringe experiences, moral horror mixed with transgressive pleasure of the text and imagination.

Notwithstanding Larsson's insistence on political correctness—entitling the debut as *Men Who Hate Women*, featuring a Salander characterized as "the woman who hated men who hate women" (*Fire* 580), and concluding the trilogy with the polemics of "when it comes down to it, this story is not primarily about spies and secret government agencies; it's about violence against women, and the men who enable it" (*Hornet's Nest* 514), the repetition of sadomasochistic details betrays a subconscious thrill, a tease for heightened eroticism. First of all, Larsson's alter ego Bloomkvist lives out typical middle-age male fantasy in being irresistible to any female. His recipe of success consists of tender loving care, sincerity and loyalty to any open-ended relationship, good in bed, and "feminine" tasks of making sandwiches and coffee. It is rather narcissistic on Larsson's part to portray all males having sex as middle-aged with an expanding midriff, except Salander's brief Caribbean fling with a 16-year-old George Bland, which would make Salander a pedophile by American standards. (All the middle-aged men Salander picks up for biological needs think she is underage and thus engage in illicit sex as well.) Salander herself has been repeatedly strapped down by such males as Dr Teleborian and Bjurman and sexually violated by the latter. However, when she willingly submits to the dominatrix Miriam Wu, bondage becomes a consensual game, heightening sexual tension and release. Despite all her unfeminine habits and behavior, she flies into a rage on the concluding pages of *Dragon* when she happens on her lover Bloomkvist kissing his long-time lover Erika, instantly severing all ties until the last page of *Fire*. As a consequence, she undergoes breast implants to acquire a more desirable body and self-image. Even her girlish build can be construed as a come-on for aging males indulging in self-rejuvenation via women young enough to be their daughters. The heart of the mystery, Salander contains opposites in the vein of handicapped handymen. Supposedly unattached due to the Asperger's Syndrome, she gets jealous like anybody in love and subconsciously makes herself more attractive. Suspicious of all authorities, she sheds tears when she realizes how she has unknowingly abandoned her former guardian Palmgren, the father figure in her life. Cold and machine-like, she intuits the identity of Erika's cyberstalker amidst a sea of information. The expressionless "Mr Spock" façade endears her to readers who are led to believe that they see through her deadpan act and feel for someone who cannot feel for herself (*Fire* 117).

The Casanova Bloomkvist's exploits range from the petite 4 ft 11 in. Salander to the muscular ex-bodybuilder inspector Monica Figuerola over six feet tall. The pair reminds one of the buxom cyborg Major Motoko Kusanagi in the anime *Ghost in the Shell* (1995) reborn into the body of a teenage girl. Inspector Figuerola accosts Bloomkvist thusly: "Now, are you going to come quietly [to Figuerola's home to be undressed] or do I have to handcuff you?" (*Hornet's Nest* 338). Replete with sexual innuendos, sadomasochism turns from dehumanization and abomination to, insofar as consensual adults are concerned, lubricant for sensual ecstasy. Freest of all lovers, Bloomkvist with his arrangement of ménage a trois with Erika Berger and her husband has long fled the marital bondage. But it is obviously not against his liberal principle to try a bit of forbidden sex to maximize pleasure.

Zen keytsch is mindlessly rehearsed in contemporary culture, West and East. The novice potential cautions Neo in *The Matrix* and us that "there is no spoon," a Zen-like awakening that elevates Zen into the new millennium's silver spoon. If there is no silver spoon, then there is no Zen, only the human longing for transcendent magic. In place of true deliverance, popular culture recycles shattered fragments of allegedly preternatural power. In Joan Acocella's "Man of Mystery," review of Larsson's novels in the January 10, 2011 issue of *The New Yorker*, the magazine's famed illustrator features Larsson in a film noir private eye get-up with a black hat and coat, its collar turned up. The dark costume sports a coiling dragon design, which re-emerges in red above and behind his head. The striking contrast of black and red is complemented by three yellow bees, all images from the trilogy. The color contrast, the waves of cloud, and the dragon's curving lines evoke Japanese printmaking style. This illustration in *Japonisme* testifies to Oriental images as discursive handymen, mysterious yet kitschily functional in inducing an aura of awe, ever so elusive while dutifully serving at the pleasure of the West. It matters little that Larsson's trilogy does not bear on Japan or "dragon-infested" East Asia. Like the Batman searchlight, the dragon tattoo has been projected onto the night sky over the global Gotham, coming in handy for virtually all problems of the twenty-first century.

Notes

1   Alfred Hitchcock describes "MacGuffin" in a 1939 lecture at Columbia University: "[We] have a name in the studio, and we call it the 'MacGuffin.' It is the mechanical element that usually crops up in any story. In crook stories it is almost always the necklace and in spy stories it is most always the papers." The mystery and thriller genre deploys MacGuffin as the mover of plot, a treasure or secret protagonists and antagonists vie to obtain.

2   See Ferdinand de Saussure's *Writings in General Linguistics* on the anatomy of the "sign."

3   While melancholy has always been one of the romantic traits, Romanticism as a movement is characterized by the desire of overreaching, often beyond individual human capabilities, which necessarily results in a sense of inadequacy and melancholia.

4   For Orientalist themes in film noir and detective fiction, see Sheng-mei Ma's "Anal Apocalypse," chapter 1 to *East-West Montage* (2007).

5   In *Detective Fiction*, Charles J. Rzepka uses the word "hunt" to describe investigation in the detective genre.

6   Robert Hans van Gulik's Judge Dee mysteries are followed by the date of the English edition, not the original Dutch edition.

7   Janwillem van de Wetering quotes van Gulik commenting to a fellow novelist: "I *am* Dee" (77).

8   This is one of many four-word maxims and phrases this film uses, consistent with the Chinese habit for such expressions, which are watered down and simplified in English subtitles. Another example is the translation of Fanyanna into four words, despite the fact that only three are needed. The film locates its dialogue between modern vernacular Chinese and classical Chinese to give the sense of a faraway, mythical time. The English translation not only fails to capture the occasionally archaic usage but approximates a running commentary for the visually impaired. Tsui Hark's Chinese script resembles the concocted archaic-sounding language of *Lord of the Rings*.

9   Among many other reports, Joan Acocella in "Man of Mystery: Why Do People Love Stieg Larsson's Novels?" cites Eva Gedin, editor at Larsson's Swedish publisher Norstedts, who claimed that *Men Who Hate Women* was the title Larsson absolutely insisted (73). It was changed to *The Girl with the Dragon Tattoo* in the English translation, either by translator Steven Murray under the pseudonym of Reg Keeland or someone else at Knopf and Vintage. But the English titles of the three installments give the trilogy more coherence, starting from the "key" symbol of "the dragon tattoo."

Works cited

Acocella, Joan. "Man of Mystery: Why Do People Love Stieg Larsson's Novels?" *The New Yorker* January 10, 2011: 70–4.

Alfredson, Daniel. Dir. *The Girl Who Kicked the Hornet's Nest*. Perf. Michael Nyqvist and Noomi Rapace. Music Box, 2009. DVD.

—dir. *The Girl Who Played with Fire*. Perf. Michael Nyqvist and Noomi Rapace. Music Box, 2009. DVD.

Asperger, Hans. "'Autistic Psychopathy' in Childhood." Trans. and Annotated Uta Frith. In *Autism and Asperger Syndrome*. Ed. Uta Frith. Cambridge: Cambridge University Press, 1991. 37–92.

Biggers, Earl Derr. *Five Complete Novels*. New York: Avenel, 1981.

Burdett, John. *Bangkok 8*. New York: Vintage, 2003.

Calinescu, Matei. *Five Faces of Modernity: Modernism, Avant-Garde, Decadence, Kitsch, Postmodernism*. Durham: Duke University Press, 1987.

Chaplin, Charlie. Dir. *A Countess from Hong Kong*. Perf. Marlon Brando and Sophia Loren. Universal Pictures, 1967. DVD.

Christie, Agatha. *The Body in the Library*. 1941. New York: Dodd, Mead and Company, 1942.

—*Poirot in the Orient*. New York: Berkley, 2005.

Frazier, Charles. *Cold Mountain*. New York: Atlantic Monthly P, 1997.

Genette, Gérard. *Paratexts: Thresholds of Interpretation*. 1987. Trans. Jane E. Lewin. London: Cambridge UP, 1997.

Gibson, William. *Neuromancer*. New York: ACE, 1984.

—*All Tomorrow's Party*. New York: ACE, 1999.

Gosselin, Adrienne Johnson. *Multicultural Detective Fiction: Murder from the "Other" Side*. New York: Garland, 1999.

Gulik, Robert Hans van. trans. *T'ang-yin pi-shih (Parallel Cases from under the Pear Tree)*. Leiden: Brill, 1956.

—*The Chinese Bell Murders*. New York: Perennial, 1958.

—*The Chinese Gold Murders*. New York: Harper, 1959.

—*The Red Pavilion*. Chicago: University of Chicago Press, 1964.

—*The Monkey and the Tiger*. Chicago: University of Chicago Press, 1965.

—*The Willow Pattern*. Chicago: University of Chicago Press, 1965.

—*The Gibbon in China: An Essay in Chinese Animal Lore*. Leiden: Brill, 1967.

—*The Lore of the Chinese Lute: An Essay in the Ideology of the Ch'in*. 1940. Tokyo: Sophia University, 1968.

—trans. *Dee Goong An (The Cases of Judge Dee)* 1949. New York: Dover, 1976.

—*Sexual Life in Ancient China: A Preliminary Study of Chinese Sex and Society from ca. 1500 B.C. till 1644 A.D.* 1961. Leiden: Brill, 2003.

Horne, Marc. *Tokyo Zero*. New York: Creative Commons, 2004.

Huang, Yunte. *Transpacific Displacement: Ethnography, Translation, and Intertextual Travel in Twentieth-Century American Literature*. Berkeley: U of California Press, 2002.

Hulsewé, A. F. P. "Nécrologie: R. H. van Gulik (1910–1967)." *T'oung Pao*, 2nd Series, 54.1/3 (1968): 116–24. Web. 19/03/2011.

Lach, Donald F. "Introduction." In *The Chinese Lake Murders*, by Robert van Gulik. 1960. Chicago: University of Chicago Press, 1979. 1–12.

Larsson, Stieg. *The Girl with the Dragon Tattoo*. 2005. New York: Vintage, 2009.

—*The Girl Who Played with Fire*. 2006. Trans. Reg Keeland. New York: Vintage, 2009.

—*The Girl Who Kicked the Hornet's Nest*. 2007. Trans. Reg Keeland. New York: Knopf, 2010.

Marquand, John P. *Mr. Moto's Three Aces*. Boston: Little, Brown and Company, 1938.

The Matrix. Dir. Andy and Larry Wachowski. Perf. Keanu Reeves, Laurence Fishburne, and Carrie-Anne Moss. Warner Bros, 1999. DVD.

The Matrix Reloaded. Dir. Andy and Larry Wachowski. Perf. Keanu Reeves, Laurence Fishburne, and Carrie-Anne Moss. Warner Bros, 2003. DVD.

Oplev, Niels Arden, dir. *The Girl with the Dragon Tattoo*. Perf. Michael Nyqvist and Noomi Rapace. Music Box, 2009. DVD.

Randolf, Cox, J. "The Detective Novel." In *The Facts on File Companion to the American Novel*. Ed. Abby H. P. Werlock. New York: Facts on File, 2006. 1434–7.

Rendell, Ruth. *The Speaker of Mandarin*. London: Hutchinson, 1983.

Rzepka, Charles. *Detective Fiction*. Cambridge, England: Polity, 2005.

—"Race, Region, Rule: Genre and the Case of Charlie Chan." *PMLA* 122.4 (2007): 1463–81.

Saussure, Ferdinand de. *Writings in General Linguistics*. London; New York: Oxford University Press, 2006.

Scott, A. O. and Manohla Dargis. "Gosh, Sweetie, That's a Big Gun." *The New York Times* A&L May 1, 2011: 8, 10.

Tsui, Hark. Dir. *Detective Dee and the Mystery of the Phantom Flame*. Perf. Andy Lau and Carina Lau. Huayi Brothers, 2010. DVD.

Van de Wetering, Janwillem. *Robert van Gulik: His Life, His Work*. New York: Soho, 1987.

Welles, Orson. *A Touch of Evil*. Perf. Orson Welles, Janet Leigh, Charlton Heston. Universal Pictures, 1959. DVD.

8

Knowing the unknowable: detecting metaphysics and religion in crime fiction

Kim Toft Hansen

Secret societies were the tune of the 18th century. Throughout no other historical period has that many and varied cult societies for initiated members only seen the light of day. Though, the light of day was precisely what they never saw. They remained a dark, intangible undercurrent beneath the Enlightenment's strive for light and clarity. As if one would not do without the other, as if one could not appear without the other.

ARNE DAHL, *MÖRKERTAL* (2005 255)[1]

Arne Dahl's Swedish novel *Mörkertal* [*Hidden Numbers*] (2005) deals with the disappearance of a teenage schoolgirl during a school camp. To intensify the investigation, the so-called Intercrime Team is summoned and—as time passes and the possibility of finding her alive fades—slowly a gloomy picture of a local pedophilia ring appears. The police question a suspect associated with this ring, and the suspect ends up talking about the relationship between reality and virtual reality. The online world acts, in his view, as a release for the decadence in the real world because here it is possible to live out the innermost self to a degree that covers up certain perversions and secrets. "You have to understand what hidden numbers I'm talking about," the suspect says in that connection, "almost everybody is somehow in on it, nothing of importance takes place in the real world." "Hidden numbers," he says as the police ask, are "that which is not detectable in statistics" (Dahl 2005, 245). "Hidden numbers" usually indicate unregistered crimes and are, hence, often used to estimate the extent of a certain type of crime while still maintaining awareness that not everything sees the light of day. In Dahl's novel this expression by default does not include the crimes of the local pedophilia ring, but is a more abstract evaluation of general pedophilia accessible through virtual networks, an even bleaker view.

Throughout the novel, the Swedish term *mörkertal*—literally meaning *dark figures*—is used as a consistent metaphor for aspects of human life that are out of the ordinary. The pedophiles are portrayed as creatures of the night, as vampires, that perform "the old well-known grab by the throat" (260), while the pedophiliac instinct is described as a need that "must be met so that he can live on ... for without it he will die" (261). At the moment when the suspect realizes that the police team is close on his heels he is given "a message from the dark" (262). The attempt to enter the vanished girl's computer becomes, in addition, much easier when a police officer recalls the word "Mistah" which he found written on a note in the girl's room: "Mistah Kurtz, he nodded in approval. From *Heart of Darkness*. That's what the blacks call the self-proclaimed dictator Kurtz" (175). The journey into the girl's computer and, furthermore, the search for what fate had in store for her—as Marlow's journey into Kurtz' Congo—is a journey *into the heart of darkness*. In the final chapter of the novel a female officer makes her entrance into a clandestine S&M club where the password is—*mörkertal* (392).

Altogether the term *dark figures* (and its linguistics link to *hidden numbers*) is a central metaphor through which the novel articulates hidden needs of humans, the disguised, the unconscious, the suppressed and not least, the various aspects that social relations have disqualified and failed to appreciate. The eighteenth century, as highlighted by the opening quote, displayed a significant interest in secret, occult and esoteric societies that—staying within metaphors of light and darkness—never really saw the light of day (cf. Gilhus/Mikaelsson 1998). In *Hidden Numbers* the police investigate a secret lodge in Stockholm, which is the cue for Dahl to discuss the general cultural symptoms of Enlightenment: the general spiritual tendency of the eighteenth century, writes Dahl, "remained a dark, intangible undercurrent beneath the Enlightenment's strive for light and clarity" (255)—a strive that later triggers the attention towards human profanity, historicity and ultimately, secularism in modernity. Consequently, the title is also a metaphor for everything that Enlightenment and modernity denied the existence of in the search for rational frameworks for human understanding and sense of self that results in the loss of metaphysics, religion and the supernatural as sober conceptualizations of the characteristics of reality; accordingly, these frameworks are dislodged into private and hidden societies. *Hidden Numbers* is then not necessarily a crystal-clear metaphor in Dahl's novel: on the one hand it puts decried crimes such as pedophilia on display, but on the other hand it reveals certain opportunities for man to act out basic needs and desires within private and relatively fixed boundaries. The novel is thus not just a story about a crime, but a story that shows how modern society in itself has skeletons in its cupboard. The final chapter of the novel shows that furtive societies still exist as externalizations of internal lives. This fact may be good just the same if the novel's last word—"Welcome"—is any indication (392).

In much the same way, this essay draws attention to the backside of crime fiction and narratives of detection. While several scholars highlight in various ways a present cultural transformation towards the revitalization of metaphysics and religion in so-called *post-secular conditions* (Sigurdson 1999; Schanz 1999; Habermas 2008) this essay shows that this move is in itself nothing new. The history of crime fiction and stories about investigating crime—in this case up until the Second World War—are fleetingly pierced by an undercurrent of irrationality and an interest vested in metaphysics, religion and the supernatural. The notion of an *undercurrent*, as used by Dahl in his novel about the backlash towards Enlightenment, primarily obtains its meaning from a current beneath the water level going in a different direction than the upper stream and, as a result, becoming dangerous. Figuratively speaking, though, the word carries the sense of something hidden, a strong and pervasive feeling, tone or tendency, which does not quite manifest itself, but is nevertheless perceived as essential.

Leaving the psychoanalytical undertone aside, this relationship between two interdependent currents is also used in Edgar Allan Poe's essays about literature. He explicitly uses it as an operational narrative model explaining the search for a solution in, for instance, crime fiction, and therefore he names stories in which this relationship is most unmistakably expressed "tales of ratiocination" (Poe 1984, 573). A distinctive feature of such tales in particular and epistemology in general is it that "a strong undercurrent of suggestion runs continuously beneath the upper stream of the tranquil thesis" (571). Poe spells out the suggestive nature of the undercurrent as

"indefinite of meaning" (24): even though the detective in "tales of ratiocination" has an alleged tranquil thesis about the state of things, a suggestive
challenge of the truth persistently runs beneath, which may be a significant
contributory cause to the suspense of crime fiction. The clues discovered by
the detective are transitorily "indefinite of meaning" until the investigation
reaches the point where the upper stream and the undercurrent run in the
same direction—the burden of proof is at this time so compelling that the
truth appears self-evident. Poe calls this narrative moment "dénouement"
(13) which in French means solution, outcome, adjudication, and ending.
Crime fiction therefore most often ends with the denouement. Furthermore,
with the undercurrent running continuously, Poe drops a strong hint that
this epistemological conclusion does not go for every facet of life which
makes the structural relationship between upper streams and undercurrents
particularly interesting for culture analyses: concurrently, this epistemological model is a helpful illustration of how Enlightenment and modernity
have marooned—as Dahl phrases it—"a dark, intangible undercurrent" in
its search for reason and rationality.

With precise attention to this undercurrent, this essay, then, covers two
aspects of interest: Firstly, I will uncover various instances throughout the
long history of crime fiction that in total will characterize this undercurrent
of disqualified elements. Secondly, I will—as a frame of reference—pinpoint
existing theories and treatments of metaphysics and religion in crime fiction.
Consequently, this essay is a historical overview of the backside of crime
fiction—the hidden numbers of the genre—as well as a meta-theoretical
scrutiny into perspectives on crime fiction on the one side and it its relation
to metaphysics, religion and the supernatural on the other.

However, the notion of an undercurrent could prove to be inexpedient
if it produces an unequivocal dichotomy between modern society and its
Other. It may appear as something merely suppressed and oppressed, which
would make out a rigid, simplified and distorted picture of the Age of
Enlightenment and its rational consequences for modernity. Enlightenment
already proved to be motley circumstances where the surreptitious affairs
as such were not merely hidden away, but rather Enlightenment is said to
be a result of the affairs in question. Margaret C. Jacob goes as far as to
say that the philosophy of the Enlightenment is particularly indebted to
European Freemasonry of the eighteenth century which though—according
to Thomas Bredsdorff—is an overestimation of the heyday of hidden
societies (Jacob 1981, 109ff; Bredsdorff 2003, 107ff). This is, however,
not a discussion that I will have time to resolve here, but I note that both
underscore that darkness was not just the enemy of Enlightenment, but
implicated in it: "To strive for the light", writes Bredsdorff, "does not mean
that darkness is denied, only that you are attempting to shed light into it"
(12). Perhaps this is why darkness is so ambiguously framed by Arne Dahl.
I do not mean to suggest an unambiguous Enlightenment or modernity

giving birth to a countercurrent that Bredsdorff identifies as a simplifi-
cation caused by Romanticism. Instead, an undercurrent in water may
have major consequences for the surface—as anyone who has been caught
by an undercurrent in water knows. Hence, I rather use undercurrent as a
concept to indicate that historically there has been a tendency that has not
been as obvious and consistent as the main stream—in my case the often
retold narrative of rational crime fiction—but this does not imply that the
undercurrent has had no influence on mainstream crime fiction. Very much
as the hidden numbers of crime statistics may stay slightly disregarded, the
actions themselves are not without impact. Keeping Enlightenment and
modernity on the one side and metaphysics and religion on the other has
resulted in an unfortunate dichotomy between modernity and metaphysics
qua more or less defensible attempts towards clarity. Post-secular sociology
and philosophy challenge these assumptions in saying that they both have
had distinctive influence on each other—and they still have (Sigurdson
2009).

Christianity, and the paternity of crime fiction

Various cultures and authors have over the years paid alimony to this
difficult question: Where and why did crime fiction occur? The case of
what Fedwa Malti-Douglas calls *the paternity of the detective genre* has
never really been solved and the genre history has in itself an incorporated
mystery (Malti-Douglas 1988, 59): it would be unconvincing to ascribe the
genre to a particular culture or author without ample evidence to support a
certain provenience. Here, I draw attention to a range of interesting assertions in an attempt to test their validity. This examination makes it possible
for me to trace specific cultural components integrated in crime fiction
while also demonstrating that the history of crime fiction does not insist on
a clear separation of the epistemological interest of the investigation and
perspectives extending beyond. I do not intend—neither do I believe it to
be feasible—to anchor an obvious hotbed of crime fiction. If anything, a
dialogical relationship between several different components within crime
fiction comes into evidence.

The intersection between crime fiction and religion is particularly underlined when Christian cultures get the paternal custody: "The crime novel
is one of the few literary genres that we do not know from pre-Christian
Antiquity", states Trond Berg Eriksen. "This in particular would suggest
that the genre has Christian preconditions" (Eriksen 1989, 334). Referring
to the inviolability of the individual in evangelical doctrines, Johannes
H. Christensen claims that without Christianity we would have no crime
fiction: "In murder we are all equal", he says while highlighting that

"the notion of the absolute value of man and the unconditional equality of all people originates from Christianity," which is why "the genre emerges in the Christian world. Outside it does not exist" (Christensen 2006, 2ff). I see no reason here to doubt Christian charity as a morally metaphysical conception of human equality, but above all Eriksen's and Christensen's assertion slights that Stoicism in particular produced the idea of *natural rights* before Christianity. Throughout history of philosophy, though, natural rights is not a particularly precise concept, but the Stoics maintained that the universe was "a rational whole regulated by the laws of reason which was both natural laws and binding regulations of actions" (Lübcke et al. 2010, 504) which is why this mentality "underlies much of future ethics and political philosophy, including ... human rights" (665). It is certainly debatable to what extent this philosophy had a tangible impact on living conditions, but this goes for several Christian institutions as well, meaning that they have not always administered charity for the benefit of everybody. Additionally, Graham Murdock points out—with a certain amount of generalization—that 900 B.C. until A.D. 200 was a time where the principle of "concern and compassion for others" gained currency (Murdock 2008, 42). This means that Eriksen's and Christensen's historical arguments form a shady basis for claiming that crime fiction is a solely Christian genre.

What we may gain from these assertions that crime fiction represents equal rights for everybody in instigating criminal investigations regardless of the status of the victim in question—is the emphasis on moral metaphysics and ethical essentialism. This is, then, reflected in the narrative structure of crime fiction where the common objective is the elimination of the disorder fostered by the criminal act. Considering genres such as crime fiction, westerns and thrillers, J. I. Packer reaches a similarly dubious conclusion when he claims that these are "stories of a kind that would never have existed without the Christian gospel," but interestingly enough he also takes the question of narratives into consideration: "Culturally, they are fairy tales, with savior heroes and plots that end in what Tolkien called a *eucatastrophe*—whereby things come right after seeming to go irrevocably wrong" (Packer 1985, 12). John G. Cawelti highlights a matching contention, claiming that "mystery has been far more important as a subsidiary principle in adventure stories" (Cawelti 1976, 43). The comparison with fairy tales is appealing and the structure of fairy tales—where the hero is brought out of his safe environment to solve a problem in order to return home in an altered frame of mind—indicates that crime fiction also draws heavily upon a cross-cultural framework for narrative development. W. H. Auden considers the central problem within crime fiction to be "the ethical and eristic conflict between good and evil, between Us and Them" which, in a way, points out a similar narrative attention, but also ties into the dualism that is often found in classical crime fiction (Auden 1963, 147). Auden eyes a relationship between the narrative structure of crime stories and biblical perspectives: "The fantasy, then, which the detective story addict indulges is the fantasy of being restored to the Garden of Eden" (158). Though the idea is appealing and attractive, it may be exceedingly speculative to lay crime fiction into the hands of a universally human longing for Paradise, but if we contrast the number of crime narratives that wrap up the stories with a more or less certain epistemological closing with crime narratives that leave the readers in the dark we would undoubtedly find a majority of order narratives. Hence, several scholars draw attention to biblical texts as interesting precedents of crime fiction. Charles Lock claims that Cain's murder of Abel is originary (Lock 2010, 9) while John Scaggs mentions the apocryphal excerpts "Bel and the Dragon" and "Susannah" from the book of Daniel as biblical stories with investigational structure (Scaggs 2005, 8). William David Spencer goes one step further in claiming that "the figure of Daniel in both tales, *Bel and the Dragon* and *Susannah*, is an archetype of the hard-boiled mystery hero," because Daniel "alone attacks the solutions everyone else has found satisfactory, wreaking havoc without a qualm" (Spencer 1989, 29).

Here and in other precedents we find striking similarities with crime fiction which—reasonably and temptingly—then lead scholars to bring out crime fiction under Christian or biblical trademarks: "Once the genesis of the detective story is attributed to a historical period," writes Malti-Douglas, "theories are developed to account for its presence in this period" (Malti-Douglas 1988a, 89). She finds that Siegfried Kracauer's *Der Detektiv Roman* (1971) is a good example of this model of inference: "For Kracauer, the whole system of the detective novel replaces that of Christianity, and major elements of the novel can be understood in precise Christian ritual terms, with the detective replacing the priest" (Malti-Douglas 1988a, 90). Comparatively, a pastor in the novel *Falne engler* (*Fallen Angels* [no English translation]) (1989) by the Norwegian author Gunnar Staalesen says to the detective: "In a way we're in the same – boat" (Staalesen 1989, 241). These arguments, following Malti-Douglas, do in fact resemble a classical inductive fallacy where we—within a Christian culture—locate a suitable number of cases and from out of these conclude that crime fiction per se must be Christian. However, as we shall see, a reassessment of this argument does not mean that crime fiction within Christian cultures renounces its interest in Christian faith.

Arabic and Chinese crime fiction

Before reaching further into Christianity, the question is of course what we may find if we look outside western and/or Christian cultures. Fedwa Malti-Douglas has studied the Arabic crime fiction tradition and she traces, for instance, proper detective stories—based on authentic caliphs who also served as detectives—back to the twelfth century. These stories, writes Malti-Douglas, are "restricted to the events relating directly to the crime and its investigation" (Malti-Douglas 1988a, 62) where the investigation comprises the ability to combine "knowledge of human nature and behavior with observation and analytical skills" (64)—a talent she compares with Poe's detective Dupin and Doyle's detective Holmes. Additionally, Malti-Douglas draws attention to a long-term Arabic narrative tradition for telling stories about theft, though they do not pose as crime fiction with an investigational focal point, but they do underline an Arabic interest in stories about crime and a flair for finding just solutions to ethical and juridical transgressions—an interest that seems to be cross-cultural and found in every era and in several forms of narrative (cf. Malti-Douglas 1988b). Julian Symons, for example, refers to *Arabian Nights* where "The Tale of Three Apples" revolves around the elucidation of a murder (Symons 1972, 20). Malti-Douglas discusses this story as well and points out that "there is no detective in the story," and hence it "does not fit the detective mode" (Malti-Douglas 1988a, 77f). That may be so since the investigator Ja'afar, instead of actually doing detective work, puts his faith in justice without his influence because he fears his afterworld punishment if he lays the blame on the wrong suspect. Thus while Malti-Douglas is right that no actual investigation takes place in the story, but nevertheless an alternative interpretation would be that it deals with divine intervention based on the fact that Ja'afar succeeds by investigating nothing. Moreover, Malti-Douglas may have missed that the story is structurally framed as crime fiction and it does in fact uphold a reader-oriented suspense, which means that the reader searching for the solution becomes the detective who expects a final denouement—and gets it. Contrary to Malti-Douglas, Roger Allen—translating the Arabic title of the story into "The Tale of a Murdered Young Woman"—designates the story as "a quintessential murder mystery" (52) and "a finely crafted mystery story" (58) and refers, then, to the significance of the reader's "curiosity as to who killed the girl" (54). He concludes by noting that links between Arabic and Western genres "have been little investigated" (Allen 1984, 59). "The Tale of Three Apples" is, in other words, an interesting place to start when it comes to crime fiction (cf. Hansen 2009).

If we take this Arabic connection a step further, though, it may prove irrelevant to the task of this essay given that the supernatural, writes Malti-Douglas, "is almost completely absent in the corresponding Arabic literature" (Malti-Douglas 1988a, 82). Religion and metaphysics as a link to moral essentialism is by all means present in "The Tale of Three Apples" and, hence, it does have some relevance, but I include the Arabic perspective as a gradation of seeing crime fiction as particularly Christian. Still with reference to Kracauer, Malti-Douglas concludes, with specific attention to Islam, that the "coexistence which we have seen of the detective and a flourishing Abrahamic religion makes Kracauer's association more difficult to demonstrate" (90). With attention to the above mentioned Johannes H. Christensen and his claim that crime fiction is Christian, Peter Kirkegaard criticizes him from the same stoic angle as I have mentioned, but highlights furthermore: "We certainly find only few Muslim crime stories at the book shop" (Kirkegaard 2010, 119). Could it be that Kirkegaard has visited the wrong bookshops? Could the reason why we find so few Muslim crime novels in Western bookshops be that they are simply not translated? For that reason, it is of course difficult for readers without Arabic linguistic abilities to enroll Arabic crime fiction in the world history of crime fiction when so few works are available in Western languages.

However, the international history of crime fiction has a remarkable parallel to the Arabic tradition in Chinese crime fiction—a genre that originally goes by the name of *gongan*, commonly translated as *court case fiction*. The Chinese tradition for writing crime fiction can be located as early as the seventh century, perhaps earlier, but it develops as a literary form in writing during and beyond the twelfth century—up until this point the *gongan* was orally passed on. Chinese crime fiction differs in some areas from the Western tradition, but the pivotal similarity is that these narratives deal with the investigation of crime by means of contemporary detective techniques most often personified by the local parochial prefect who was both investigator and judge. The long history of Chinese crime fiction may presumably be traced throughout the history of Chinese dynasties, where it has functioned as affirmative narrative, but never without doubting the purity of the prefect in stark contrast to the dirty character of the misdoings. Morality and law were formalized ethics metaphysically accepted and underlined by the absolution of the emperor, which in narratives was channeled into the spotless prefect. Contemporarily, it also had great significance that the stories—often of anonymous origin—were written (down) by the judges themselves, who in many cases recorded their own experiences throughout and after the juristic and investigational engagement. The best known piece of so-called authentic Chinese crime fiction in the West is Robert van Gulik's translation of *Dee goong an*—available as *The Celebrated Cases of Judge Dee* (1976)—a narrative about the authentic and legendary Judge Dee (630–700). It is uncertain at which time this story was written down, but there is reasonable substance in claiming that the book found its written form in the eighteenth century. This missed chapter about Chinese crime fiction is of course of great importance in the international history of crime fiction because the Chinese and the Arabic crime stories may be the earliest established traditions for writing about the investigation of crime. Throughout the thirteenth century the Chinese *gongan* starts to have an impact on many other written and performed genres, mainly chant fables and Chinese opera while Wolfgang Bauer points out that several prefects were appreciated for literary talent within this court case tradition (Bauer 1974, 435).

Within the scope of this essay the *gongan* is particularly interesting perhaps to a greater extent than the Arabic tradition considering the predilection for the supernatural in Chinese crime fiction. Among the miscellaneous differences between Western and Chinese crime fiction mentioned by Gulik we find the fact that "the Chinese have an innate love for the supernatural," which then "clashes with our principle that a detective novel should be as realistic as possible" (Gulik 1976, iii). In the above mentioned novel Judge Dee is aided by a *restitutory* visit at a Taoist temple by the interpretation of dreams and by the helpful assistance of ghosts whose supernatural powers decidedly contribute to Dee's investigation. This is specifically in evidence in the "The Case of the Strange Corpse"—one of three coherent stories—where Dee communicates with the corpse in question. The use of metaphysics and religion in recent Western crime fiction may imply a reopening of such sensibilities in late modern societies while we rediscover this interconnection in classical Chinese crime fiction—here, primarily expressed through the employment of the supernatural and the religious undercurrent in visiting a temple. Furthermore, Anne Wedell-Wedellsborg finds a "deliberate blurring of borderlines between fantasy and reality" in recent Chinese fiction (Wedell-Wedellsborg 2005, 22). She not only sees this as a new weighting of a relationship between the fantastic and the real but concurrently explains the literary changes by referring to the revitalization of older Chinese genre traditions, for example, the *gongan*, which was prohibited during Mao. She mentions, for instance, the Chinese writer Wang Shuo and his novel with the English title *Playing for Thrills* (1989)—a novel that takes inspiration from hard-boiled American detective fiction while the author also "occasionally weaves tantilizing scraps of fantasy into his narrative" (24). Wedell-Wedellsborg concludes with a plausible reason for what she calls *haunted fiction* as a modern fantastic allegory:

> In China and in the West, the modern fantastic allegory can be read as a reaction to modernity. It is a site of difference, one that privileges the alien, the illusory, and the irrational in contrast to a vision of modernity that subsumes everything under a rubric of ideological homogeneity, rationalism, and materialism. The fantastic inherently recognizes the complexity and unknowability of the modern world. (31)

Here, Wedell-Wedellsborg implies a complex picture of Chinese as well as Western fiction, reflecting that modern society and modernity do not necessarily preclude a relationship towards the supernatural, metaphysics and the irrational—at least not anymore. In my case this serves as an interesting perspective on how a realistic world view may coexist with the involvement of metaphysics which in contemporary philosophy have been dubbed *self-constrained modernity* (cf. Hansen 2010 and 2011b). Modernity has come to realize that it cannot deliver answers to urgent existential questions and, hence, it becomes self-constrained (Schanz 2008).

From divine to secular omniscience

The Arabic and the Chinese traditions are central to an international intercultural interest in revising the literary history of narratives about detecting crime. In a Western frame of reference it remains rewarding to look back at the prehistory of crime fiction before Edgar Allan Poe's three seminal detective stories in order to revise how the criminal and methods of detection were applied in a literary context.

Dubbing his view on crime fiction *a counter-history*, Maurizio Ascari—again with a choice of words referring to paternity—treats the acceptance of Poe as the point of origin of the detective story as a *foundation myth*: "one could say that a 'foundation myth' identifying Poe as the father of detection was created to support a normative view of the genre" (Ascari 2007, 10). Ascari does not concern himself with either Chinese or Arabic crime fiction, but nevertheless reaches some highly relevant conclusions—in other words it appears problematic to claim that Poe as such is "the undisputed father of the detective story" (Symons 1972, 29) or that Poe's detective Dupin is the "father of them all" (Holquist 1971, 140). A response to this claim may be that the metaphor of paternity is usually backed by antecedents and Poe is by all means the pivot when it comes to literary kinship. However, Holquist claims that the detective story does not appear before the nineteenth century for "the obvious reason that you cannot have detective fiction before you have detectives" (139), but this argument, firstly, includes a less than reliable assertion that it would be impossible to write about what does not exist in reality, an unnecessary complication for several genres. Secondly, the assertion that detective fiction emerges no earlier than the nineteenth century must be modified for "the obvious reason" that China *had* detectives long before the West—and the literary representations of these gave rise to a conspicuous genre throughout Chinese literary history (cf. Hansen 2011a). Through references to numerous examples until and after Poe Ascari qualifies a wider and more nuanced perception of the prevailing comprehension of crime fiction by adjusting the notion of investigation. At first he accentuates that during "the nineteenth century the paradigm of rational inquiry did not completely eradicate the search for a higher design ruling the fiction of law and order" by way of which Ascari implies a general ambivalence within modernity which was powerful at that time as modernity rose against Romanticism considering the variance of Romanticism. He continues, then, by suggesting that "it may well be argued that the enjoyment of readers depended on the interplay between natural and supernatural elements, which engendered a fruitful tension between the domain of the intellect and that of the emotions" (Ascari 2007, 10). In contrast to granting crime fiction the custody of simply incorporating rationalism and empiricism, he underlines a wide variety of domains that directly or indirectly may have had a dialectic rather than a dualistic influence on the relationship between modern rationalism on the one side and the quest and the urge for assimilating supernatural, religious and metaphysical elements in the narratives on the other.

He identifies dreams as an investigative tool in solving a murder in Geoffrey Chaucer's "The Nun's Priest's Tale" from *The Canterbury Tales* from the fourteenth century (19). He finds ghosts and hauntings contributing to bringing down a murderer, for instance in Shakespeare's *Hamlet*. These and other examples, though, do not mean that Ascari fails to spot the variations that modernity brings along, but instead make room for varying an unambiguous dichotomy between reason and supernaturalism. Hence, he notes the transition from *the eye of God*—"traditionally inscribed within the perfect shape of a triangle"—to *the eye of the police* which was at first accentuated by the application of the eye as a symbol of detection by the French police in 1791 (43). Ascari restricts himself to only implying the striking symbolism of using a Christian symbol in what he calls "secular omniscience" (42) personified by the police force. The actual and symbolic use of religious components, supernatural elements and pseudoscientific mentalities leads Ascari towards the contention that "gothic fiction anticipated detective fiction" (49) given that the Gothic backlash against Enlightenment seeks into "a nightmarish view of omniscience" (45) which in its own way becomes an indication of the omnipresence and omniscience of the supernatural. Arne Dahl shows an awareness of the anticipation in question in *Hidden Numbers* by an almost verbatim emphasis on the search for light and clarity of the Enlightenment. Ascari's analyses, then, describe an interesting Western cultural prehistory of why the paternity of crime fiction should be ascribed to not just one person but a wide variety of features.

The way in which crime fiction surfaces as a literary and socio-philosophical result of modernity in the first half of the nineteenth century is sufficiently described (Scaggs 2005; Thompson 1993; Hansen 2011b). Here, I focus on mostly well-known Western examples from unconventional approaches. On the one hand there are good reasons to keep our minds on Poe's version of crime fiction where, especially in "The Murders in the Rue Morgue," materializes a condensed format for the Western, rational modern detective story, but Holquist has on the other hand demonstrated that Poe's biography and remaining authorship delves into anything but rational clarity and light. Personally, Poe was sunken into alcoholism and drug abuse and he "died on an uncompleted journey, after being found wandering the streets of Baltimore in a raving delirium." Hence, it is, continues Holquist,

> ... in the very depths to which he experienced, and was able to capture in words, the chaos of the world, that we must search for the ordered, ultra-rational world of the detective story.
>
> It was in this powerful impulse towards the irrational that he opposed the therefore necessarily potent sense of reason which finds its highest expression in *The Murders in the Rue Morgue* and *The Purloined Letter*. Against the metaphors for chaos, found in his other tales, he sets, in the Dupin stories, the essential metaphor for order: the detective. (Holquist 1971, 141)

"First reasoning in order to escape feeling," Joseph Wood Krutch joins in, "and then seizing upon the idea of reason as an explanation of the mystery of his own character, Poe invented the detective story in order that he might not go mad" (Krutch 1926, 118). Concordantly, Poe can be viewed as a biographical metaphor for the contemporary cultural cross-section from which he and crime fiction emerge, from which were a situation—perhaps too rigidly—marked by an emotional reality of Romanticism in contrast to, and gradually succeeded by, the developing rationality of modernity. Directionally, Poe builds a literary bridge between past and future, between a metaphysical sensibility and a rational frame of mind which does not unerringly make him the *father* of crime fiction, but a hub of attention passing on erstwhile historical roots.

Danish literature presents a fascinating case with some similitude to Poe. The writer Steen Steensen Blicher found himself in a comparable cross-section between Romanticism which he could not reconcile and, for him, a more acceptable type of realism that was simultaneously developing. Blicher and his short story "Præsten i Vejlbye" ("The Rector of Veilbye") (1829) is worthy of note not least on account of the subtitle "A Story of a Crime" which at that time was a Danish name for entertaining literature based on real cases.[2] The story deals with the murder of the coachman Niels with the main suspect the parish rector in Veilbye. The shire bailiff Erik—though he deems himself incapable since he is the rector's future son-in-law—has to investigate the murder that in the end turns out to be a deception, but the rector is by then convicted and executed. Niels survived the rector's violent strokes upon their disagreement, but Niels' brother Morten—who himself was courting the rector's daughter—wanted to frame the rector in the light of his rejection. Firstly, "The Rector of Veilbye" is obviously remarkable on the grounds of its publication twelve years before Poe's first short story about Dupin and must be considered a detective story based on Erik's definition of detection as investigational effort. Secondly, the story is interestingly similar to the Chinese *gongan* in its display of the linkage between executive and judicial powers (Hansen 2011a). At first, Erik investigates the murder of Niels and, subsequently, he condemns the rector to death. Not until increasing modernity in the wake of the American and French revolutions in late eighteenth century do Western societies implement a separation of judge and detective that was not in effect in Denmark before the 1849 constitution—the year after the death of Blicher. Thirdly, Blicher's short story is, here, a thematically convincing example of what William David Spencer calls *clerical crime fiction*—a subgenre where a "great division of the clerical crime novel might well be tales that feature crimes by a cleric" (Spencer 1989, 12) which, at least until the innocence of the rector is proven, is a fitting description of "The Rector of Veilbye." Regarding a religious mind frame, the short story presents a priest who willingly accepts his guilt and death sentence because in his view both are fair verdicts. In total, Blicher's story is at any rate a historically interesting phenomenon within the search for early Western examples of crime fiction while it also provides a significant picture of a Danish society where evidential investigation and religious belief may go hand in hand.

Desacralization of crime fiction

Usually, though, cultural transformations take some time and do not occur in such clean breaks as the passage from pre-modern to modern is often considered. The "passage from tragedy and epic to detective fiction," writes Ascari, "entailed a '*secularization of mystery*'" (Ascari 2007, 55) which is a wide-ranging progression that we may recognize from Peter Brooks' analyses of how tragedy turns into melodrama—a process that he calls "a process of desacralization" leading into the "post-sacred era" of the nineteenth century (Brooks 1976, 15). This gives rise to questions in relation to discussions of secularization that revolve around, firstly, if this desacralization took place so extensively that we should name an era post-sacred and, secondly, whether or not the spiritual sensibilities tiptoed somewhere else. Still focusing on crime fiction, Ascari writes that that "this process did not completely rule out a certain amount of interaction between detection and the supernatural in nineteenth-century literature" (Ascari 2007, 55). Comparatively, Brooks points out that this process directs limited metaphysics and senses of the holy into another form of expression which in this case appears as the dualisms of melodrama and what Brooks terms *the moral occult*. Here, Brooks attaches his concept to the etymological meaning of 'occult'—in the sense of something 'hidden'—which again places metaphysics and the supernatural as an undercurrent claiming a certain influence on human existence: "We might say that the center of interest and the scene of the underlying drama reside within what we could call the 'moral occult,' the domain of operative spiritual values which is both indicated within and masked by the surface of reality." Brooks continues, with the separation from the pre-modern in mind: "The moral occult is not a metaphysical system; it is rather the repository of the fragmentary and desacralized remnants of sacred myth" (Brooks 1976, 5). First and foremost, this definition emphasizes how crime fiction at this time unquestionably took part in a larger cultural process where religion and metaphysics was to the greatest extent guided into the private sphere. However, the metaphysical sensibilities at the same time found new ways of expression that momentarily appear in the history of crime fiction and popular culture.

Likewise, this perspective on crime fiction underlines the melodramatic elements of the genre, "its easier effects" (xii), which Ascari treats under the subject of sensationalism, where the exotic and the occult are significant varieties (Ascari 2007, 110ff). "The melodramatic mode in large measure exists to locate and articulate the moral occult," says Brooks (Brooks 1976, 5), even though, writes Ascari, "the role of God as the ultimate agent of justice is reasserted ... It may be argued that a new attention towards the link between crime and the supernatural was fostered by the public interest in spiritualism" (Ascari 2007, 57). Thus, implicitly referring to Brooks, Ascari concludes that this "melodramatic imagination also represented a conservative antidote to modernity, whose aesthetic fruit was realism and whose ideological fruit was positivism" (58). When Ascari, then, mentions "a ghost denouncing his own murder" (57), dreams as "a principle of order" (58), "simultaneous presence ... of gothic and modernity" (61) which all "re-entered the genre through the back-door" (62) we find apparent socio-logical parallels in Ingvild Sælid Gilhus and Lisbeth Mikaelsson's sociology of nineteenth century religion where "occult societies maintained a belief that man was developing into a higher spiritual stage alongside preserving an interest in hidden forces" (Gilhus/Mikaelsson 1998, 37). This fostered "tentative combinations of scientific mentalities and ... mysticism" (42) in such a way that people within this generally popular nineteenth century undercurrent could be "placed as the hub of the mysterious co-operation of forces, spirits and linkages" (53). Modernity is often explained within a simplified model as "the triumph of the scientific method and a materi-alist approach to reality," Ascari concurrently writes, "but this cultural phase was ambivalent, involving an interest in the spiritual and the occult" (Ascari 2007, 66)—which also had an effect on the configuration of popular culture and, hence, crime fiction. Backstage, however, authors also found an interest in these spiritual trends which I return to later.

Before going into biographical considerations I will include a small digression about Wilkie Collins' novel *The Moonstone* (1868) which is often noted as a historical link between Poe's and Doyle's respective detective stories while being an interesting case given that it triggers two very dissimilar analyses. According to Karsten Wind Meyhoff the novel has a "downright criminalist nature" and, in addition, he quotes T. S. Eliot saying that it is "the first, the longest, and the best of modern English detective novels." "The story is constructed," Meyhoff continues, "in the style of the best British golden age detective fiction"; it is about "stealing valuable gems" while a police sergeant "is needed to make the pieces fall into place" (Meyhoff 2009, 32f). Here, Meyhoff is clearly writing from the point of view of the model launched by Poe a few decades earlier and, thus, he places *The Moonstone* within what Ascari calls a *foundation myth*: only those elements that can be placed fittingly within Poe's format are included in the characterization while Ascari's own analysis of Collins' novel points toward the pseudoscientific such as "phrenology, mesmerism and spiritualism" (Ascari 2007, 71) by way of which "Collins clearly refused to attribute an absolute value to rational detection" in favor of "divine detection ... ensuring the triumph of divine ... justice" (72). These two analyses can seem like the readings of two different novels, but when taken together, they underline the ambivalent character of the novel and contemporary responses to cultural change. Dealing with crime fiction in the light of popular theology, Robert S. Paul portrays the cultural landscape as "a climate deeply imbued with the rational ideals of the Enlightenment but increasingly inspired by a new romantic belief in the capacity of the human spirit" (Paul 1991, 35).

Indicatively, the biographical Doyle and several stories alongside the Holmes canon arrive on the scene as an amazingly ambiguous embodiment of the cultural transformations. Even though all of Doyle's detective stories wrap up the narrative with a neat denouement, a lesser number of stories incorporate whiffs of the supernatural—often exemplified by *The Hound of Baskerville* (1901/1902). Scholars have, hence, shown a wider interest in Doyle's complete writings, which display an extensive attention towards spiritualism and supernaturalism. Ascari refers to the short story "Lot No. 249" about a resurrected mummy, but points out that the story at the same time combats "'uncanny' forces that it perceives as 'other' although they belong to its own past" (Ascari 2007, 81). Stephen Kendrick treats a "religious undercurrent moving through the investigation" in the greater part of the detective stories (Kendrick 1999, 12). As a point of departure, he zooms in on a statement by Holmes—"There is nothing in which deduction is so necessary as in religion" (5)—and uses Doyle's crime narratives to reread religious discussions. Holmes' statement is by all means ambiguous: on the one hand it may imply the secularization thesis that deduction will remove the sound basis for religion while on the other hand it may be interpreted as an expression of rational elements within religion itself which—in its own point of view—is maintained by theology. Backed by the next sentence in the story—"It can be built up as an exact science by the reasoner"—Kendrick chooses the latter of the two. This, then, launches

Kendrick's detailed exposition of so-called *holy clues* in Doyle's narratives in an attempt to find clues towards Holmes'—and Doyle's—religiosity. For instance, Kendrick calls attention to how Holmes in 14 out 60 detective stories communicates forgiveness and "somehow manages to free the guilty" (138). In conclusion, Kendrick identifies that "detective fiction at its best can be a spiritual guide to the administration of mercy, not merely justice" (136).

However, he does not uphold his Christian frame of reference, but highlights that Holmes "carries about him the aura of a Zen teacher, a guru of awareness and observation" (18). Holmes has a unique phenomenological talent for "the moment of perception before our thoughts take over, before our concepts and notions intervene" which Kendrick recognizes from the spiritual teachings of Buddhism. In other words: "Bare attention is seeing things as they exactly are" (26). On one hand, by increasingly drawing on religious sources rather than Doyle himself, Kendrick's analyses show an arguably speculative tendency, but on the other hand Kendrick throws out a lifeline for himself by including Doyle's writings besides detective fiction as well as his biography. It is a well-known fact that Doyle was an acknowledged spiritualist, says Kendrick, but he personified a spiritualist of a particular kind. Doyle's autobiographical *The Stark Munro Letters* (1895) provides Kendrick with an exhaustive picture of the writer and "the picture of Doyle that emerges here is not of a credulous innocent tumbling into Spiritualism but of a man whose spiritual quest was really a form of the scientific method" which according to Doyle himself would lead to "the grand religion of the future" (104). What Doyle was searching for, insists Kendrick, was "a new world religion that was compatible with science and personal experience" (105) comparable to "the New Age movement today" (106). It is rather unclear what Kendrick means by New Age, but the twentieth century development towards a belief in a divine force rather than a personal God is, according to Kendrick, suggested in Doyle's spiritual writings and incorporated into his rationalist detective fiction. Consequently, Doyle's conception of God is

... somehow peculiarly acceptable to the modern sensibility, in which God somehow seems missing in action, a void, a shadow, a presence evoked by the whiff of retreating incense. For so many people ... the notion of the Kingly God who judges all and presides over the cosmos is becoming more and more problematic. (51)

The various theological implications in Doyle's writings may be contested, but it remains surprisingly interesting how the spiritual framework of faith Kendrick locates bears noticeable resemblance to the notion of a *self-constrained modernity*, where modernity and religion remain in dialogue rather than being each other's antitheses. Investigating Doyle's spiritualism,

Robert S. Paul reaches a very similar conclusion and characterizes an author who "undoubtedly reflects the optimistic deterministic attitude of science at that time; and in some measure religion, if it was to retain credibility among intelligent people, would have to come to terms with it" (Paul 1991, 53). Whether or not Kendrick's and Paul's selections of religious disputes hold water may require a more extensive theological discussion, but both approaches pave the way for alternative readings of an author who today seems entirely known for his detective fiction. It is, then, possible to draw a historical parallel between Doyle and Poe (perhaps besides the eccentricity of Poe) which together shows a biographical and literary association between spirituality and crime fiction. In both cases crime fiction was in a way a personal laboratory where certain interest could be test run in a formalized as well as a culturally reflexive configuration.

Crime fiction takes the place of religion

The existing tension between modern society and spirituality—and, more broadly, metaphysics—does clearly *not* involve the disappearance of the spiritual from the public sphere (Habermas 2006), though the most stringent modernity has had this as it distinctive goal. It is, nevertheless, worthy of note that spirituality has been particularly represented in closed, private lodges, a placement that indicates how modernization has had an unquestionable influence on perceptions of religion at the turn of the century. Kendrick writes, for instance, that "the decline of religious myths in our time could serve to explain the tremendous popularity of murder fiction" (Kendrick 1999, 12f) which is an assertion that Nicholas Blake—pseudonym for the crime writer C. Day Lewis—agrees with:

> We may imagine some [anthropologist] of the year 2042 discoursing on "The Detective Novel – the Folk-Myth of the Twentieth Century." He will, I fancy, connect the rise of crime fiction with the decline of religion at the end of the Victorian era ... When a religion has lost its hold upon men's hearts, they must have some other outlet for the sense of guilt.
> This, our anthropologist of the year 2042 may argue, was provided for us by crime-fiction. He will call attention to the pattern of the detective-novel, as highly formalized as that of a religious ritual, with its initial necessary sin (the murder), its victim, its high priest (the criminal) who must in turn be destroyed by a yet higher power (the detective) ... He will note a significant parallel between the formalized dénouement of the detective novel and the Christian concept of the Day of Judgment. (Blake 1946, 399f)

There are several stimulating as well as problematic aspects within Blake's argument which is why Michael Holquist—quoting the above passage as well—polemically notes that "Lewis has completely missed the point about detective stories, particularly the ones he had in mind" (Holquist 1971, 145). This may be, but Holquist does neither explain "the point about detective stories" nor "the ones he had in mind," but leaves the problems unresolved. The basic problem is, though, that Blake presupposes a number of facts that do not seem to be true. Firstly, the anthropologist looking back from the twenty-first century (in a way, as we are here) would ascertain that contemporary religion is not losing its hold, but is only changing. Secondly, it is presumably uncertain that the atheist would seek out an "outlet for the sense of guilt" in crime fiction rather than within a social structure that punishes the guilty party.

Blake's analysis does, nonetheless, appear relevant in that he is precocious in his discussion of the fictional and cultural transformation in the nineteenth and early twentieth century that emerges as increasingly lucid separation of rational investigation and its secreted Other. Crime fiction, then, springs up in one way or another as a replacement of *something* that religion up until now has vouched for—or perhaps rather as an *expression* of a sensibility that previously was formalized within religious frameworks. By comparison, Risto Saarinen considers crime fiction to express an alleged *secular theodicy*. In other words, the problem of evil is adapted in crime fiction in much the same way as it has been discussed in theology: simplified, the question "*how can we defend the good of God while there is still evil*" is rephrased into the question "*how can we defend the good society while there is still evil*" (Saarinen 2003, 132). Within Lutheran traditions, Saarinen outlines a certain inclination towards "a *Deus absconditus*, a hidden God, whose goodness remains a mystery for us" (134). This turns around in the secular theodicy of crime fiction, says Saarinen, where authors "openly admit that we cannot understand the demonic drive within human beings. Crime authors outline a *homo absconditus*, a humanity whose real intentions remain hidden" (134). This jointing of the sensibilities of a hidden goodness of God and a hidden humanity, or lack thereof, has distinct similarities with Kendrick's and Doyle's attention to "a God missing in action." This metaphysically indicates *a* God, but leaves a blank when it comes to *explaining* this godly presence which in secular societies becomes symbolic incorporation within our attention towards state and society. Saarinen, though, is not the only one who takes a specific Protestant notion of godliness into account.

Referring to the British development of a Protestant reformation, Erik Routley argues that crime fiction may be read as a *secular Puritanism*, which above all, forms a theoretical tie to Blake's notion of such a development during late British Victorianism. Routley, then, supports his view by way of the discrepancy between crime fiction and the supernatural:

"Secular puritanism insists that make-believe is for women and children: for men, the world of reality is their field of conquest and their faculties must not be blunted by fantasy" (Routley 1972, 57). This goes hand in hand with puritan values such as a tidy distinction between right and wrong, law and disorder, while leaving "little room for romance" (124)— which in total constitutes a reappearance of a dualistic interpretation of crime fiction. This is often attached to rational modernity and makes sense in several canonical instances where the right and wrong side of the law appear clearly distinguished, though Routley's inclusion of Doyle may seem muddy in the light of his inclination for setting the guilty party free if he feels like it—nevertheless, it would seem wide of the mark to hope for enticing romances in the midst of Holmesian deductions. In concluding remarks, Routley ties the link between secular puritanism and crime fiction to a general "puritan form of fiction" revolving around "urbanism, rationalism, distrust in supernatural elements, protestant work ethics, and masculinity" (224). Yet, with the moral relativity of the twentieth century influencing particularly the police procedural, it becomes gradually easier to find exceptions to Routley's secular puritanism. As touched upon above, proving that religious roots gave birth to crime fiction can be difficult. The inclusive level of social analysis within the scope of secular theodicy as a defining frame for modern crime fiction becomes much more applicable. If we, however, direct our attention towards the interest in fundamentalism in recent crime fiction, especially in the wake of 9/11, Graham Murdock points out that puritanism—understood as "a refusal to accommodate uncertainty, ambiguity, pluralism and difference," hence without a precise reference to its Protestant counterpart—again emerges as a present discourse within "popular imagination" (Murdock 2008, 39). What is specifically conspicuous in these cases is that the focalization of puritanism has gone from being the ideals of the investigator—as in Routley's examples—to being represented as the fault of the criminal terrorist. All in all, while these references draw a picture of crime fiction replacing the role of religion, they do serve as a theoretical backdrop in explaining why we see religious symbols and biblical references to an extent that cannot be coincidental.

Persuasively, William David Spencer also enters into this discussion of replacement with special attention to religious, and specifically Christian, roots of crime fiction. Initially, he opens his readings with the assertion that "the story of Jesus is a murder mystery" and asks the question: "Why did Jesus have to die?" (Spencer 1989, 1). Apparently without intending to do so, Spencer points towards the development out of puritanism that crime fiction goes through in the twentieth century as it moves in the direction of social engagements by, for example, partly revealing the narrative through the criminal. By "focusing on the reasons behind the act" the narrative transitions from the *whodunit* towards the *whydunnit* (Scaggs 2005, 112).

This is, furthermore, a perspective included by Johannes H. Christensen in his view on crime fiction where "every human life is ascribed limitless value however miserable it may be" (Christensen 2006, 3). Though Christensen surprisingly misses this, the same goes for the criminal—"Truly I tell you, today you will be with me in paradise," says Jesus to one of the crucified criminals on Calvary. It is just as unexpected that Spencer also misses this parallel since his main interest is to show how the grand *mysterium*— "this instance of spiritual detecting [in order] to pierce through to God's intention"—is embedded within the *secularized modern mystery* of crime fiction:

> Perhaps the prior claim of God's law on human law, God's justice on human enforcement, God's enigma in human secrets, God's revelation on detection and exposure informs the secularized modern mystery genre as well. Because these tales are mysteries by designation, they point back to the great mysterium of existence. They are images of the hidden enigma of God. They stand in the way of affirmation, they image a truth in the nature of God about the eternal order, the primal goodness, justice, love, and mercy which human existence in the images of God reflects. (Spencer 1989, 9)

Spencer's claim that divinity is embedded in crime fiction may appear hard to confirm, but very much in line with Blake, Saarinen, and Routley he accentuates that crime fiction passes on something which this far has been managed by religion:

> As the literature of the mystery genre became a secularization of the concealing/revealing quality of the great mysterium, God as orderer and focal point of unity was displaced by secular society, priests displaced by police, and the sacred act of repentance and reconciliation displaced by indictment and punishment. (10)

It is in conclusion characteristic that three out of four—imbued in the concepts—note the secular elements of crime fiction: *secular theodicy*, *secular puritanism*, and *secular mysterium*. The ecclesiastical authority for conviction is replaced by profane institutions, but this does not, according to Spencer, imply that crime fiction forgets "the sacred mysterium behind the secular mystery" (11). If such interpretive frameworks have become secular without losing the power of interpretation it tells us a lot about how late modern societies still are woven into their cultural and religious roots.

Ministers and metaphysics

In Spencer's view, the subgenre most indicative of a cultural entanglement in religion is what he calls *the clerical crime novel* (Phillip Grosset's website *Clerical Detectives* hints at the magnitude of this type of fiction). Spencer typologizes the subgenre into three categories where the *first* one is "any tale that involves the clergy and crime." He admits that this may be too wide a category mostly because "the line between dealing with sin and crime is a slim one." This assertion is, of course, highly debatable, but basically this category—according to Spencer—covers "every tale about active ministers." For him, then, the next two types are to be understood as specifications of the literary field in question. The *second* type involves a "crime by a cleric" (Spencer 1989, 12) where Blicher's "The Rector of Veilbye" serves as the obvious example. The *third* and, for Spencer, most significant type is about "mysteries solved by the cleric" which specifically means that "the clerical crime novel focuses on clerics solving mysteries—not creating them" (13).

Spencer delves into copious examples with the earliest being "Susannah" and "Bel and the Dragon" as well as G. K. Chesterton's stories about Father Brown, and the latest being Andrew M. Greeley's and Isabelle Holland's respective crime fiction. Spencer rounds off these various perspectives by synthesizing general tendencies within clerical crime fiction in which "the cleric stands as the servant of the savior, the bearer of good tidings, the bringer of reconciliation" (304). The clerical detective, he continues, "like the mediator Christ, stands in the gap between the questing mystery and the revealing mysterium, a detecting human filled with God's perspicacity" (305). The result is a clerical crime fiction that maintains rational investigative methods, but does not en route evade theological reflections. However, Spencer demonstrates that the notion of compassion does not uphold its similarity with the evangelical conception, but instead "often reveal[s] a grim interpretation of what mercy is. Justice in the clerical crime novel is primarily retributive rather than distributive," where "the bulk of the clerical sleuths ... have no compunction about turning perpetrators over to the police" (305). Hence, the role of the ministers in some sense becomes the counterpart of the investigation of private detectives while theological disputes seep in through the cracks of the plot. Clerical crime fiction may present itself as a compelling example of a post-secular coexistence of profane rationalism and ecclesiastical metaphysics.

The "metaphysical detective novel" was, furthermore, introduced by Howard Haycraft as a description of G. K. Chesterton's short stories about Father Brown in that they are "chiefly concerned with the moral and religious aspects of crime" (Haycraft 1942, 76). Haycraft also notes an interesting cross-section within the Brown stories marked by the impression that Chesterton's cultural context "had only two main classifications: increasingly heavy-handed romanticism on the one side, and the new scientificism on the other" (76). The short stories, published from 1911 to 1935 place Romanticism somewhat late, but Haycraft also points ahead into the sentimental elements that would influence the future American hard-boiled tradition—a tradition dubbed by Leonard Cassuto as *hard-boiled sentimentality*: "Inside every crime story is a sentimental narrative that's trying to come out" (Cassuto 2009, 7). Moreover, Cassuto also puts crime fiction into a complex, and in this case American, dialogue with religious expressions:

> The optimistic view of human nature joins with a nondenominational and evangelical Christianity to form the basis for the American sentimental worldview. In conjunction with a philosophical argument that elevates the value of acting on behalf of others, sentimental Christianity idealizes renunciation and celebrates personal sacrifice ... The crime novel and the sentimental novel draw on the same symbolic lexicon then, but with an important difference in religious perspective [because] hard-boiled fiction edits the sentimental lexicon to express a secular creed. (12)

Once again we come across the idea of something religious becoming secular without losing the religious frame of meaning. In Cassuto's view it goes both ways: "The move in hard-boiled fiction toward sentimental men who actively and violently guard the community ... also enables the secular to move into the place of the religious" (15). In a sense, this is not *loss* of religion, but a transformation of the perception of religion.

Father Brown is a recurring figure in critical treatments of the relation between crime fiction and religion—and in several cases a subversive dissociation of an uncritical assumption of supernaturalism. "Father Brown's stories," writes Ascari, "actually combine detection with an orthodox view of religion, refuting every 'irrational' approach to reality as a form of superstition" (Ascari 2007, 160). Put otherwise, then, the theological contributions of Chesterton's stories reflect the rational, self-critical and self-reflexive components featured in various ways within philosophy of religion and metaphysics which, furthermore, matches the investigational process of crime fiction. In the Brown stories, continues Ascari, "crime is typically presented at first as the result of supernatural agencies, but this transitory explanation is soon deconstructed by the humble hero" and consequently, "thanks to miraculous intuitions that could be better described as *abductions*, Father Brown can re-establish the realm of reason" (160). Robert S. Paul even argues that Brown's position as a priest is a contributory cause to his extraordinary flair for detection given that "his personal method is his ability to identify himself with the thought processes that make a criminal perform a criminal action" (Paul 1991,

72). For this reason, Ascari's definition of a "realm of reason" in detective fiction does not conflict with Brown's clerical duties, but Father Brown "engages in detection not in spite of being a priest," says Paul, "but ... he is a detective *because* he is a priest" (73). Brown's conceded social sensibility may largely be tied to his clerical obligations.

By way of the piercing rationality, Chesterton's short stories are an interesting preamble to the inter-war British Detection Club where the supernatural seriously—and literally!—was renounced. This goes for S. S. van Dine's rules for writing detective stories that prohibit "the world of spirits" and "the fourth dimension of metaphysics" (Dine 1946, 190) and together with the oath of the Detection Club this has probably nowhere else been so intensively phrased:

> "Do you promise that your detectives shall well and truly detect the crimes presented to them using those wits which it may please you to bestow upon them and not placing reliance on nor making use of Divine Revelation, Feminine Intuition, Mumbo Jumbo, Jiggery-Pokery, Coincidence, or Act of God?" (cited in Brabazon 1981, 144f)

In relation to the jointing of detection and theology it may seem contradictory that Chesterton in 1930 became the first president of the Detection Club, but if the oath is inspected closer it turns out to be solely about the process of investigation—not what otherwise could be thematized in the stories. Though Brown's intuition seems like a borderline case, Chesterton was probably not in danger of exclusion despite his "metaphysical detective stories." Distinctively, this also says a lot about how the concept of metaphysics at this time was shifting meaning in the light of the rising secular forces in society where metaphysics increasingly was contemplated as "Mumbo Jumbo" rather than a rational and reasonable interpretation of essential sensibilities.

Several detective stories—including Doyle and Chesterton—were, then, symptomatic of the development in what has been labeled classical detective fiction, suggesting that crime fiction may have room for supernatural tendencies, but this will usually be disclosed as something completely natural. With attention to Agatha Christie, Ascari writes that:

> ... although the canonical tradition of detective fiction that Christie came to embody as the "queen of crime" emphatically relied on rational investigation, it never completely detached itself from the supernatural dimension that characterized the counter-canon of crime fiction. Like Doyle and Chesterton before her, Christie reduced the supernatural to the subsidiary role of transitory explanation, but at the same time she also exploited it to conjure up an ominous atmosphere of mystery that lures the public into reading and is progressively cleared away by the investigation. (Ascari 2007, 172)

Even though it may absorb Gothic forms, religious conceptions, revenge dramas, etc., in this way classical crime fiction becomes a narrative metonymy for credence in elimination of the supernatural and the spiritual by way of reason and secular values. At the same time the Chesterton case underlines that reason and secularism does not involve a unilateral loss of religiosity, even if religion seems to relinquish its epistemological influence on investigation.

The (post)modern prism

The outlined cultural transformation implies a more blatant and growing desire to separate two spheres of metaphysics. On the one hand, the transcendent metaphysics, the question of the highest being, and the divine does not lose awareness, but it is tentatively directed more and more into the private sphere by critiques of metaphysics. On the other hand, this leaves room for immanent metaphysics discussing profane absolutes. In sum, theological considerations within crime fiction are detached disputes about the highest being while the investigational process in and by itself is a version of profane metaphysics specified as trust in the powers of acknowledgment and the ultimate existence of guilt—this is, in fact, what Umberto Eco calls *the detective metaphysic*:

> The fact is that the crime novel represents a kind of conjuncture, pure and simple. But medical diagnosis, scientific research, metaphysical inquiry are also examples of conjuncture. After all, the fundamental question of philosophy (like that of psychoanalysis) is the same as the question of the detective novel: who is guilty? To know this (to think you know this), you have to conjecture that all events have a logic, the logic that the guilty party has imposed on them. (Eco 1984, 54)

That events *have* a logic refers to a metaphysical essentialism reflected in the act of imposing guilt. In cases where the essential logic refers to God, as is the case with Blicher's "The Rector of Veilbye," it may be viewed as transcendent metaphysics: the rector accepts his guilt and sentence in the light of his trust in God. In cases where guilt is profanely imposed, metaphysics become immanent—and for most readers of crime fiction it is clear that only few popular pieces of crime fiction abandon the plot unresolved, though a range of deconstructed examples certainly exist.

Nevertheless, the lack of a denouement does not make crime fiction less metaphysical, but the result is that these cases rather explore a defeatist affiliation with metaphysics. The notion of a metaphysical detective story scrutinized by Patricia Merivale or Susan Elizabeth Sweeney is in many ways the contrary to Eco's essentialism: "The metaphysical detective story is distinguished ... by the profound questions that it raises about narrative, interpretation, subjectivity, the nature of reality, and the limits of knowledge" (Merivale/Sweeney 1999, 1). Such metaphysical crime fiction points to a greater extent into a postmodern uncertainty which is phrased unmistakably by Holquist: "the new metaphysical detective story finally obliterates the traces of the old which underlie it. It is non-teleological, is not concerned to have a neat ending in which all the questions are answered, and which can therefore be forgotten" (Holquist 1971, 153). Where Eco's metaphysics refers to the acknowledgment of an underlying essentialism Holquist, Merivale, and Sweeney more specifically refer to a particular lack of essentialism: "its telos is the lack of telos, its plot consists in the calculated absence of plot. It is not a story—it is a process," continues Holquist (153). The questions raised by the postmodern metaphysical detective story contradict the attempt to establish, interpret and sustain an absolute precondition for guilt in an effort to deconstruct essentialism. This, in fact, underlines the imbued metaphysics in deconstruction, namely the absolute nature of the process, but at the same time it discloses the trans-formation that metaphysics goes through in the wake of modern critique of metaphysics. It may, then, seem paradoxical that postmodernism breaks with the main essences included in the most ruthless versions of modernity and, through that, slowly relaunches metaphysics. The resignation of metaphysics in the history of modernity, hence, leads to a dissimilar metaphysics of uncertainty which may be seen as prelude to late modern interest in metaphysics and particularly religion: a renewed and unsettled involvement with and reevaluation of metaphysics and religious practice in late twentieth and early twenty-first century.

Holquist and Merivale agree that the inter-war hard-boiled American tradition anticipates the development of uncertainty. As Holquist writes, Raymond Chandler and Dashiell Hammett "attempt to break away from the rigid conventions of detective fiction," while Merivale points out that both authorships "suffer from a surfeit of clues, a shortage of solutions, and thus a distinct lack of narrative closure" (Merivale 1999, 102). In reworking Haycraft's concept of the metaphysical detective story, Merivale highlights this type of crime fiction as an "important parodic pattern" (Merivale 1967, 210). In Chandler's and Hammett's writings we do find a clearly expressed challenge to classical crime fiction which may be dubbed parodic, but Merivale aims to greater extent at post-war postmodern crime fiction. In Merivale's juxtaposition of metaphysical and postmodern (or so-called anti-) detective stories, this becomes manifest with the prefix "anti" underlining the defeatist attitude (Merivale 1999, 101). In her view, defining "The Mystery of Marie Roget" as "a proto-postmodernist detective story" Poe provides a historical precedent based on the lack of a narrative solution to the initial case. In other words, what Holquist,

Merivale and Sweeney defines as metaphysics essentially bears the mark of the postmodern prism that they are looking through and, for the same reason, it is very likely that they would find proto-examples—the window pane affects what we may notice on the other side. Metaphysics is much more than merely discussing—or even resigning from—narratives, identity and knowledge given that metaphysics also comes across as an accentuation of the need for essential frameworks of existence. This indicates that metaphysics—and the metaphysics of uncertainty in writings by, for instance, Alain Robbet-Grillet, Paul Auster, and Jorge Luis Borges—does not have to give up narratives, subjectivity, and epistemology. Nonetheless, this quarrel leaves a trace within popular culture where it becomes defensible to discuss absolute preconditions of existence be they immanent or transcendent.

This essay has scratched the surface of the backside history of crime fiction well into the twentieth century and gazed into later and contemporary crime fiction. Basically, I stress that metaphysics—in various interpretations—is no stranger in the field of crime fiction, though it appears less frequently. The prehistory of crime fiction shows a noteworthy coexistence of rational investigation on the one hand and metaphysics, religion and supernaturalism on the other—and in some cases under the influence of one another. Late twentieth and early twenty-first century present a growing interest in especially religious discussions in crime fiction and popular culture in general. Predominantly, the aspects of crime fiction touched upon here and its history of critique may explain why that happens: it has been running along as an undercurrent or side stream the whole time. Correspondingly, the variety of critical attention that I continually refer to conveys a vocabulary that will aid our description of crime fiction in the light of recent interests in the relationship between crime fiction and metaphysics—a tendency that has received an especially heightened awareness following Dan Brown's *The Da Vinci Code* (2003). Furthermore, these perspectives make the incentives of post-secular philosophy and the fundamental notion that secularism has never really come about seem increasingly plausible which then motivates *post-secular crime fiction*. Religion is a substantial part of the public sphere, public communication, and—perhaps incited by—the popular cultural tendencies within which we locate contemporary crime fiction. Religion, metaphysics and supernaturalism which savage modernity and hard secularism, have strived to cleanse from the public sphere are a powerful and weighty part of society and popular culture—and have apparently been an undercurrent in the history of crime fiction since before the concept of crime fiction was invented.

Notes

1 English translations are mine if not otherwise biographically indicated.

2 "The Rector of Veilbye" was translated into English as early as 1909 and included in Julian Hawthorne's ten volume *The Lock and Key Library Classic Mystery and Detective Stories*. Here, I quote directly from the Danish version.

Works cited

Allen, Roger. "An Analysis of the 'Tale of Three Apples' from *The Thousand and One Nights*." In *Logos Islamikos – Studia Islamika in Honorem Georgii Michaelis Wickens*. Roger M. Savory and Dionisius A. Agius (eds) Pontifical Institute of Mediaeval Studies, 1984.

Ascari, Maurizio. *A Counter-History of Crime Fiction – Supernatural, Gothic, Sensational*. New York: Palgrave MacMillan, 2007.

Auden, W. H. "The Guilty Vicarage." In *The Dyers Hand and other essays*. London: Faber and Faber, 1963.

Bauer, Wolfgang. "The Tradition of the 'Criminal Cases of Master Pao' *Pao-kung-an (Lung-t'u kung-an)*." *Oriens* 23, 1974.

Blake, Nicholas. "The Detective Story – Why?" In *The Art of the Mystery Story – A Collection of Critical Essays*. Ed. Howard Haycraft. New York: Simon and Schuster, 1946.

Blicher, Steen Steensen. "Præsten i Vejlbye" ["The Rector of Veilbye"]. In *En Landsbydegns Dagbog og andre Noveller*, Copenhagen: Gyldendals bogklubber, 1995.

Brabazon, James. *Dorothy L. Sayers: a Biography*. New York: Encore Editions, 1981.

Bredsdorff, Thomas. *Den brogede oplysning*. Copenhagen: Gyldendal, 2003.

Brooks, Peter. *The Melodramatic Representation – Balzac, Henry James, Melodrama, and the Mode of Excess*. New Haven and London: Yale University Press, 1976.

Cassuto, Leonard. *Hardboiled Sentimentality – The Secret History of American Crime Stories*. New York: Columbia University Press, 2009.

Cawelti, J. G. *Adventure, Mystery, and Romance*. Chicago: The University of Chicago Press, 1976.

Christensen, Johannes H. "23. søndag efter trinitatis." Sermon given in the Church of Skovshoved, Denmark, November 19, 2006, unpublished.

Dahl, Arne. *Mörkertal* [*Hidden Numbers*]. Stockholm: Månpocket, 2005.

Dine, S. S. Van. "Twenty Rules for Writing Detective Stories." In *The Art of the Mystery Story. A Collection of Critical Essays*. Ed. Howard Haycraft. New York: Simon and Schuster, 1946.

Eco, Umberto. *Postscript to the Name of the Rose*. Trans. by William Weaver. New York: Heatcourt Brace Jovanovich, Inc., 1984.

Eriksen, Trond Berg. "Riter uden myte – det postmodernes historie," In *Nietzsche og det modern*. Oslo: Universitetsforlaget, 1989.

Gilhus, Ingvild Sælid and Lisbeth Mikaelsson. *Kulturens refortrylling –
Nyreligiøsitet i moderne samfunn.* Oslo: Universitetsforlaget, 1998.
Grosset, Philip. *Clerical Crime Fiction.* Website: http://www.detecs.org (visited
January 2011).
Gulik, Robert van. *The Celebrated Cases of Judge Dee – An Authentic
Eighteenth-Century Detective Novel.* Translated and Introduced by Robert
van Gulik. New York: Dover Publications Inc., 1976 (reissue of *Dee goong an:
Three Murder Cases Solved by Judge Dee* from 1949).
Habermas, Jürgen. "Religion in the Public Sphere." *European Journal of
Philosophy* 14.1, 2006.
—"Notes on Post-Secular Society." *New Perspectives Quarterly* 25.4, 2008.
Hansen, Kim Toft. "Fra synd til skyld – krimiens kulturelle rødder." *Bogens
verden* 1, 2009.
—"Recherches philosophiques et roman policier – Le roman policier autoréflexif
de Henning Mortensen." *Etudes Germaniques* 4, 2010.
—"Chinese court case fiction – A corrective for the history of crime fiction."
Northern Lights 9, 2011a.
—*Mord og metafysik*, Aalborg: Aalborg University Press, 2011b, in
preparation.
Haycraft, Howard. *Murder for Pleasure – The Life and Times of the Detective
Story.* Surrey: The Windmill Press, 1942.
Holquist, Michael. "Whodunit and Other Questions: Metaphysical Detective
Stories in Post-War Fiction." *New Literary History* 3.1, 1971.
Jacob, Margaret C. *The Radical Enlightenment: Pantheists, Freemasons and
Republicans*, London: George Allen & Unwin, 1981.
Kendrick, Stephen. *Holy Clues – The Gospel According to Sherlock Holmes.* New
York: Vintage Books, 1999.
Kirkegaard, Peter. "A Fucking Tragedy – Krimien som vor tids tragedie?" In *Den
skandinaviske krimi – Bestseller og Blockbuster.* Gunhild Agger and Anne
Marit Waade (eds) Gothenburg: Nordicom, 2010.
Kracauer, Siegfried. *Der Detektiv Roman* – Ein philosophischer Traktat. Frankfurt
am Main: Suhrkamp Verlag, 1971.
Krutch, Joseph Wood. *Edgar Allan Poe, A Study in Genius.* New York: Russel &
Russel, 1926.
Lock, Charles. "Tidlige spor af detektivlitteratur." In *En verden af krimier.* Pia
Schwartz Lausten and Anders Toftgaard (eds) Aarhus: Klim, 2010.
Lübcke, Poul, ed. *Politikens filosofileksikon.* Copenhagen: Politiken, 2010.
Malti-Douglas, Fedwa. "The Classical Arabic Detective." *Arabica International*
35, 1988b.
—"The Classical Arabic Crime Narratives – Thieves and Thievery in *Adab*
Literature." *Journal of Arabic Literature* 19, 1988a.
Merivale, Patricia. "The Flaunting of Artifice in Vladimir Nabokov and Jorge Luis
Borges." In *Nabokov – The Man and His Work.* Ed. L. S. Dembo. London:
The University of Wisconsin Press, 1967.
—"Gumshoe Gothics – Poe's 'The Man in the Crowd' and His Followers."
In *Detecting Texts – The Metaphysical Detective Story from Poe to
Postmodernism.* Patricia Merivale and Susan Elizabeth Sweeney (eds)
Philadelphia: University of Pennsylvania Press, 1999.

Merivale, Patricia and Susan Elizabeth Sweeney. "The Game's Afoot – On the Trails of the Metaphysical Detective Story." In *Detecting Texts – The Metaphysical Detective Story from Poe to Postmodernism*. Patricia Merivale and Susan Elizabeth Sweeney (eds) Philadelphia: University of Pennsylvania Press, 1999.

Meyhoff, Karsten Wind. *Forbrydelsens elementer*. Copenhagen: Informations forlag, 2009.

Murdock, Graham. "Re-enchanctment and the popular imagination: fate, magic and purity." *Northern Lights – Film and Media Studies Yearbook* 6, 2008.

Packer, J. I. "Tecs, Thrillers, and Westerns." *Christianity Today*, November, 1985.

Paul, Robert S. *Whatever Happened to Sherlock Holmes? Detective Fiction, Popular Theology, and Society*. Carbondale and Edwardsville: Southern Illinois University Press, 1991.

Poe, Edgar Allan. *Essays and Reviews*. New York: The Library of America, 1984.

Routley, Erik. *The Puritan Pleasures of the Detective Story – From Sherlock Holmes to Can der Valk*, London: Victor Gollancz Ltd., 1972.

Saarinen, Risto. "The Surplus of Evil in Welfare Society: Contemporary Scandinavian Crime Fiction." *Dialog: A Journal of Theology* 42.2, 2003.

Scaggs, John. *Crime Fiction*. London and New York: Routledge, 2005.

Schanz, Hans-Jørgen. *Selvfølgeligheder – Aspekter ved modernitet og metafysik*. Aarhus: Forlaget Modtryk, 1999.

—*Modernitet og religion*. Aarhus: Aarhus Universitetsforlag, 2008.

Sigurdson, Ola. *Det postsekuläre tillståndet – Religion, modernitet, politik*. Munkedal: Glänta Produktion, 2009.

Spencer, William David. *Mysterium and Mystery – The Clerical Crime Novel*. Carbondale and Edwardsville: Southern Illinois University Press, 1989.

Staalesen, Gunnar. *Falne engler* [*Fallen Angels*], Oslo: Gyldendal Norsk Forlag, 1989.

Symons, Julian. *Bloody Murders – From the Detective Story to the Crime Novel*. New York: Mysterious Press (3rd rev. edn), 1992.

Thompson, Jon. *Fiction, Crime, and Empire. Clues to Modernity and Postmodernism*. Urbana and Chicago: University of Illinois Press, 1993.

Wedell-Wedellsborg, Anne. "Haunted Fiction: Modern Chinese Literature and the Supernatural." *The International Fiction Review* 32.1–2, 2005.

9

African initiation narratives and the modern detective novel

Amadou Koné

The novel, as a literary genre, was born in Africa fairly recently. One of the reasons for this late birth is that the novel is essentially a written genre whereas writing was not practiced on a wide scale in pre-colonial Africa. It is also the case that the novel is a genre of the individual, whereas the traditional African literary genres are more adapted to communities than the individual. I have attempted to explain at greater length and in more detail the reasons for the late birth of the novel in Africa in other texts.[1] In addition, if the historical novel and the novel of realist tendencies came about almost immediately, the detective novel has remained extremely rare in African novel production.[2] In our view this rarity would seem to be explained by the fact that the modern African novel could be considered as the inheritor of the traditional oral narrative tradition. In effect, the African novel, as well as modern poetry, has placed since its origins an emphasis on the didactic function and on efficacy.

   Literature has sought to contribute to the liberation struggle against colonialism. The historical novel has attempted to reestablish the image of a glorious African past and the realist novel has in general proposed images that contrasted with the caricature of colonialist exoticism. It seems then that for African writers the detective novel has been considered somewhat as an inadequate or ill-adapted genre in this context. Finally, at the level of the structures of fiction, the literary genres of this African oral tradition do not seem to accord importance to the development of intrigue and the management of suspense which are the fundamental givens of the detective novel in general and of other genres that are originally written. Oral narration would seem to place an accent on a performance before a public of listeners rather than on constructing a complicated mystery.

That being said, is it the case that motifs of detectives are totally absent in the African oral tradition? The response to this question in my view is no. And in provocative fashion, I will attempt to show that it would be pertinent to compare certain elements in African initiation narratives and detective narratives. Such a parallel might seem surprising at the outset or strange to some, but in studying up close the narrative structure of initiation stories one becomes aware that this type of narrative functions in reality by using motifs that are similar or at least analogous to the motifs of detective stories. The initiation narrative, it must be said very clearly, is not a detective story. But one could maintain and even prove that certain elements of these two types of narrative coincide in a certain way. For example, the initiation narrative is a quest that progresses through an investigation. The candidate for initiation is questing for something either material or spiritual. The ending is also fundamental here. This is the ultimate stage that provides closure to the story through the success of the hero.

Taking up the Fulani initiation narratives translated by Âmadou Hampâté Bâ, I will attempt to demonstrate a homology between the characters of these stories and those in the detective novel. Evidently, these characters are very different from the characters who appear in detective novels. Their actions seem to be very limited to the point where it is difficult even to call them actors (*actants*). In the same way, the narrative "functions," in the sense given by Roland Barthes, would not seem to present themselves as in the detective narrative. There are catalysts or indices that permit the action to progress rather than the traditional narrative links. In this article, I will utilize three Fulani initiation narratives presented by Hampâté Bâ, but I will focus more specifically on the *Kaïdara* initiation narrative.[3] I will try to show that in this narrative where the characters (actors or agents) act very little, there are nevertheless indexes (*indices*) that play the same role the principle functions play in the detective novel.

Âmadou Hampâté Bâ is certainly one of the greatest African tradition-alists. His works on the African oral tradition possess authority. In addition to his works of research, he has collected and translated into French the traditional oral narratives of his Fulani ethnic group. I will mention here three of the stories from the *jantol* genre, even though I will deal in depth with only one in this essay.[4]

Koumen, Texte initiatique des Pasteurs Peul recounts the initiation of the first Fulani shepherd (*pasteur*), Silé Sadio.[5] Silé is led by his master initiator, Koumen, through 12 clearings. This voyage is an initiation during which Silé, who is following the instructions of his master, will pass through different stages until attaining an encounter with Foroforandou, the wife of Koumen. All along the voyage, questions are posed to Silé Sadio. But it is his master initiator who responds to these questions, and in many different ways, so these responses remain mysterious and incomprehensible to Silé, who is not yet initiated, and to the reader (listener) who reads the text. It is Koumen who responds to the serpent's question; it is he who responds to the frogs and to the spirits; it is Koumen who allows Silé to avoid the traps set by Foroforandou and to successfully accomplish the initiation at the end of which Silé becomes a *silatigi*, that is to say "he who has the initiatory knowledge of pastoral matters and the mysteries of the brush" ("celui qui a la connaissance initiatique des choses pastorales et des mystères de la brousse") (*Koumen* 21). Thus, Silé accomplishes his initial objective which he had proclaimed to Koumen, at the beginning of the narrative: "I desire the knowledge that will add to my qualities as a shepherd and my wisdom as a *silatigi*" ("Je désire le savoir qui augmentera mes mérites de pasteur et mes connaissances de *silatigi*") (35).

Kaïdara is the second story of this triptych. Three characters, Hammadi, Hamtoudo and Dembourou, meet at a crossroads. Their goal seems clear at the outset. We know that they will undertake a voyage to the country of the dwarf-genies (pays de génies-nains). The objective seems to be to reach Kaïdara, the god of gold and of knowledge. They will have to pass through 11 subterranean layers that correspond to 11 symbols and 11 challenges to be in the presence of the supernatural being who will give them the sacred metal. But the encounter with Kaïdara and the acquisition of the gold are not the true ending to the story. Once they have acquired the gold, the three companions need to return home and wisely utilize this gold. Here is the recommendation that Kaïdara makes in giving the gold to the three companions:

> The gold that I just gave you, use it well.
> You will find everything there, if your actions are right;
> Even the ladder that will take you to the heavens
> And the stairs that lead to the center of the earth.
> [L'or que je viens de vous donner, employez-le bien.
> Vous y trouverez tout, si vos actes sont droits;
> Même l'échelle qui vous conduit aux cieux
> Et les escaliers qui mènent au sein de la terre.] (79)

Kaïdara imposes this condition which has a very precise meaning. The good utilization of the gold must lead to the understanding of the symbols encountered during the voyage. But each of the three friends interprets the words of Kaïdara in his own way. For Dembourou, using the gold well consists in utilizing it to acquire political power. As he says:

> Governing the villages well, I will be a great leader.
> They will repeat my words, they will sing my praises;
> All will fear me, I will accept no equals.
> [Gouvernant bien des villes, je serai grand seigneur.
> On répètera mon dire, on chantera mes louanges;
> Tout le monde me craindra, je n'accepterai pas d'égal.] (81)

Hamtoudo for himself wants to become a merchant. He wants to further increase his wealth. So Dembourou manifests his ambitions for power and the futilities of human glory while Hamtoudo aspires to material ease, the opulence for which he will have the spirit of lucre and the necessary egoism. Only Hammadi seems to understand what Kaïdara meant by using the gold well (bien utilizer l'or). To use the gold well means being able to find the sense of the symbols encountered during the voyage. Because Hammadi knows that as long as he has not resolved the mystery of the symbols observed during the voyage, the initiation will be incomplete. Now the goal of the initiation is the acquisition of knowledge. Therefore, for many years he will search for the master capable of decoding the signs for him. At the end of the narrative, the master initiator, whom he seeks for many years, will arrive and will give him this knowledge. Hammadi will have searched for and acquired knowledge. But in truth, the story continues in the last volume of the triptych.

In effect, in *Layatere Koodal, L'éclat dans la grande étoile*, what the grandson of Hammadi is seeking is the conduct of men, the conduct of the city, in other words politics.[6]

Hammadi had utilized the gold and power to acquire knowledge. Diôm-Diêri, his grandson, wants wisdom. He wants to know how to utilize knowledge to lead his people appropriately. This is what his master Bagoumawel will teach him in this *jantol*.

This very rapid overview of three Fulani initiation narratives recounted by Âmadou Hampâté Bâ seems to suggest that this type of narrative is very distant from the detective narrative in Western literature. One would apparently find more points of divergence than points in common between the two literary forms. The initiation narrative is not a story brought about by a crime someone has committed; there is no detective who must resolve the crime; there are no suspects, etc. There is however at the formal level, it seems to us, if not a homology between these narratives and those regarding

detectives at least some elements of correspondence which have some perti-
nence in our current problematic.

There is to begin with the mystery that is extremely important in the
initiation narrative, even if the type of mystery that one finds in the initiation narrative is different from the mystery in the detective novel. There
is the mystery that stems from the places the action takes place, from the
characters in the narrative, from the scenes that one witnesses during the
story. The place where Hammadi, Hamtoudo and Dembourou meet is said
to be mysterious in the text itself:

> It was in the mysterious, faraway country of Kaïdara
> That no man can locate exactly.
> [Ce fut au mystérieux, lointain pays de Kaïdara
> Que nul homme ne peut situer exactement.] (*Kaïdara* 21)

The initiatory voyage of the three companions takes place under the earth
where Kaïdara, the god of gold, dwells. It is the intermediary country
between the country of clarity (pays de clarté) where the visible members
of all species live and the country of profound night (pays de nuit profonde)
where the dead sojourn along with those yet to be born. The country of
Kaïdara is a shadowy world where the hidden (cachés) ones live, invisible
spirits capable of incarnating themselves and of transforming themselves
into every sort of being or thing. In this mysterious country, anything can
happen and one can encounter the most unusual characters. The space, the
characters and the actions contribute to the enchantment that is proper to
these initiation narratives. At a certain point when the three companions
witness an exchange of leaves between two trees, Hamtoudo observes:

> There is not the shadow of a doubt;
> We have become involved in a land of miracles.
> The eyes see phenomena
> That reason cannot comprehend.
> [Il n'y a pas l'ombre d'un doute;
> Nous voici engagés au pays des miracles.
> Les yeux voient des phénomènes
> Que la raison ne comprend pas.] (55)

If it is not a matter here of resolving the mystery of a crime committed, it
is a matter nevertheless of resolving a global mystery related to knowledge.
At the beginning of the narrative the objective is not very well defined. But
it becomes clear that for Hammadi the goal is to encounter Kaïdara and
to obtain the signification of the symbols observed all along the journey.
The comprehension of these symbols will constitute the acquisition of a
profound knowledge within this society. The quest for knowledge is for

Hammadi the ultimate goal of the voyage.[7] There is thus an investigation, or at the very least a quest; a mystery to resolve; a system of knowledge to master. This system seems to be an ensemble of clues that one must patiently decode. We do not have here, as in the modern novel, those functions that influence the overall action, but rather indexes (*indices*) as Barthes would say.[8] In effect, Hammadi and his two companions at first encounter a chameleon once they descend the stairs that lead them beneath the earth. Here is what Hammadi exclaims when he perceives the chameleon:

> Oh you! Yes, you children of my own mother,
> come! come see this fantastic animal!
> he moves hesitantly between advance and retreat!
> he changes color, rolls his eyes and looks
> in every direction without moving his head.
> [O vous! Oui vous fils de ma propre mère,
> venez! venez voir l'animal fantastique!
> il se déplace hésitant entre l'avance, le recul!
> il change de couleur, roule des yeux et regarde
> de tous cotés sans remuer la tête.] (*Kaïdara* 67)[9]

The three companions will encounter successively animals that naturally constitute curiosities whether because of their normal physical constitution (the bat, the scorpion, the sand skink (*le scinque*)), or the action that they are undertaking (the billy-goat, the cock that transforms into a ram and the ram that becomes a bull). Confronted by these metamorphoses, Dembourou says:

> Where are we then we others, oh sons of my mother?
> The cinders then respond and say: You have reached
> An extraordinary country that troubles visitors;
> Reached the entrance of a troubling, fantastic county.
> [Où sommes-nous donc nous autres, ô fils de ma mère?
> Les cendres alors répondirent et dirent: Vous êtes parvenus
> Au pays extraordinaire qui trouble les visiteurs;
> Parvenus à l'entrée du pays troublant, fantastique.] (67)

The three voyagers also encounter some objects that participate in this symbolic system that demand to be interpreted. They are surprised by the pond with the limpid, fresh waters guarded by a variety of venomous serpents; they are also amazed by a little hole that succeeds in supplying them abundantly with water and refreshing them; they are stupefied by the two trees that reciprocally exchange their foliage, etc.

The goal of the voyage for Hammadi clearly becomes to reach his encounter with the mysterious Kaïdara in order to understand what these symbols signify. It is not a matter of unraveling a crisis in a definitive manner, such as identifying who has committed a crime. It is rather a matter of achieving an understanding of the elements of the global mystery of the functioning of the world and society.

To attain initiation in general, and to inquire into the signification of the symbols, one must adopt a comportment that is approved by the master initiators, the identification of whom is in itself a test. In *Koumen*, Silé Sadio clearly states his great desire: "I desire the knowledge that will add to my qualities as a shepherd and my wisdom as a *silatigi*" ("Je desire le savoir qui augmentera mes mérites de pasteur et mes connaissances de *silatigi*"). And Koumen leads him to understand: "You would not have gone further, if you had demanded anything else" ("Tu ne serais pas allé plus loin, si tu avais demandé autre chose") (*Koumen* 35).

In *Kaïdara*, when he has the occasion, Hammadi speaks of "the hunger for knowledge which is always a burning fire" ("la faim de connaître qui est un feu toujours ardent") (71). And when he and his companions will have reached Kaïdara, it is not the gold he receives that interests him. It is knowledge:

Oh Kaïdara, I beg you, agree to explain to me each
of the signs that we saw
on the route that leads to you.
[Ô Kaïdara, je t'en supplie, accepte de m'expliquer chacun
des signes que nous vîmes
sur la route qui mène jusqu'à toi.] (*Kaïdara* 79)

The initiation narrative is different from the detective narrative in the fact that there is no detective. But there is a neophyte who seeks to understand. There is something of the detective in the aspiring initiate. He pays attention to the indexes (*indices*) or the indexes are revealed to him. In *Kaïdara*, the three companions know that the animals they encounter, such as the chameleon or the bat, or the strange scenes they witness such as the metamorphosis of the cock, are symbols that have a hidden sense. They profoundly signify something else than what is immediately perceived. The quest cannot be definitively accomplished until such time as these symbols will have been interpreted. It must be noted that the neophyte must have the intrinsic disposition to be able to accomplish the initiation. In *Kaïdara*, once they have come to Kaïdara, Dembourou and Hammadi no longer preoccupy themselves with the symbols they have encountered during their voyage. Their goal seems to be to reach Kaïdara and to receive the gold that he gives them. For them, the future lies in increasing the bounty of that gold and to become even more rich (Hamtoudo) or to utilize that gold to acquire political power (Dembourou) (81). These two characters are not worthy of initiation. Only Hammadi remains preoccupied with knowledge.

He knows that his initiation is incomplete until he manages to decode the symbols:

> [Hammadi] decided in his heart to learn
> The signification of the symbols and their cause.
> Even if he had to use all his gold, he would comprehend
> Their ultimate sense and satisfy his curiosity.
> [[Hammadi] décida en son cœur de connaître
> La signification des symboles et leur cause.
> Dût-il employer tout son or, il en comprendrait
> Le sens ultime et dissiperait sa curiosité.] (81)

Hammadi is equally someone who seems to have the proper comportment and the worthiness to procure the knowledge that he seeks. First of all, he needs to identify the master initiator capable of giving him the instruction he needs. If, in *Koumen*, the master initiator presents himself easily to Silé Sadio, in *Kaïdara*, Hammadi must identify his master initiator. He has the vague sense that certain characters that he encounters during the voyage are exceptional characters. For example, after having left Kaïdara, the three companions encounter an old man in dirty clothes. Hammadi speaks respectfully to the old man while his companions treat him as a monster, crazy and mute (87). The reason is that Hammadi closely observes the oldster and understands that he is not just any ordinary man and that he is not there by chance.

> He went up to the little old man and observed him.
> ...
> He saw that the torso of the little old man surpassed
> By two times the length of his limbs
> And that the right thigh was thicker than the left.
> His chin measured twice the normal length
> And that his turned-in feet were deformed:
> One was equine, the other a talus.
> His eyes looked in different directions: one fixed on the ground
> The other more prominently gazed toward the sky. (91)

Not only does Hammadi act respectfully toward the old man, but what is more, he washes the rags of the old man, he massages his body gently and he wants to give him a little gold so he can buy something to eat. But the little old man doesn't want charity. So Hammadi will ask him for some counsel. The price of the three pieces of advice is exorbitant. Hammadi gives all his gold to the old man for three pieces of advice that seem futile. That Hammadi recognizes that this old man is a master initiator is very important to the narrative. Dembourou and Hamtoudo, who have not listened to the old man's counsel, are going as a consequence to lose their lives. The three pieces of advice will reveal themselves to be essential, will save the life of Hammadi and permit him to be reunited with his family. In the same way, it is due to his perspicacity and his respect for the values of his society that Hammadi will succeed in finding the master, so long sought after, who will finally interpret all the symbols at the end of the narrative.

So, the neophyte is not a detective. But he has one or more master initiators. In fact, it is not one or more suspects that the candidate for initiation must identify or interrogate. It is he/she or they who will guide him on his initiatory journey. Hammadi, Hamtoudo and Dembourou ask themselves questions regarding the encounters they have. Sometimes it is a voice that simply responds to their interrogations; sometimes it is also the symbol itself that speaks. Sometimes it is an old man who is engaged. At the end of the narrative it becomes clear that all the symbols are none other than the manifestations of a sole being: Kaïdara. Hammadi had to prove his perspicacity in identifying the Old Man with the deformed feet. He is also the only one who is going to be capable of identifying the master who will give him the instruction for which he has waited so long, the profound sense of the symbols observed in the country of the dwarf-genies. In effect, one day, a beggar presents himself at the gates of Hammadi's palace. The beggar refuses the alms that the guards want to give him and demands to see Hammadi:

I don't want any alms! I want to see
and to encounter the king in order to dine with him!
My hand and his in the same vessel,
So I can communicate with him my lice and my fleas.
[Je ne veux point d'aumône! Je désire voir
et rencontrer le roi pour déjeuner avec lui!
Ma main et la sienne dans le même vase,
Que je lui communique mes poux et mes puces.] (127)

The guards find this demand excessive and are ready to treat the old man rudely. But Hammadi, whose attention has been drawn to the scene, accepts the demand of the old beggar. When the latter crosses the threshold of the palace, he pronounces a formula that seems remarkable to Hammadi:

By the fourteen boreal regions minus my senses!
Oh those openings of my physical being!
[Par les quatorze boréales moins mes sens!
Ô les ouvertures de mon être physique!] (129)

Hammadi will also observe that before eating, the old beggar washes his hands back to back (dos contre dos). These are the indexes (indices) that permit Hammadi to comprehend that the beggar is not really a beggar.

Venerable old man, I would have us speak a while.
In effect what you said upon entering my door
And also your manner of washing your hands have convinced me
That you are in no wise a weak beggar; of that I am sure.
[Vieil homme vénérable, je voudrais que nous causions.
En effet ce que tu as dit en traversant ma porte
Et aussi la manière de te laver les mains m'ont convaincu
Que tu n'es point un faible mendiant; de cela je suis sûr.] (131)

The beggar will reveal to Hammadi that he is the supreme master initiator. He is each of the symbols, each of the beings and the elements encountered during Hammadi's voyage. He is Kaïdara, himself. And he explains at length the symbols and instructs Hammadi in the knowledge for which he has so thirsted.

So, the neophyte has a guide who presents himself and whom he must identify. This master knows what the neophyte is looking for. This is clear in *Koumen* and in *L'éclat de la grande étoile* (*The brilliance of the great star*). At the outset of the initiatory voyage of Silé Sadio, Koumen responds directly to the first questions posed by Silé. In the first clearing, it is Koumen who replies to the enigmatic questions of the serpent. It is also he who will respond to the frogs in the second clearing (39). Koumen will explain what attitude Silé must adopt when faced with Foroforondou. He will also teach him the magic formula Silé needs to successfully conquer the lion whose hide will allow him to have the dream in which the name of the sacred bovine will be revealed to him, which constitutes the last stage of his initiation.

So, if there is not a suspect in the initiation narrative, there is a questioning of different things. The final question is never who has committed such and such a crime. The question is: What do the different elements signify and together what do they all mean at the end? There are many questions throughout the story. The symbols to be decoded replace the suspects. The questions sometimes come from character-obstacles scattered along the route of the candidate for initiation; but they are more often and ultimately posed by the neophyte to his master initiator, who is his guide and who, from the outset, knows what his student is looking for. But, if the unveiling of the symbols takes so much time, and so the story continues, it is because the student must deserve the knowledge. The candidate for initiation must have all kinds of experiences and he must pass through numerous stages to see and retain what the master will explain for him later. One of the voices in *Kaïdara* says to the three companions:

You will know when you know that you don't know!
When you can wait to learn, you will know.

[Tu sauras où quand tu sauras que tu ne sais pas!
Quand tu pourras attendre pour savoir, tu sauras.] (31)

Here, as in the detective narrative, the unveiling is delayed until the end of the narrative. But this delay is not played out for suspense. It is rather a matter of letting the neophyte discover more signifying elements. Silé Sadio must cross through 12 clearings. Each one represents something significant in the traditional Fulani universe.

The Fulani *jantols* are texts that are complex, esoteric, and that explain with great profundity traditional African values. Social values, moral values, political values, even religious values. The comparison of certain motifs or structural elements does not mean that we are assimilating these two kinds of narratives. In fact, it seemed of interest to see how two genres that are so distant from one another could nevertheless present similarities or a relation of homology.

Detective narratives contain a certain number of elements, topoi that contribute to the particular nature of these narratives and even determine their structure. If there is a crime, we need a detective to investigate and find the criminal. The detective must interpret indexes (*indices*), interrogate witnesses or suspects.[10] The narrative plays with suspense. The examination of the African initiation narratives has shown that these topoi are not necessarily utilized exclusively by detective narratives and can be found in narratives of a very different nature. These initiatory narratives expose a candidate for initiation to a great number of indexes (*indices*) to which he must find the meaning in order to understand the profound functioning of a society. Here it is the student who poses the questions to the master initiator who reveals himself or must be identified. There is no suspense raised here. The interest resides in a general interpretation of symbols and not in the final identification of a guilty party.

Translated from the French by Peter Baker

Notes

1   Most notably in *Du Récit oral au roman, études sur les avatars de la tradition héroïque dans le roman africain modern.* Abidjan: Ceda, 1976.

2   A rare example is *L'archer bassari*, by Modibo Sounkalo Kéita. Paris: Kathala, 2001.

3   Hampâté Bâ and Lilyan Kesteloo. *Kaïdara, récit initiatique peul.* Paris: Armand Colin, 1968.

4   In their Introduction to *Kaïdara*, the authors explain that "the *jantol* is a very long narrative in which the characters are human or divine; its subject could

be a mystical adventure, an exemplary story either didactic or edifying, an allegory of initiation ..." ("le jantol est un récit très long dont les personnages sont humains ou divins; son sujet peut être une aventure mystique, une histoire exemplaire didactique ou édifiante, une allégorie initiatique ...") (7–8).

5   Âmadou Hampâté Bâ and Germaine Dieterlen. *Koumen. Texte des Pasteurs Peul*. Paris: Mouton et Cie, 1961.

6   Âmadou Hampâté Bâ, *Layatere Koodal, Léclat dans la grande étoile*. Paris: Armand Colin, 1974.

7   Once the group has encountered Kaïdara, the goal will be different for each of the three companions.

8   Roland Barthes, "Introduction à l'analyse structurelle des récits." In *Communications* 8, Paris: Le Seuil (1966): 1–27.

9   The chameleon is the first symbol that Hammadi and his companions encounter in the land of the dwarf-genies. Its symbolic significance will be explained at length by Kaïdara at the end of the narrative (135–9). The color of the chameleon, its physical constitution and its behavior are interpreted and placed in relation to the behavior of people in society.

10   This chain is logical in the *possibles narratifs*, as Claude Bremond would say. "La logique de possibles narratives." In *Communications* 8, Paris: Le Seuil (1966): 60–76.

Works cited

Barthes, Roland. "Introduction à l'analyse structurale des récits." In *Communications* 8, Paris: Le Seuil (1966): 1–27.

Bremond, Claude. "La logique des possibles narratives." In *Communications* 8, Paris: Le Seuil (1966): 60–7.

Hampâté Bâ, Âmadou. *Laaytere Koodal, L'éclat de la grande étoile*. Paris: Armand Colin, 1974.

Hampâté Bâ, Âmadou and Germaine Diéterlen. *Koumen. Texte des Pasteurs Peul*. Paris: Mouton et Cie, 1961.

Hampâté Bâ, Âmadou and Lilyan Kesteloot. *Kaïdara, récit initiatique peul*. Paris: Armand Colin, 1974.

Kéita, Modibo Sounkalo. *L'archer bassari*. Paris: Kathala, 2001.

Koné, Amadou. *Du Récit oral au roman, étude sur les avatars de la tradition héroique dans le roman africain moderne*. Abidjan: Ceda, 1976.

INDEX